STARZ *Spartacus*

D1610309

Screening Antiquity

Series Editors: Monica S. Cyrino and Lloyd Llewellyn-Jones

Screening Antiquity is a cutting-edge and provocative series of academic monographs and edited volumes focusing on new research on the reception of the ancient world in film and television. Screening Antiquity showcases the work of the best-established and up-and-coming specialists in the field. It provides an important synergy of the latest international scholarly ideas about the conception of antiquity in popular culture and is the only series that focuses exclusively on screened representations of the ancient world.

Titles available in the series:

Rome *Season Two: Trial and Triumph*
Edited by Monica S. Cyrino

Ben-Hur: *The Original Blockbuster*
By Jon Solomon

Cowboy Classics: The Roots of the American Western in the Epic Tradition
By Kirsten Day

STARZ Spartacus: *Reimagining an Icon on Screen*
Edited by Antony Augoustakis and Monica S. Cyrino

Forthcoming Titles:

Broadcasting Ancient Greece on Television
Edited by Fiona Hobden and Amanda Wrigley

STARZ *Spartacus*

Reimagining an Icon on Screen

Edited by Antony Augoustakis and
Monica S. Cyrino

EDINBURGH
University Press

Edinburgh University Press is one of the leading university presses in the UK. We publish academic books and journals in our selected subject areas across the humanities and social sciences, combining cutting-edge scholarship with high editorial and production values to produce academic works of lasting importance. For more information visit our website: edinburghuniversitypress.com

Edinburgh University Press Ltd
The Tun – Holyrood Road, 12(2f) Jackson's Entry, Edinburgh EH8 8PJ

First published in hardback by Edinburgh University Press 2017

Typeset in 11/13 Sabon by
Servis Filmsetting Ltd, Stockport, Cheshire
and printed and bound in Great Britain by
CPI Group (UK) Ltd, Croydon CR0 4YY

A CIP record for this book is available from the British Library

ISBN 978 1 4744 0784 7 (hardback)
ISBN 978 1 4744 3256 6 (paperback)
ISBN 978 1 4744 0785 4 (webready PDF)
ISBN 978 1 4744 0786 1 (epub)

Contents

Series Editors' Preface

Screening Antiquity is a new series of cutting-edge academic monographs and edited volumes that present exciting and original research
on the reception of the ancient world in film and television. It provides an important synergy of the latest international scholarly ideas
about the onscreen conception of antiquity in popular culture and is
the only book series to focus exclusively on screened representations
of the ancient world.

The interactions between cinema, television, and historical representation is a growing field of scholarship and student engagement; many Classics and Ancient History departments in universities
worldwide teach cinematic representations of the past as part of their
programmes in Reception Studies. Scholars are now questioning how
historical films and television series reflect the societies in which
they were made, and speculate on how attitudes towards the past
have been moulded in the popular imagination by their depiction in
the movies. Screening Antiquity explores how these constructions
came about and offers scope to analyse how and why the ancient
past is filtered through onscreen representations in specific ways.
The series highlights exciting and original publications that explore
the representation of antiquity onscreen, and that employ modern
theoretical and cultural perspectives to examine screened antiquity,
including: stars and star text, directors and *auteurs*, cinematography,
design and art direction, marketing, fans, and the online presence of
the ancient world.

The series aims to present original research focused exclusively on
the reception of the ancient world in film and television. In itself this
is an exciting and original approach. There is no other book series
that engages head-on with both big screen and small screen recreations of the past, yet their integral interactivity is clear to see: film
popularity has a major impact on television productions and for its
part, television regularly influences cinema (including film spin-offs

of popular television series). This is the first academic series to identify and encourage the holistic interactivity of these two major media
institutions, and the first to promote interdisciplinary research in all
the fields of Cinema Studies, Media Studies, Classics, and Ancient
History.

Screening Antiquity explores the various facets of onscreen cre-
ations of the past, exploring the theme from multiple angles. Some
volumes will foreground a Classics 'reading' of the subject, analysing
the nuances of film and television productions against a background
of ancient literature, art, history, or culture; others will focus more
on Media 'readings,' by privileging the onscreen creation of the past
or positioning the film or television representation within the context
of modern popular culture. A third 'reading' will allow for a more
fluid interaction between both the Classics and Media approaches.
All three methods are valuable, since Reception Studies demands a
flexible approach whereby individual scholars, or groups of researchers, foster a reading of an onscreen 'text' particular to their angle of
viewing.

Screening Antiquity represents a major turning point in that it signals a better appreciation and understanding of the rich and complex
interaction between the past and contemporary culture, and also of
the lasting significance of antiquity in today's world.

Monica S. Cyrino and Lloyd Llewellyn-Jones
Series Editors

Editors' Acknowledgments

We would like to thank the authors for their enthusiasm in embracing this project and for their inspiring contributions to this volume. Special thanks are owed to Carol Macdonald at Edinburgh University Press for her support of this volume from the beginning, and to her editorial staff, Ellie Bush and Rebecca Mackenzie, for their assistance in the production process. We have greatly benefitted from the feedback provided by the two anonymous reviewers: their comments and suggestions made this into a stronger and much improved volume. We would also like to extend our gratitude to Lloyd Llewellyn-Jones, the series co-editor. Finally, we would like to thank our families, students, and colleagues who continue to inspire us to explore classics and popular culture. This volume is dedicated to them.

Contributors

Antony Augoustakis is Professor of Classics at the University of Illinois, Urbana-Champaign, USA. His research interests include Roman comedy and historiography, Latin imperial epic, women in antiquity, classical reception, and gender theory. He is the author of *Motherhood and the Other: Fashioning Female Power in Flavian Epic* (Oxford, 2010) and *Statius, Thebaid 8* (Oxford, 2016). He is the editor of the *Brill Companion to Silius Italicus* (2010), *Ritual and Religion in Flavian Epic* (Oxford, 2013), *Flavian Poetry and its Greek Past* (Brill, 2014), *Oxford Readings in Flavian Epic* (Oxford, 2016), and co-editor of the *Blackwell Companion to Terence* (2013). He has published numerous articles and book chapters on various topics of the literature and culture of Greco-Roman antiquity. He is the editor of *The Classical Journal*.

Monica S. Cyrino is Professor of Classics at the University of New Mexico, USA. Her academic research centers on the reception of the ancient world on screen, and the erotic in ancient Greek poetry. She is the author of *Aphrodite* (Routledge, 2010), *A Journey through Greek Mythology* (Kendall-Hunt, 2008), *Big Screen Rome* (Blackwell, 2005), and *In Pandora's Jar: Lovesickness in Early Greek Poetry* (Rowman & Littlefield, 1995). She is the editor of *Rome, Season Two: Trial and Triumph* (Edinburgh, 2015), *Screening Love and Sex in the Ancient World* (Palgrave Macmillan, 2013), *Rome, Season One: History Makes Television* (Blackwell, 2008), and co-editor of *Classical Myth on Screen* (Palgrave Macmillan, 2015). She has published numerous articles and book chapters and often gives lectures around the world on the representation of classical antiquity on film and television. She has served as an academic consultant on several recent film and television productions.

* * * * * * * * * *

Gregory N. Daugherty is the Shelton H. Short III Professor in the Liberal Arts and Chair of the Department of Classics at Randolph-Macon College in Ashland, Virginia, USA. His research focuses on the reception of classics in American popular culture, especially representations of Cleopatra. He is the co-author of *To Be A Roman: Topics in Roman Culture* (Bolchazy-Carducci, 2007). He has been president of the Classical Association of the Middle West and South, and the Classical Association of Virginia.

Alison Futrell is Associate Professor of Roman History at the University of Arizona, USA. Her abiding interest in the symbols and rituals of power led her to explore Roman spectacle in her books *Blood in the Arena* (Texas, 1997) and *The Roman Games* (Blackwell, 2006). She is also fascinated with the way the ancient Mediterranean is reconfigured in popular culture and has published articles on *Spartacus*, *Xena: Warrior Princess*, *Troy*, and *Rome*.

Hunter H. Gardner is Associate Professor of Classics at the University of South Carolina, USA. She is the author of *Gendering Time in Augustan Love Elegy* (Oxford, 2013), and is a horror film enthusiast. She is currently working on a monograph on plague narratives in Latin literature and their impact on representations of contagion in Western literature, film, and visual arts.

Juliette Harrisson is Lecturer in Ancient History at Newman University in Birmingham, UK. She is the author of *Dreams and Dreaming in the Roman Empire: Cultural Memory and Imagination* (Bloomsbury, 2013), and co-editor of *Memory and Urban Religion in the Ancient World* (Bloomsbury, 2012). Her current projects include a co-authored book on screen representations of Roman Britain and a textbook on religion in ancient Rome.

Lisa Maurice is Senior Lecturer of Classical Studies at Bar-Ilan University, Israel. Her research interests center on Roman comedy and the reception of antiquity in popular culture. She is the author of *The Teacher in Ancient Rome: The Magister and his World* (Lexington, 2013), and the editor of *The Reception of Ancient Greece and Rome in Children's Literature: Heroes and Eagles* (Brill, 2015). Her current work explores the connections between ancient Roman and early Jewish pedagogical practice.

Alex McAuley is Lecturer in Hellenistic History at Cardiff University in Wales, UK. His research interests center on localism and cultural pluralism in the Hellenistic World, and he has published articles on royal women, dynastic ideology, and civic government. He has several current and forthcoming articles and book chapters in the field of reception studies, with a particular focus on how 9/11 and the War on Terror have influenced onscreen depictions of antiquity.

Amanda Potter is a Research Fellow in Classical Studies with the Open University, UK, where she completed her PhD on viewer reception of classical myth in *Xena: Warrior Princess* and *Charmed*. Her research interests include the classical world on film and television, and classics and gender, and she has published on Greek mythology in the television shows *Xena: Warrior Princess*, *Charmed*, and *Torchwood*. She is currently working on Greek myth in *Doctor Who*.

Meredith D. Prince is Associate Professor of Classics at Auburn University, USA, where she teaches Latin, Greek, and ancient Greece and Rome in film. She has published numerous articles on Augustan Age poetry, including Ovid's *Metamorphoses*, but now focuses on the reception of antiquity in film and television. She currently is working on a book chapter on Agrippina the Younger as model for Cersei Lannister in the HBO series *Game of Thrones*.

Stacie Raucci is Associate Professor of Classics at Union College in Schenectady, New York, where she teaches a course on the ancient world in the cinema. Her academic research focuses primarily on the reception of the ancient world in popular culture and Roman love elegy. She is the author of *Elegiac Eyes: Vision in Roman Love Elegy* (Peter Lang, 2011). She has published articles and delivered papers on the popularization of antiquity, Medusa Barbie, Roman orgies in film, and the HBO series *Rome*.

Nuno Simões Rodrigues is Professor of History of Classical Antiquity at the University of Lisbon, Portugal. He holds a PhD in Classical History with a thesis on the life of Jews in first-century Rome. His research focuses on politics and society in ancient Rome as well as ancient Greek culture. Among other publications, he has translated Euripides (*Alcestis* and *Iphigenia among the Taurians*) and Plutarch (*Coriolanus*) into Portuguese.

Anise K. Strong is Assistant Professor of History at Western Michigan University. Her research centers on Roman social history, gender and sexuality in the ancient world, and the reception of classical culture in modern mass media. Her book *Prostitutes and Matrons in the Roman World* was published by Cambridge University Press (2016). Recent articles include analyses of the myths in *Monty Python's Life of Brian* and *Agora* and the treatment of ethnic intermarriage in Herodotus' *Histories*.

Illustrations

Episode Listing

Readers can consult http://www.starz.com/originals/spartacus/ and http://spartacus.wikia.com/wiki/Spartacus_Wiki for synopses of each episode.

SEASON 1, *SPARTACUS: BLOOD AND SAND* (2010)

Episode 101, "The Red Serpent," written by Steven S. DeKnight, directed by Rick Jacobson

Episode 102, "Sacramentum Gladiatorum," written by Steven S. DeKnight, directed by Rick Jacobson

Episode 103, "Legends," written by Brent Fletcher, directed by Grady Hall

Episode 104, "The Thing in the Pit," written by Aaron Helbing and Todd Helbing, directed by Jesse Warn

Episode 105, "Shadow Games," written by Miranda Kwok, directed by Michael Hurst

Episode 106, "Delicate Things," written by Tracy Bellomo and Andrew Chambliss, directed by Rick Jacobson

Episode 107, "Great and Unfortunate Things," written by Brent Fletcher and Steven S. DeKnight, directed by Jesse Warn

Episode 108, "Mark of the Brotherhood," written by Aaron Helbing and Todd Helbing, directed by Rowan Woods

Episode 109, "Whore," written by Daniel Knauf, directed by Michael Hurst

Episode 110, "Party Favors," written by Brent Fletcher and Miranda Kwok, directed by Chris Martin-Jones

Episode 111, "Old Wounds," story by Dan Filie and Patricia Wells, directed by Glen Standring

Episode 112, "Revelations," written by Brent Fletcher, directed by Michael Hurst

Introduction:
Reimagining a New Spartacus

Antony Augoustakis and Monica S. Cyrino

The acclaimed and highly successful television series *Spartacus*, airing on the premium cable network STARZ, attracted a large fan base around the world, starting with its initial season *Spartacus: Blood and Sand* (2010).[1] The first season was followed by the prequel season *Spartacus: Gods of the Arena* (2011), the second season *Spartacus: Vengeance* (2012), and the third and final season *Spartacus: War of the Damned* (2013), which narrates the last stand of the revolution organized by the Thracian slave, gladiator, and rebel leader Spartacus.[2] This new reception of the centuries-old icon of Spartacus, both reimagined and distinctively idealized for a new millennium, draws from many of its predecessors on the big and small screen, most significantly Stanley Kubrick's 1960 film *Spartacus*,[3] just as it pays visual and narrative homage to other incarnations and appropriations of ancient warrior and revenge-seeking figures, such as those depicted in *Gladiator* (2000) or *300* (2007); but STARZ *Spartacus* also evokes the thematic tropes of the critically lauded HBO series *Rome* (2005–7), on which it draws extensively for its portrayal of ancient Roman politics, society, women, and sexuality.[4] Viewers of the new *Spartacus* are invited to appreciate the extreme sexualization of both the male and female characters, the nexus of complicated relationships formed among slaves or between slaves and masters, the surreal and gory representation of warfare, and the bloody, CGI-enhanced violence of the gladiatorial shows in the arena. To be sure, this is an utterly new and reimagined Spartacus, as the hero of the slave revolt is recast for a contemporary twenty-first-century audience. Modern spectators are invited to reimagine the Spartacus legend and connect with antiquity in novel and manifold ways. Moreover, the series vigorously follows the earlier Spartacus reception thread by highlighting the topic of slavery, a perennially favorite theme in the media that has recently surged as a "hot" topic for current onscreen entertainment:[5] the fight for freedom continues to fascinate. The sociopolitical and economic context here is key to understanding the reception of the Spartacus story: in light of the global economic crisis, it can be argued that freedom is indeed acquiring a "post-political" dimension.

STARZ Spartacus: Reimagining an Icon on Screen is a collection of essays written by scholars in the fields of Classics, History, Gender Studies, and Film and Media Studies, who have come together to offer an extraordinary exploration of a wide range of topics, narratives, and characters. Individual chapters address various provocative themes, cinematic conventions, and visual tropes as they are portrayed in the series, such as slavery and freedom, society and class, economics and politics, material culture and aesthetics, gender and sexuality, violence and spectacle, and fan reaction and reception. The contributors to this volume pose the question: How is the story of Spartacus recreated to suit the expectations of a twenty-first-century audience, a full fifty years after Kubrick's famous and groundbreaking 1960 epic film? While it is clearly the product of a long reception trajectory, STARZ *Spartacus* is also a vibrant and innovative creation of its own time that reflects the dynamic entertainment context of the modern premium cable medium, as it participates in the same powerful visuality and intensity of language that are characteristic of recent successful series on HBO such as *Rome*, *Deadwood* (2004–6), and *Game of Thrones* (2011–), or Showtime's *The Tudors* (2007–10) and *The Borgias* (2011–13). With its hauntingly beautiful episode titles and the Latin-grammar-styled cadences of its characters' dialogue, this *Spartacus* strives to tell a new story.

SCREENING A NEW *SPARTACUS*

The story of Spartacus, the historical Thracian gladiator who led a slave uprising against the Roman Republican army from 73 to 71 BC, has inspired numerous receptions over the centuries in a variety of different media, while the figure of the rebel slave leader has often served as an icon of resistance against oppression in modern political movements and popular ideologies.[6] STARZ *Spartacus*, the four-season original television series from the US-based premium cable channel, was created by Stephen S. DeKnight, who also served as executive producer and head writer for the series. The show's other executive producers included Sam Raimi and Rob Tapert, longtime collaborators who also produced *Hercules: The Legendary Journeys* (1995–99) and *Xena: Warrior Princess* (1995–2001). The series was filmed on location in New Zealand and employed numerous local actors and crew. Heavily marketed and initially shown in the United States on pay television channels starting in January 2010, *Spartacus: Blood and Sand* attracted an enormous fan base and spawned a prequel, *Gods of the Arena*, as well as two sequels, *Vengeance* and *War of the Damned*. The series also aired internationally on various broadcast networks around the world. Soon after each season was broadcast, the DVD and Blu-ray disc sets were released for home video purchase in the US, UK, and Australia.

Producers of the series decided that the first season would elaborate on the shadowy events of the early life of Spartacus leading up to the historical records.[7] The first season, *Spartacus: Blood and Sand*, tells of the capture of Spartacus in Thrace, his enslavement, and his training as a gladiator in the *ludus* of Quintus Lentulus Batiatus in Capua. The premiere season was then followed by *Gods of the Arena*, a miniseries prequel to the first season, which fills in the back-story of the rise of the *lanista* Batiatus in the gladiator business. The third installment – technically known as the second season – of the series, *Vengeance*, depicts the aftermath of the slaves' bloody escape from the *ludus* and the development and progress of the gladiator rebellion. The final season, *War of the Damned*, focuses on the decisive conflict between the rebel army led by Spartacus and his gladiator-troops and the Roman Republican army led by Marcus Licinius Crassus and a young Julius Caesar. The "disclaimer" that begins every episode throughout the entire STARZ *Spartacus* series is extraordinary both for its bold claim to historicity as well as its unapologetic stance on the explicitness of its subject matter: "*Spartacus* is a Historical Portrayal of Ancient Roman Society that Contains Graphic Violence and Adult Content. Viewer Discretion is Advised."[8]

STARZ *Spartacus* engages with earlier onscreen receptions of antiquity as it breaks new ground. In some respects the *Spartacus* series is highly derivative, as it was clearly intended to appeal to a ready-made audience who had enjoyed recent films and television series set in the ancient world. *Spartacus* uses the slow-motion combat sequences and visual stylization from Zack Snyder's fantasy film *300*, the nudity, sexuality, and focus on strong female characters from the HBO series *Rome*, and the exciting arena sequences filled with physically striking fighters from Ridley Scott's *Gladiator*. But more nudity, more sex, more violence, and more blood than had ever been seen together on mainstream television, mixed with gripping plotlines and a focus on the lives of the slaves as well as their masters, made this *Spartacus* feel entirely new. While STARZ *Spartacus* gained immediate notoriety for its heady mix of highly stylized, CGI-enhanced violence with an unprecedented amount of onscreen nudity and graphic sexual acts, the series also offered viewers new visual, narrative, and thematic aesthetics for the depiction of the Spartacus story and its received meanings. Audiences noted that the STARZ series both nodded to earlier Spartacus receptions, especially Kubrick's 1960 film, as well as other recent popular onscreen recreations of antiquity, such as Snyder's *300* and HBO's *Rome*. Yet at the same time the series applied innovative techniques of interrogation to current issues such as love and sexuality, race and class, and violence and spectacle.

As ancient Rome has always been a preferred cinematic locus for the display of various types of sexual extremes and decadent erotic practices, the STARZ *Spartacus* television series, in terms of representing sexuality, follows some earlier conventions while also blazing new trails of onscreen eroticism.[9] STARZ *Spartacus* both promised and delivered plentiful nudity and sexual situations, in graphic scenes which were remarkable not only for their exotic nature, but also for their quantity, frequency, and explicitness. Like earlier cinematic depictions of ancient Rome, sexual excess and perversion in *Spartacus* are also regularly equated with the extreme hunger for power and the use of excessive violence. The *Spartacus* series utilizes several tropes to expose sexual excesses that are explicitly coded as Roman-style "deviance," including group sex and other non-private sexual acts; sex that crosses class hierarchies or sex with slaves; sexual compulsion, abuse, and non-compliance; lesbianism and homosexuality; masturbation, voyeurism, incest, and sado-masochism.[10] While these tropes may have been hinted at or even shown in earlier screenings of ancient Rome, the STARZ *Spartacus* series escalates each trope to an extraordinary degree of expression in response to the desires of the increasingly affect-hungry viewers watching at home.

The first season of the series, *Spartacus: Blood and Sand*, premiered in January 2010 and unfolded in thirteen weekly episodes.[11] The series' first season follows the aftermath of Spartacus' capture in Thrace and his training as a gladiator in the *ludus* of the *lanista* Batiatus. As Spartacus becomes an immediate superstar in the arena, he achieves the status of "Champion of Capua." The first season also introduces the *lanista* Batiatus as the financially strapped owner of a gladiator school vying for prominence in the saturated and ultra-competitive human spectacle market of Campania. Batiatus and his steadfast wife, Lucretia, will do anything for prestige and social advancement, as they claw and scrape their way to achieve place among the elite ranks of Roman citizens. So Batiatus stakes his future and that of his *ludus* on the raw talents of Spartacus, the brooding Thracian slave who agrees to fight and become a champion gladiator when Batiatus promises to reunite him with his enslaved wife, Sura. But when Sura is returned on the point of death, Spartacus, furious, vows revenge on Batiatus and the *ludus*. The thirteen-episode arc ends in a brutal bloodbath in their *atrium*, where Batiatus is slain and Lucretia critically injured (but not killed), followed by the famous escape of the gladiators from the *ludus*. So the next season, if there was one, was to follow the runaway gladiators and slaves as they wreaked havoc on the slopes of Mount Vesuvius and attempted to fend off the Roman military.

When the first season premiered in January 2010, the outlook could not have been brighter. In December 2009, STARZ had already given the green light for a second season of the bloody gladiator series, a full month before the show debuted to critical praise and record ratings.[12] The new *Spartacus* was the upstart network's first true breakout hit: the series' premiere episode, "The Red Serpent" (101), set a record for STARZ with over half a million viewers, and audiences increased steadily over the rest of the opening season, with an average of 1.27 million viewers per show, which is a remarkable achievement for a network that reaches only about 17 million homes. But then in March 2010 lead actor Andy Whitfield (Figure I.1),

Figure I.1 Spartacus (Andy Whitfield) in episode 102
("Sacramentum Gladiatorum"). STARZ.

who played Spartacus in the first season with both sensitivity and strength and to much critical acclaim, was diagnosed with early stage non-Hodgkin's lymphoma. This somber news delayed the filming of the series' Season Two, so in a bid to keep the popular franchise going while Whitfield underwent treatment, the network decided to produce a six-episode miniseries prequel.

Spartacus: Gods of the Arena, also known in the press somewhat ominously as *Spartacus Minus Spartacus*, premiered in January 2011 and aired six weekly episodes. The prequel focuses on the rise of the House of Batiatus in the city of Capua before the arrival of Spartacus, as it traces the career of the Celtic gladiator Gannicus, the first fighter in the *ludus* of Batiatus to become the "Champion of Capua." Although the prequel was born of a sad situation – lead actor Whitfield's cancer later returned, forcing him to leave the series altogether, and he eventually died in September 2011[13] – *Gods of the Arena* with its back-story narrative allowed the literal resurrection of several compelling characters from the first season and proved to be enormously successful, receiving positive critical reviews and audience reception. Set within a flashback as Batiatus lay bleeding in the *impluvium* of his house after the attack and escape of the gladiators under the leadership of Spartacus, the prequel takes the audience back about five years, as it explores Batiatus' rough relationship with his father, his constant struggles with the other businessmen and politicians of Capua, his interactions with his original stable of gladiators, and his deeply loyal emotional bond with his wife Lucretia in the early days of their marriage. *Gods of the Arena* reveals how Batiatus and Lucretia develop into the gritty, striving characters that are presented in the first season, as the prequel illuminates why the stakes are so high for them, and how they become so ruthless in seeking to attain their goals. Furthermore, gladiators like Gannicus rise to prominence during this prequel, and thus their role for the future development of the rebellion in the following seasons is foreshadowed. Throughout the narrative of the six prequel episodes, numerous low-angle and point-of-view shots show the glorious new stone arena that is being erected in Capua to replace the rickety old wooden stadium: these camera glimpses serve as a visual parallel to the growing aspirations of Batiatus and Lucretia in their relentless desire to promote their gladiators, their *ludus*, and themselves.

The second season of the series, *Spartacus: Vengeance*, premiered in January 2012, and presented ten weekly episodes. While it is quite rare for a continuing television series to recast its leading role with a different actor, Whitfield gave his blessing for the series to

Figure I.2 The "replacement" Spartacus (Liam McIntyre) in episode 205 ("Libertus"). STARZ.

carry on without him and for the role of Spartacus to be recast with Australian actor Liam McIntyre (Figure I.2).[14] The second season picks up immediately after the bloody escape of the gladiators from the *ludus* of Batiatus that had concluded the first season. As the gladiator rebellion begins to devastate the countryside around Capua, and as Spartacus and his generals free more slaves and gather more recruits to join their rebel army, the citizens and politicians of Rome become acutely terrified. The military praetor Claudius Glaber, the Roman officer who had originally captured Spartacus and his wife and sold them into slavery at the beginning of the first season, is dispatched with his troops first to Capua and then to the area around Mount Vesuvius to subdue Spartacus and his band of freed slaves. Meanwhile, back at the house of Batiatus, his widow Lucretia engages in a deadly game for social ascendancy and control over her aristocratic rival, Ilithyia, Glaber's wife, which results in both of their deaths in the last episode of the season. But the main plot of *Vengeance* underscores Glaber's personal vendetta to kill Spartacus, as he becomes increasingly obsessed with finding and capturing the rebel leader. Aided by his fellow gladiators, including former champions Gannicus and Crixus the Gaul, the gladiator trainer Oenomaus, and Agron the German, Spartacus defeats the Roman army in numerous clashes, and finally satisfies his own need for vengeance by killing Glaber. With his dying breath Glaber defiantly promises that his death will draw down the full power and wrath of the Roman legions and that Spartacus and his rebel slave army are doomed.

After the airing of the second season in the spring of 2012, STARZ announced that the third season of the *Spartacus* series would be the final one. The series' third and final season, *Spartacus: War of the Damned*, premiered in January 2013 and offered up ten weekly episodes. The narrative of the final season enters into territory that portrays individuals and events well attested in the ancient historical sources, as *War of the Damned* follows the bloody conflict and final conclusive struggle between Spartacus and his gladiator troops on the one side, and on the other the Roman army raised and led by Marcus Licinius Crassus, whose enormous wealth was matched only by his extraordinary political ambition. Just as in Kubrick's 1960 film, the final season of *Spartacus* also introduces Julius Caesar, who is depicted as a young but ruthless and experienced soldier, and who seeks to increase his own political power by enlisting Crassus as a financial patron and by proving himself in the campaign against Spartacus. Crassus relentlessly pursues Spartacus, but the gladiator leader wins several skirmishes against the Roman forces as they become increasingly frustrated by their inability to defeat the rebellious slaves. After the rebels are betrayed by the Cilician pirates and after Crassus massacres Crixus and his army, Spartacus strains to keep morale high among his followers, as they learn that more Roman troops under Pompey and Lucullus are on their way to southern Italy to support Crassus' campaign against him. In the series finale, "Victory" (310), Spartacus decides to turn his forces to face the legions of Crassus and Caesar in a final stand at the Battle of the Siler River, where Crassus gains a decisive victory.[15] Although he nearly beats Crassus in hand-to-hand combat, Spartacus is mortally wounded by three Roman soldiers and is carried from the battlefield by Agron, while Gannicus is captured and crucified along with thousands of the rebel slave prisoners: the series is thus more authentic to history than the 1960 Kubrick film, which has Spartacus dying Christ-like on a cross with his fellow rebels.[16] Pompey arrives after the battle yet steals credit for the defeat of Spartacus, thereby sowing the seeds of the power struggle between himself, Crassus, and Caesar that would ravage Rome for the next two decades, as it also provides an evocative link to the narrative material of the first season of the HBO series *Rome*.

ABOUT THIS VOLUME

STARZ Spartacus: Reimagining an Icon on Screen surveys the various dimensions of the *Spartacus* series by engaging with a fascinating array of topics, themes, and characters. In addition to drawing connections between this new version of the story and previous receptions and media incarnations of the Spartacus legend, the essays in this volume examine the creative freedom enjoyed by the producers of the show who succeeded in delivering a four-season series that is both captivating and aesthetically pleasing. As the individual chapters attest, STARZ *Spartacus* challenges our perceptions of ancient society in provocative ways, while it proves that the practice of classical reception speaks to contemporary aspirations, tastes, and anxieties.

The first part of the volume, "Heroes and Heroism," opens with Alison Futrell's chapter "Memories of Storied Heroes," in which she explores how the slaves of Batiatus' *ludus* rebuild their individual identities by redefining categories of value and connection, gender and family, as they are stripped of their past and end up becoming a band of brothers with their own loyalties and narratives of meaning. As Futrell shows, a number of these narratives are embedded within Roman artifacts, such as the herms in Batiatus' villa or the *rudis* of Gannicus: for instance, the amphitheater of Capua functions as a visible expression of imperial prestige, deployed as a tool of local power that resonates all the way to the city of Rome. In the second chapter, "From Kubrick's Political Icon to Television Sex Symbol," Nuno Simões Rodrigues starts from the iconic 1960 film as he compares the two *Spartacus* versions to demonstrate how the political and ideological nature of the Spartacus figure re-emerges in the twenty-first century, reinvented and far more sexualized than its predecessor. STARZ *Spartacus*, Rodrigues argues, has an altogether different set of objectives, placing special emphasis on the glorified and eroticized image of mostly male – but also female – bodies. Rodrigues concludes that Kubrick's Spartacus is transformed from a political icon, representing freedom, equality, and independence, into a new Spartacus who also becomes the image of a hypersexualized masculinity.

In the third chapter, "The Life and Death of Gannicus," Juliette Harrisson turns to another hero in the series, Gannicus, as she discusses the portrayal of the messianic death given to this character. Harrisson argues that Gannicus experiences an anti-heroic journey as he resists the role of rebel or leader until the very end of the series; as such, he is sharply juxtaposed to both Spartacus and Crixus but also complements these other characters in underscoring their very deficiencies. Harrisson analyzes Gannicus' symbolic death by crucifixion to demonstrate how his death showcases the transformations of the rebel leader, Spartacus, by complicating and multiplying the paradigm of the single hero, just as audiences are invited to rediscover the true meaning of freedom. In the fourth chapter of this section, "A New Crassus as Roman Villain," Gregory N. Daugherty examines the historical Crassus as reimagined in the STARZ series by means of clever adaptations and modifications. Daugherty argues that Crassus undergoes a transformation, as he is sexualized by the addition of a tender romance with a slave woman, Kore, an affair turned bitter by the machinations of an invented son named Tiberius, and by his glad-iator-style physical conditioning regimen. The result is a compelling characterization that is not a product of its literary and cinematic predecessors but is remarkably consistent with the ancient source material and respectful of at least some of the realities of period.

The second part of the volume, "Social Spaces," starts with Monica S. Cyrino's chapter "Upward Mobility in the House of Batiatus," which considers the depiction of the ambitious, ruthless couple Batiatus and Lucretia and their scheming aspirations to turn their *ludus* into the foremost gladiator spectacle business in Capua. Although their plans for upward mobility utilize violence, sexual manipulation, and multiple murders, Cyrino claims that this does not diminish the characters' appeal to viewers, due to a pair of robust and sympathetic performances by the actors who play them. This chapter argues that the series successfully uses visual and narrative strategies to do something innovative within both the epic cinematic tradition and the Spartacus reception tradition: STARZ *Spartacus* invites the audience to transfer their allegiance away from the Roman elite and the rebel slaves, and identify with the cunning bourgeois boot-strappers at the head of the House of Batiatus.

In the sixth chapter, "Social Dynamics and Liminal Spaces," Stacie Raucci focuses on those liminal spaces that highlight the power struggles of the series' main characters. Specifically, Raucci examines the obvious liminality of concrete physical thresholds, such as cliffs and balconies, and then moves on to spaces that function as gateways to change while being physically more self-enclosed. These spaces in-between and at the margins, as Raucci shows, reveal and facilitate acts of transgression, transformation, and resistance. Such liminal spaces ultimately reflect Spartacus' own journey, as he finds himself in spaces of transition and transformation, with each place present-ing special challenges. The seventh chapter, Lisa Maurice's "Building a New Ancient Rome," investigates how the world of ancient Rome is portrayed onscreen in the *Spartacus* series by assessing the phys-ical sets – including the buildings and cities, interior design, and furniture – as well as the art direction in terms of color and costume design. In her analysis of the distinctive look of the physical settings of the series, especially the villas and the cities (Capua, Sinuessa, and Rome), Maurice concludes that *Spartacus* offers a vision of a dark and turbulent new Rome that owes as much to contemporary thinking as to its past, both historical and cinematic.

The third section of the volume, "Gender and Sexuality," begins with Anise K. Strong's chapter, "The Rape of Lucretia," which looks closely at the dominant female character of the first three seasons of the series, Lucretia, the wife of the gladiatorial *ludus* master Batiatus. Strong maintains that Lucretia's sexual choices and, in particular, her relationship to the act of rape as portrayed in the series present an ongoing reflection on the depiction of rape in modern historical fiction to assert power and to demean women. As Strong argues, the question of rape in *Spartacus* is fraught with issues of power and its abuse, and she exposes how the series creators make a significant and meaningful distinction between implicit rape, which is depicted non-violently and often performed silently by extras, and the violent, explicitly abusive rape of named characters.

In the ninth chapter, "The Others," Antony Augoustakis details the series' frank presentation of what contemporary viewers would call "second-class" citizens, namely the male and female slaves in the villa and the *ludus* of Batiatus. Augoustakis also calls them "the *others*," that is, those figures who are normally given little or no voice in the historical sources on the society and civilization of antiquity. In his analysis, Augoustakis discusses how audiences might perceive and comprehend the role of the non-elite women depicted in STARZ *Spartacus*, taking into consideration the extent to which modern scholarship on gender in classical antiquity now informs our understanding of love, sexuality, familial relationships, and marriage in the ancient world, whether they are accurately or approximately depicted on the small screen. And in the tenth chapter, "Fan Reactions to Nagron as One True Pairing," Amanda Potter considers the same-sex couple, Agron and Nasir, also known by the popular *portmanteau* "Nagron," as she examines the reception of this ground-breaking representation by gay and straight fans alike. In her survey of numerous fan sites and the many comments posted online about the characters, Potter concludes that although "Nagron" is a positive step forward for the representation of gay relationships on television, the centrality of this relationship to the main text left little for writers of slash fiction to explore in their writing.

The final section of this volume, "Spectacle and Violence," opens with Alex McAuley's chapter, "Base Pleasures, Spectacle, and Society," which takes a closer look at Spartacus' engagement with Roman spectacle as a fighter and entertainer. Beyond the series' intense focus on sexuality and the problems of slavery, McAuley argues that the creators also emphasize the multimodal representation of the Roman culture of performance and spectacle in the arena. The new *Spartacus* series, McAuley claims, offers a complex image of Roman spectacle in terms of spatial materialities, spectacular aesthetics, and social realism: the amphitheater is conveyed as a microcosm of Roman society and the central point of reference for Roman "popular" culture in the sense of mass entertainment. In the twelfth chapter, "Draba's Legacy and the Spectacle of Sacrifice," Meredith D. Prince explores how STARZ *Spartacus* reworks and inverts the pivotal scene of the private fight between Spartacus and Draba for Crassus' viewing pleasure in Kubrick's iconic 1960 film. While the new series omits the figure of Draba, Prince argues that his influence reveals that, in contrast to the elite Romans in the earlier film, the Romans of the series – ruthlessly ambitious Batiatus, and vengeance-minded Lucretia and Ilithyia – are far more base in their political scheming and sexual desires. Prince examines the series' staging of two bespoke fight exhibitions that draw on the Draba scene to present a narrative of decline that highlights the degeneracy of the Roman spectators and ultimately leads to rebellion.

In the final chapter, "Violence and Voyeurism in the Arena," Hunter H. Gardner and Amanda Potter explore the different forms of violence portrayed in the series, principally the gladiatorial violence in the arena, violence in the streets including beatings and murders, and sexual violence perpetrated on slaves but also on Roman citizens. Gardner and Potter point out that through scenes of graphic bodily dismemberments and eviscerations, the series asks its audience to contemplate the difficult distinction between morally justified bloodshed and the fetishized conventions of gore, conventions popularized in various subgenres of the horror film, in particular the "splatter film" and the "meat flick." Despite its slippery tendency to celebrate violence both attached and unattached to a moral perspective, Gardner and Potter maintain that the series offers a unique window on the embodiment of violence in the ancient world.

All the contributors to this volume, who are both scholars of classical receptions in modern popular culture and also fans of its ongoing expression in contemporary media, earnestly and justifiably consider the STARZ *Spartacus* series a valuable and entertaining contribution to understanding how specific threads of reception are constantly being rewoven to suit current predilections.

NOTES

1 The first episode of the series, "The Red Serpent" (101), aired in the United States on 22 January 2010. Note that each season of the series starts with the name *Spartacus* in its official title.

2 The final episode of the series, "Victory" (310), aired in the United States on 12 April 2013.

3 On the 1960 Kubrick film, see the collection edited by Winkler (2007a).

4 On HBO *Rome*, see the volumes by Cyrino (2008a) and (2015).

5 Films contemporary with the STARZ *Spartacus* series that focus on the history of slavery and emancipation in the American South include *Lincoln* (2012), *Django Unchained* (2012), *12 Years a Slave* (2013), and *Belle* (2013).

6 On the Spartacan slave wars, see Shaw (2001); on the reception thread, see Urbainczyk (2004).

7 Sources for the Spartacus narrative include the writings of Plutarch, Appian, and other ancient historians; for more details, see Rodrigues in this volume.

8 Note the forceful capitalization of words as the disclaimer appears on the title card.

9 On the steep trajectory of Roman cinematic sexual depravity, see Cyrino (2014).

10 For recent examinations of the multiplicities of new sexual and erotic modes in the series, see Augoustakis (2013), Raucci (2013), and Strong (2013).

11 Tucker (2010).

12 Stransky (2011).

13 Hibberd (2011b).

14 Ross (2012: 28).

15 The series finale on 12 April 2013 delivered one of the show's best ratings ever: see Hibberd (2013).

16 See the interview in Ross (2013), where DeKnight discusses his vision for the "gut-wrenching" last two scenes of the series.

PART I

Heroes and Heroism

1 *Memories of Storied Heroes*

Alison Futrell

The story of Spartacus, retold in many forms in culture high and low, is an "age-old" story of the struggle for freedom, a story of resistance to imperial oppression. STARZ *Spartacus*, however, presents a more complicated vision of the gladiatorial institution. Its Roman world is a system of profound constraint that operates upon all levels of society. This problematizes the notorious sexual and political license of Roman elites, just as it nuances the choices of the gladiators, who struggle to achieve agency even at the lowest levels of the hierarchy. Stripped of their past, the slaves of the gladiatorial *ludus* rebuild individual identity by redefining categories of value and connection, gender and family, becoming a band of brothers with their own loyalties and their own narratives of meaning, their own arena stories. The parables of past and current champions unfold in the Spartacus arenas to explain the society of the *ludus* and, at the same time, challenge that society, mislead the spectators, and put the lie to the Roman past.

A number of these narratives are embedded within ancient artifacts, as the producers create access to imperial "truths" through an archaeological pathway, tweaking methods of memorialization used in antiquity to reveal truths about the systems of power that bind the characters and channel their life choices. The sculpted portraits in the house of Batiatus represent the champions – the "gods" of the arena – the "storied heroes" whose narrowly expressed narratives both symbolize the family honor and shape its ambition. The long process of the series arc deconstructs the abusive power embedded in these representations, undercutting the ideals celebrated. Visualized counter-narratives also unpack these contrived arena identities, as when graffiti come to animated life to subvert the combat stories and play out the agonized choices driving the fights. The *rudis* of

Gannicus, the wooden sword awarded for unusual gladiatorial success, likewise carries a "commemorative" inscription that is freighted with failure and loss.

In many ways, the producers' choice reflects the complicated relationship with the past crafted by ancient monuments. Roman public spaces were filled with visual rhetoric that reinforced official claims about duty and triumph, with statues, reliefs, and large-scale paintings that commemorated the achievements of individuals and of the community as a whole. Such monuments framed the social and political actions that took place in those spaces, inspiring generations of citizens to emulate their worthy forebears just as they, potentially, reminded them of their present inadequacies in contrast to past glories.[1] Private homes were also venues for this kind of polyvalent memorialization. In the atrium of the elite Roman household, visitors might confront the *imagines* of family ancestors: sculpted portraits, perhaps originally based on wax death masks, with lists of the deceased's major accomplishments appended to them. These individualized images were meant to evoke filial and general respect, to emphasize the generations of achievement that endorsed the family's status. They could also, however, be configured to cast unflattering shadows on less worthy descendants, who aspired now to decadence and entitlement rather than duty and excellence.[2] Other domestic spaces found other purposes for similar images: painted representations invited dinner guests to imagine impossible conviviality, while those invited into the garden found their pastoral leisure informed by the abbreviated likenesses of philosophers, idealized heads mounted on inscribed pedestals in the style of Athenian herms.[3] Objects and representations that crystallized human actions in visual form, whether displayed in public or private spaces, were the acknowledged fabric of collective memory; some Romans likewise were uneasily aware that new monuments or the "restoration" of memorials had the capacity to revise and refocus history.[4]

This use of objects to tell stories fits well into modern habits of representing the ancient past; "faithful" recreations of artifacts in nineteenth-century history painting were perceived to carry a particular kind of authenticity that was valued by increasingly bourgeois audiences and readily embraced by early film studios.[5] The sequential nature of film narratives also enabled object significance to be mobilized to enhance the narrative. Props used by characters in one scene could carry visual resonances forward into multiple contexts, offering to the attentive viewer a richer understanding of the emotional journey of the characters as represented by these items.[6] In the popular imagination of Spartacus, ancient objects likewise have particular weight; archaeological evidence has been valued as a counterbalance to the elite-centered textual tradition hostile to the rebels, as bearing a "hidden" truth that gives the lie to the victor's history.[7]

THE *LUDUS* OF COMMEMORATION

In the villa of Batiatus, portrait heads mounted on quadrangular inscribed pedestals represent the heritage of the family as creators and controllers of the gladiatorial school or *ludus*.[8] In form, these resemble herms, a type of monument particularly associated with Athens, developed initially as images of the god Hermes that marked gateways, roads, and boundaries.[9] The direct gaze of the herm confronted and engaged the viewer, creating a commonality of being, a communication of equals, particularly appropriate to the citizens of a democracy. An erect phallus carved on the front surface of the quadrangular pedestal was the sole corporeal sign of the herm; it likewise represented the mature authority of Athens' citizen body and its capacity to reproduce that authority. Eventually, the heads of herms took on the features of historical leaders, generals, philosophers, and athletes, each with their significance to the confirmation of state values.

The herms in the house of Batiatus, however, veer from this tradition in the selection of targets of commemoration and in the placement of the monument in the domestic interior. Note also that although they bear male genitalia on the front surface of the squared pedestal, as was traditional for herms, these are not vigorously ithyphallic, an absence that connects to the problematic masculinity of the gladiators.[10] Nor are they Roman-style *imagines*, as their location might suggest: these do not represent overachieving male members of the elite family, but of the gladiatorial *familia*, men "created" to play out interactions resonant with Roman values, subordinate to Roman structures of power. The house of Batiatus is centered on these monuments, introduced in a striking visual sequence in which light sweeps over isolated sculpted faces then passes on, concealing and revealing in a dynamic chiaroscuro the "storied champions" of the *ludus* (episode 2). We hear behind this visual the rising roar of the arena spectators, building to rhythmic chants of "Kill! Kill!" as the camera scans up an inscribed herm, revealing only partly the carefully crafted text that binds the stories. Light and shadow, sight and its absence, script abbreviated and read in reverse, these monuments edit, invert, and slide past the hero stories that charge the *ludus*. The room becomes

Figure 1.1 Batiatus (John Hannah) enraged before a herm in episode 2 ("Missio"). STARZ.

a key location for significant action in the series and the monuments become emblematic of the arena stories that are built and rebuilt in the teleplay (Figure 1.1).

We see how this reworking of the "official" story functions in "Legends" (episode 103), in which we enter the hero's narrative of Barca, the so-called "Beast of Carthage," through a visual counterweight to the herm of the champion: a graffito scrawled on the walls of the *ludus*.[11] The graffiti invert the herms in important ways. Located in the space of the gladiators, these are representations created by the champions themselves, crude in form and the product of spontaneous commission. Furthermore, these are energetic figural scenes, depicting the bodies of the gladiators in whole, rather in part. Instead of the static frontal gaze of the herm, graffiti combatants square off against each other, dynamically posed and, as is typical of ancient gladiatorial graffiti, caught at a decisive moment of the event.[12] The camera closes in on Barca, seated in a moment of rare calm, and the graffito on the wall next to him. As the frame zooms in, the graffito transforms into an animated scene that combines live action with superimposed, crude coloration. A voice-over conversation between Varro and Spartacus gives a kind of play-by-play for the match. Barca is literally painted as the survivor of a horrific tournament organized by the Roman victors after they sacked the city of Carthage, center of that Other Empire.[13] Captured Punic prisoners were forced into the arena to fight to the death in a parody of regime collapse, the last matched pair being a young Barca and Mago, the former lord of the Punic "throne of blood." Further moral meaning is assigned to this combat, meaning that doubles to some extent the message of Roman victory: this is a showdown between flourishing youth and strength set against the wisdom of age and experience. Barca "triumphs" over Mago, youth over experience, but also, we learn, son over father, as Barca is made to execute his sole surviving family member, sole compatriot, to stand alone as victorious victim, complicit now in the utter destruction of his social and cultural world and in the structure of the arena narrative. "Is it true?" Spartacus asks, appalled. The response is resoundingly equivocal: "In the world of the gladiator, a man's fame and glory constructs its own truth."

Crixus rises from the stones of the arena, quite literally: he is first recruited by Batiatus from the workers brought to Capua from across the empire to build its amphitheater, the "marvel of the age."[14] His face obscured by tangles of hair, his body hunched over as he trudges to his tasks, Crixus at first sight seems to be just another unskilled laborer. His sole distinction is his habitual anger, as he draws the attention of Batiatus by brawling with another slave.[15] Batiatus claims, however, to see promise in Crixus' eyes, a "spark smoldering in his breast to be ignited on the sands," as he articulates the truth of this seeming paradox to his companion: "Even the lowest man can rise beyond the heavens."[16] Batiatus is being disingenuous in this assessment; his true goal in purchasing Crixus is to draw the eye of Tullius, aspiring local powerbroker and soon-to-be rival of Batiatus. A parallel reading of Crixus' "heart" is offered by Crixus' fellow *tiro* trainee in the *ludus*, Ashur, who claims that the new recruit is "a man with dreams of blood and glory." Nor is Ashur's assertion meant to be taken at face value; the character Ashur schemes his way throughout the series, using many-layered deceptions to secure his own position and survival. The former stoneworker, however, soon embraces the possibilities represented by these arena narratives that are still prospective at best, lies at worst, declaring he "will not die a faceless slave forgotten by history" (episode 2)

The audience knows that, by the time of the first season, Crixus will be the leading champion of the *ludus*, and he will be "Crixus, the Undefeated Gaul!" The painful irony of that "undefeated" epithet is revealed in his back-story in the prequel. In training, the *tiro* Crixus has real difficulty learning to defend against the spear. His fellow gladiators find this surprising; surely as a Gaul he would be most familiar with the spear, the favored weapon of the famous Arverni warriors.[17] It is only after Crixus achieves his first combat victory, struggling against a spear-wielding *hoplomachus*, and earns the mark of the brotherhood that he confesses: as a child, he watched his entire family, fierce warriors though they were, die on the spears of the Arverni. Too young yet to defend them, Crixus was forced instead to serve those who had killed his family as a slave. His personal memories of Gaul, therefore, are haunted by defeat and suffering, tainted by their connection to an imperial trope of Gallic identity. Indeed, at the point he entered the *ludus*, Crixus was "forgotten" through the obliteration of those who knew him from birth, made "faceless" through the erasure of his former identity, his disfiguration literalized by the matted hair that hid him among the stoneworkers. Such is the truth of "the undefeated Gaul." For all those years, however, he has dreamed of honoring his dead with blood and victory, of reconnecting with an imagined warrior community. For Crixus, then, the arena serves as a place to rewrite a personal history, reverse a national tragedy, through actions that resonate outside the meanings imposed by Rome.

Oenomaus' back-story is featured in extended flashbacks (episode 202), reflecting his personal truth in a very dark mirror. Best remembered for the match that ended his gladiatorial career, Oenomaus alone, among a pack of doomed challengers, was able to survive his bout against Theokoles, "the Shadow of Death."[18] He began that career as the sole survivor from a pack of Numidians thrown into The Pit, the anti-arena.[19] Little more than a child at the time, he managed to make his size an asset against the overconfidence of his much larger and more experienced opponent, leaping nimbly onto his chest to slash and stab him. Denizens of The Pit interpreted this startling success in hostile terms: neither strategy nor technique but rather the behavior of a "rabid dog," "a demon belched from the cunt of the Underworld." The Numidian boy was deemed incapable of rather than resistant to training, resistant to the name forced on him by strangers, too stupid to follow the (better) path to swift death. The senior Batiatus, though, sees something in him; indeed, he claims that all that's needed is to "find an ember of purpose and give it breath."

The interaction between the senior Batiatus and the young "Oenomaus" is complicated. The elder Batiatus recognizes the youngster's extraordinary inner strength, but notes that in the House of Champions, one must submit to discipline, "one must learn to kneel if he is ever to rise." The most difficult task, he claims, is to find an inner purpose that drives the life of the combatant and fires the champion. More than mere personal survival, one must fight for something greater. This greater good, however, is tied here neither to the arena institution nor to the power of Rome. Batiatus suggests the will to achieve greatness must come from the individual, whether slave or free: the individual crafts the decision that leads to destiny. When Oenomaus earns his place in the *ludus* and is awarded the Mark of the Brotherhood, he tells his *lanista* that he now feels shame that he fought in The Pit, "absent honor." He has found his place, his destiny, in the arena, where legends are forged and deaths are memorialized; he has found his higher purpose, and that is to tie his life and honor to the House of Batiatus. The rumble of thunder that immediately follows undermines the loftiness of the declaration.

The visualization of Oenomaus' arena story lends retrospective weight to the end of the first season, in which the breakdown of the relationship between Doctore/Oenomaus and Batiatus is set among the herms of the *ludus* champions (episode 113). Batiatus reveals that he intends to pursue a political career, to remove himself from active oversight of the *ludus* and thus abandon, as Doctore understands it, the family legacy of honor. Batiatus hopes to entrust it to a new *lanista*, Doctore himself, who will be emancipated to assume this position. Doctore registers no enthusiasm about the idea. As we know from the narrative in the second season, Oenomaus found his higher calling by surrendering his own individuality to the idea of the House of Batiatus, as a tradition that recognized potential even among the marginal, the lost, the wild, the angry. Can he now embody that House, knowing, as he does, that the herms, the promises represented by the stories of the champions, are distorted monuments to the human spirit, wrenched into being by Batiatus' self-serving manipulation and betrayal? With the failure of the House of Batiatus, Oenomaus returns to The Pit, which represents both his source and his annihilation.

GANNICUS AND THE *RUDIS*

Among the ranks of "storied heroes," Gannicus is a cipher, a man on the edge, a quality literalized visually in his first episode as he sings and sways drunkenly along the cliffside of Batiatus' *ludus*. This is a champion whose "story" is displaced in the prequel: he is given no combat epithet for the match that introduces his character, an absence justified in the teleplay by the alleged incompetence of Batiatus' rival *lanista*, who can't even properly situate the combatants within the appropriate narrative of opposition. As becomes clear, however, his arena story has been in good part effaced by Gannicus himself, whose fatalist life view resists memory and memorialization. As he sees it, slaves' lives are, by their very nature, tremendously focused on the moment, which is, he asserts, liberating in two senses. On the one hand, their servile status means that the "burden of choice and conscience [is] equally removed" (episode 2). There is no question of moral culpability for those who operate under constraint. Furthermore, there are situations particular to the slave-gladiators in which such external constraint cannot effectively function: as Gannicus points out, they are "truly free when [they] fight or fuck." And in the prequel establishing context, that is pretty much all Gannicus does: fight and fuck, drunkenly singing "My Cock Rages On" as he teeters on the edge of imminent death.[20] Gannicus is a cocky guy, focused on immediate needs to be fulfilled. He dismisses the narrative of "destiny," of gods having guided his success: his confidence is based on his refined skill set, a combination of training and talent, and he shows a casual disregard for the discipline that binds the narratives of others.

Gannicus as champion becomes an object of desire, a sort of Helen of Capua, a prized gladiator to be featured at the *primus* event in the new arena, a token to be taken in the fatal competition between Batiatus and Tullius over status and authority in ludic Capua. Gannicus resists objectification, however, and is able to do so because of the nature of the agency granted the gladiators in the series. Champions have to perform and not just on the sands; the sexual spectacles made of – by? – the gladiators are founded on Gannicus, the first to be called to demonstrate his cocksmanship in the sexual venue crafted for the villa space. This becomes one of the key transgressive features of the STARZ series, the performance of sex that fuels multiple economies, and some of the dangers of doing so are clarified through the Gannicus story.[21] Furthermore, the choices the character makes in this sexual arena have moral consequences: they are as doom-laden as those on the sands of combat. Gannicus is compelled to couple with Melitta, one of his dearest friends and the wife of Oenomaus, his gladiatorial brother, and this utterly changes Gannicus' relationship to his cock and to his weapon. No longer able to find swift release in easy sexual encounters, Gannicus is now burdened with frustrated and guilty desire for Melitta, as their previous affection has been not just sexualized but romanticized. His bond with Oenomaus is likewise damaged by the effort to sustain the deception; he cannot support Oenomaus as grieving friend nor as new-made Doctore in the gladiatorial school. Gannicus, it turns out, cannot simply be a pawn: he is, as he drunkenly claimed, a "free" agent when he fights and fucks. Furthermore, he is a moral agent, choosing to pursue the relationship with Melitta even after the initial

Figure 1.2 The *rudis* of Gannicus in episode 6 ("The Bitter End"). STARZ.

forced encounter, fully aware that this choice brings pain in its wake. Gannicus' agency complicates the sociopolitical maneuvering of his ostensible owners and ultimately leads to Gannicus' own emancipation, a freedom that he does not entirely embrace. It also leads to a monument of his own: the *rudis* of Gannicus (Figure 1.2).

Gannicus returns to the terrorized Capua during the Spartacan revolt (episode 205). Tempted by the cash advance promised him for a comeback performance, he avers no interest in politicians or the howling mob, just in wine and women, clearly a reversion to the persona originally established for him, and equally clearly a persona that no longer gives him happiness, since he has lost the moral innocence he claimed before tragedy brought him the *rudis*. Gannicus recognizes the *rudis* as a mark of his continuing subjugation that forever binds his identity to the arena, a painful memorial of what he has lost, his own glories "long forgotten." Like the herm monuments, it tells a very selective story. The form of the *rudis*, the wooden sword, both references and mocks the life of the victorious gladiator. Historically, the *rudis* was presented to an outstanding gladiator in recognition of his career success; it marked the award of freedom from the arena's constraint but did so using a form both impermanent and useless as a weapon.[22] The STARZ *rudis* takes the anti-memorial function even further: the inscribed surface of Gannicus' *rudis* memorializes the names of those he killed, not his own name.[23] It thus suppresses his own achievement: the text inscribes the deaths of men, their final failures at the hands of a nameless "free" man, their "glories long forgotten." The object itself becomes a burden to Gannicus: it must be carried at all times, a bloody and painful past that is always on display, the story of choices he made, as Gannicus tells it, when still a slave.[24]

BECOMING SPARTACUS

The arena story of Spartacus is, of course, central to the series, with the emotional weight of that story introduced in the first moments of the first episode (101). Our main protagonist, in chains, huddles in a darkness punctuated by the screams of spectators sitting above, whose pounding feet shake sand and blood down on him: he is slowly being buried by Rome's gladiatorial power. Much of the episode is flashback, fleshing out the ancient sources' characterization of the historical Spartacus as a former Thracian auxiliary. The series hero ostensibly allies with the Romans to ensure peace through the removal of their mutual foe. From the outset, however, some questions are raised about his essential character; Sura, his wife, claims she cannot imagine her husband without a sword in hand. A vision warns her that he is destined for "great and unfortunate things." He insists, however, that he is committed to a placid life, tilling the soil and raising children. Blood and honor mandate this last campaign. He vows, with his last kiss, to "kill them all"; the kiss takes place against a carefully crafted CGI backdrop of clouds framing a baroque sunrise.

The same episode sees the establishment of the political and social function of the games for Rome's ruling elite. Far from a straightforward celebration of Roman victory, the message of the arena for those who ostensibly control it is complicated and contested.[25] In this case, Glaber is deploying spectacle as a counter-spin, to silence the Senate's critical whispers about his failed leadership in Thrace with the overwhelming roars of the crowd's approval. He offers an exotic rarity, "Thracian blood," meant to reify in performance the victory absent on the battlefield. Once Glaber wins the hearts of the crowd, it is asserted, the Senate will follow.

Expectations are overturned by the event. Our captive hero enters the arena, emerging from a *porta* littered with mutilated corpses, to find himself facing multiple, heavily armed opponents. The audience objects to these uneven odds, odds badly justified by the proclaimed magnitude of his crime: the betrayal of Rome's legions on the field of battle. When he manages to beat the odds, the crowd starts to cheer, screaming "Live! Live! Live!" to indicate their will to the *editor*, the unanimity of opinion visualized by camera shots of both the well-dressed elites and the bosomy poor. This represents a dilemma for the arena leadership. Glaber's goal had been to create the impression of impossible barbarity in Thrace, rationalizing his poor showing of leadership there. The extraordinary courage and vigorous swash of the "barbarian" has quashed that plan. Glaber grouses that they cannot simply free Spartacus; the narrative of his crime cannot be so flexible. Batiatus presents the moderate solution: the Thracian captive will be awarded neither freedom nor death but, it is implied, the deferred terminal sentence of the *ludus*, in which his survival will be a constant service to the needs of internal empire. By what name will he serve? That of "Spartacus," known for Thracian kings of old, those who first made a sinister compact with Roman power.[26] The crowd respond to the decision by shouting this false and fraught new name, a name rising to the heavens as the choral soundtrack swells.

Spartacus' arena narrative fully blooms in episode 107.[27] Batiatus has been pressuring Spartacus to commit fully to the *ludus*, a goal presented as a "comfort" in his fresh bereavement: now that his wife is dead, he can find new meaning in life by embracing the identity of the gladiatorial champion. After all, Batiatus points out, he is "the Bringer of Rain! The Slayer of Death! Behold the man as he becomes legend! In the empire of blood and glory! [His] name will be carved on the pillars of history!"[28] The latter is realized quite literally, as Batiatus has commissioned a new herm for the family collection. Spartacus points out, however, that this is *not* his name, the very loud subtext being that this is not really his story either. But, as the series emphasizes, the herms and the arena narratives do not tell the actual histories of individual gladiators. Batiatus then pushes Spartacus to surrender to a new development of his arena persona; Spartacus, he says, will be featured in the upcoming games of Mercato, a political sponsor of spectacle who plans to honor the storied history of his family by recreating his ancestor's defense of Macedonia from invading Thracians. Spartacus will arenacize the role of M. Minucius Rufus,[29] wearing the actual armor of the long-dead Roman commander, "leading" gladiators dressed as Roman legionaries. They will cut down actual Thracians, prisoners of war who will play the role of the doomed ancestors of the actual current victim/performers of the arena, both *damnati* and champion. Spartacus resists; having heard horror stories about Rufus from his father as a boy, he refuses to dress as a Roman and performatively slaughter his own people. Batiatus commands him to embrace this destiny marked for him by the gods, these "great and wonderful things," and to clear his mind of his former identity and the grief it carries.

Let us tease out the complications of these nested and mutually exclusive identities: the series protagonist, whose real name the audience does not know, is a Thracian auxiliary who refused to fight for Rome on the frontier because to do so would expose his people to attack, would betray those he is sworn to protect. Rome sees this as a betrayal and, captive, he is condemned to death, *ad gladium* in the arena. He overcomes huge odds and is victorious but cannot be forgiven his "betrayal," so he is forced to fight for Rome permanently, wielding the *gladium* in the arena instead of on the distant frontier. He has a new identity forced on him, a series of titles: he is "Spartacus," the name of the ancestral hero kings of Thrace; he is the "bringer of rain," achieved through the offering of gladiators' blood as sacrifice to the gods; and he is the "slayer of death," having killed a monster who was hired to kill champions in the arena. Now he is compelled to take on a new new identity: he is "M. Minucius Rufus," an ancestral *triumphator* of Rome, draped in his antique *phalerae*, the sculpted discs that memorialized Minucius' remarkable success in killing Thracians on the field of battle.[30] He must now execute new prisoners of war, Thracian like he was, *damnati ad gladium* like he was, who are playing the arena role of ancestral Thracians, actual ancestors shared by the condemned prisoners and by their executioner/series protagonist, ancestors who are, in fact, contemporaries of the story behind the construct "Spartacus," compatriots of the historic heroic Thracian kings who bore that name.

Spartacus at last agrees to the strong twist of his arena story, as if he has a choice in the matter, but stipulates that he will take on the role of Rufus alone, without any "legionaries." One gladiator against six *damnati* reverses the odds in his first combat, giving these prisoners the advantage. This condition is meant by Spartacus as a test of divine will: have the gods marked him for a special destiny? The teleplay (and, of course, history) confirms it: Spartacus wins, again, against extraordinary odds.

As he prepares the deathblow for the last *damnatus*, he sees that the condemned Thracian has his own face, or rather the face he wore before he joined the *ludus*, smudged and framed by tangled hair. "Don't!" his former self says. The music rises with a wordless male vocalization, the movement of the audience slows, and the camera focus is pulled to close in on Spartacus. A series of previous scenes then flash back in rapid succession, his life literally passing before his (and our) eyes as he prepares to kill ... himself.[31] In this sequence, Spartacus recognizes himself as literalized victim of the arena but also recognizes that he has assumed a certain agency in the relationship of power that plays out on the sands, and in the destruction of his former identity that involves. There is likewise recognition of his complicity now in the performance of empire and the ongoing mimesis of imperial oppression in Roman amphitheaters that supports and enables it. It is shocking and it is painful and he follows through on the killstroke.

He then turns to the audience, raises his arms to vaunt in "victory," and screams, "I am 'Spartacus'!" The word "Spartacus" echoes over the cheers of the crowd and above the soundtrack. There are cinematic echoes here as well. In the vaunting posture of the protagonist, arms raised and head high, in the framing of the audience reaction, and to a certain extent in the bitter emotional weight of the context, the series *Spartacus* mirrors a key moment in *Gladiator* (2000), when Maximus bellows at the provincial crowd in Zucchabar, "Are you not entertained?" Most obviously, the declaration "I am 'Spartacus'!" is an homage to a climactic scene in the 1960 film *Spartacus*; the surviving rebels, asked to betray their leader to the Roman general, respond by asserting their shared identity, affirming their continuing resistance to Rome by standing, one by one, to declare, "I am Spartacus!" Every subsequent reimagining of the story of the Spartacan revolt must negotiate the powerful impression left by that film, of course, but the series response here reshapes that declaration in a way that profoundly complicates imperial identities and nuances the problems of performance.

Throughout, the series commits to the fully fleshed portrayal of the gladiatorial community that a series format enables. The Spartacan narrative's paradigmatic resistance to Roman oppression is expanded to embrace the accommodation and push-back by multiple players, at multiple levels, engaging with a "Rome" that is far from unitary. Individual gladiators follow individualized paths to reach the *ludus*, finding there pain and hope in different measure, and exercising a range of options within the limitations of their world. Their stories peel back the layers of multiple motivations that drive all humans and honor the power of choices made by the lost, the angry, the defeated.

NOTES

1 See, among many others, Favro (1996: 217–51), Holliday (2002: 24–42), Gowing (2005: 132–59), Flower (2006: 115–59), Beard (2007: 143–86), Sumi (2009: 167–86). The mnemonic function of architecture is apparent in the memory-training techniques of orators which imagined public monuments in the urban landscape as a fixative framework. See

Carruthers (1990: 123–30), who points in particular to the "architectural mnemonic" in the *Rhetoric to Herennius* and in Cicero's *On the Orator*.

2 Such irony is detected, for example, by the Roman historian Sallust, *Jugurthine War* 4 and 85. On the *imagines* in the home, see Flower (1996: 185–222).

3 On interactions with painted visuals at the dinner table, see Fredrick (2003: 309–43). For the Roman use of herms, see Fejfer (2008: 228–33).

4 See, for example, Cicero's presentation (*On the Republic* 5.2) of the changing politics of the Republic as fading paintings of historical narrative, like the triumphal murals that decorated a number of public buildings in downtown Rome; see Gowing (2000: 39–64) and Gowing (2005: 1–27).

5 As claimed by Jean-Léon Gérôme (1904: 26), well-known nineteenth-century painter of the Roman arena, who attributed the success of his painting *Pollice Verso* (1874) to the fact that he had his model dress in exact duplicates of armor found at Pompeii: "my model, dressed up in them, [was] to all intents and purposes a gladiator."

6 Sometimes referred to as "McKee objects," after noted screenwriting guru Robert McKee.

7 Kirk Douglas, in the pre-production phase of *Spartacus*, was inspired by his own double reading of the "grandeur" of Roman archaeological remains, which he found redolent of the suffering of the forced labor responsible for such monumental ruins. See Douglas (1988: 304) and also Futrell (2001).

8 The ancestral masks or *imagines* one might expect to find in a Roman-inflected household do make an appearance in the series prequel for the funeral of the senior Batiatus and in the second season at the Roman home of Glaber.

9 On Athenian herms, see Osborne (1985), Fredal (2006: 134–56), and Quinn (2007).

10 Gladiators surrendered the bodily autonomy, the impenetrability, considered the essential quality of the free man by subjecting themselves to the discipline of the *ludus*. They were also targets of the audience's gaze, their bodies on display, which may have intensified their desirability. See Futrell (2006: 130–5, 146–7) and Dickson and Cornelius (2015). For the unmanly masculinity of those subject to discipline, see Parker (1999) and Alston (1998). The non-erect *phalloi* in the herms of Batiatus also likely reflect standards for visual representation, even for cable television, even for STARZ. For problematic *phalloi*, see the Gannicus section below.

11 Two other major arena stories are re-purposed in graffiti form in this episode: Crixus' bout against the Gargan Twins/Gargantuans, former pirates turned fur-clad "beasts," and Oenomaus' showdown with Theokoles, "Shadow of the Gods," represented in the animated graffito

literally as a shadow that splits asunder his terrified foes. Oenomaus goes on to "glorious," career-ending survival.

12 These moments of crisis are selected foci in most ancient arena art; what constitutes that crisis varies depending on the kind of event and the "choice" involved, as detailed in Brown (1992). On gladiatorial graffiti, see also Jacobelli (2003: 48–52) and Garraffoni and Funari (2009: 185–93).

13 The Romans destroyed Carthage in 146 BC, some seven decades before the events of the first season.

14 The existence of a formal stone amphitheater at Capua, with an elliptical arena, podium structure, and concentric vaulted seating, has been dated to the late second century BC, roughly contemporary with others at Cumae and Liternum. Recent work, however, has challenged this dating, pointing to the period of Sulla's exertions to realign loyalty after the war against her Italian allies (90–88 BC) as a more likely context for this and other amphitheater construction to have taken place. The great amphitheater there, the so-called "Campanian Amphitheater," dates to the imperial period. See Golvin (1988: 24–5, 204–5) and especially Welch (2007: 72–101), who offers much insight on the late Republican context for arena construction.

15 This may be a callout to the Kirk Douglas role in *Spartacus* (1960), who is likewise introduced as a worker in stone, likewise with a habit of rage-fueled resistance to Roman oppression, foregrounding the Spartacan rebellion in so doing. Note, however, that Crixus is fighting a fellow slave, not hamstringing a guard who prevented him from helping a fellow slave, as is the case in the earlier film.

16 Compare similar ancient maxims about lowly gladiators demonstrating surprising wellsprings of courage and discipline in the arena. See, for example, Cicero, *Tusculan Disputations* 2.17 and Pliny, *Panegyric* 33.

17 The Arverni were one of the more prominent tribal chiefdoms in pre-Roman Gaul (Strabo, *Geography* 4.2), representing an expansionist threat to neighbors and a catalyst for Rome's opportunistic warfare that eventually led to conquest. Vercingetorix, leader of the last-ditch effort to resist Caesar, was an Arverni leader.

18 The fight against Theokoles was inscribed on Oenomaus' body as well; in episode 105, Doctore reads his scars (usually hidden by the cuirass of his office) to narrate that near-fatal encounter. He does so, he says, because Crixus and Spartacus will not listen to his spoken words. The scars tell a more penetrating tale, overlaid with the echoing screams of Oenomaus' past.

19 The Pit, a creation of the STARZ series, is an inversion of the public arena, a subterranean, covert combat venue, devoid of honor, where monsters clash in horrific bloodfests; see further Shillock (2015). All combats in The Pit are *sine missione*, in this venue that owes much of its cinematic origin to Thunderdome in the third of George Miller's *Mad*

Max films (1985): two men enter, one man leaves. Pit armor involves makeshift leather, metal, and body paint. Pit fighters use improvised weapons, crafted with bone and spikes and smeared with blood and flesh, whose distribution is likewise improvised, irrespective of skill and training. This may be a reference to the "dishonorable" weapons in Plutarch (*Life of Crassus* 9) that the historical Spartacans discarded in preference for those of legionaries.

20 Every night Gannicus seeks carnal pleasures, because every day could be his last, or so he asserts in episode 1.

21 See Strong (2013: 167–82).

22 See Martial, *On the Spectacles* 39, in which the emperor Titus, as part of the games celebrating the opening of the Colosseum or Flavian Amphitheater, ostentatiously sent the *rudis* to both Verus and Priscus, combatants in an unusually long and hotly contested match; this recognition fits a pattern of extraordinary imperial generosity on display throughout Martial's book. Wooden swords were also used in gladiatorial training, which made use of retired veterans of the arena as *doctores*, specialists in certain types of weaponry.

23 If indeed "Gannicus" is his own name, rather than an arena moniker. The *rudis* prop is marked with a multiplicity of names, many of them taken from such authentic ancient artifacts as the Borghese gladiator mosaic, where can be found most of the names positioned on the last two rows of the show *rudis*: for example, Astivus, Astacius, Baccibus, Cupido, Bellerifons, Aureus, Talamonius, Melea[ger] (*CIL* VI 10206).

24 Hardly a coincidence that the problematic of the *rudis* is laid out in the episode titled "Libertus" (episode 205); here as elsewhere, freedom is not free.

25 See Futrell (1997: 29–52) and (2006: 11–51). See also Parker (1999) on the specifics of communication between *editor* and audience.

26 The reference here is to the Spartokid dynasty of Bosporus.

27 Referencing the vision of Sura, which has been iterated in multiple flashbacks by this point.

28 Batiatus repeats here Spartacus' new arena epithet, presented previously in episode 106, then, as here, surrounded by the herms. Part of this newly crafted identity involves the change of Spartacus' armory to that of a *dimachaerus*, a combat type that uses two swords. The defeated Theokoles was a *dimachaerus* and Spartacus has now "taken" his weapons as a constant visual sign of his victory.

29 Rufus was the historical proconsular governor of Macedonia in 110 BC, who triumphed in 106.

30 See Maxfield (1981: 91–5, 256) on the social and political value of these signs. Maxfield points to Marius' use specifically of his *phalerae* and scars as monuments to personal excellence that were earned, in contrast to the *imagines* of nobility, which are inherited; cf. Marius on *imagines* above with Sallust, *Jugurthine War* 85.29.

31 Note that this is a visualization of Batiatus' demand that, once he has killed the last of his countrymen, his past life dies with them, that he must embrace his fate and destiny as Spartacus, the Champion of Capua.

2 From Kubrick's Political Icon to Television Sex Symbol

Nuno Simões Rodrigues

When Stanley Kubrick presented his version of Spartacus in 1960, the film was more than just a cinematic reading of an historical event. Although this was not the first film adaptation of the story of the gladiator who led the so-called Third Slave War (73–71 BC), Kubrick's version undoubtedly established a permanent image of the Thracian in the contemporary popular imagination. A big part of this representation has to do with the political and ideological nature that Kubrick's film imprinted on the character of Spartacus. In the early twenty-first century, this image of the gladiator-slave emerged again, but the political symbolism changed toward a more sexualized meaning through the representation offered by the STARZ series. It is this metamorphosis that I aim to analyze in this chapter.

THE 1960 SPARTACUS

Much has been written about the context that led to the production of Kubrick's film.[1] This context remains crucial to our understanding of the importance of the film and what it represented for the second half of the twentieth century. As Martin Winkler notes, "To do justice to any literary or filmic text, scholars must be closely familiar with it: with its content, contexts, origin, reception, and existing scholarship."[2] Thus it is worth noting that Kubrick's film is based on the novel *Spartacus* by American writer Howard Fast, published in 1951 during the Cold War, while it is also important to recall that Fast was a leftist activist and a member of the American Communist Party from 1943 to 1957.[3] Fast's version of the Thracian slave, therefore, echoes the image developed in the nineteenth century of a hero who represented the values of Marxist ideology, as Spartacus was regarded as the leader of a slave rebellion and reflected, as a result, an archetype of social resistance and class struggle.[4] Marx's reading of Appian's Roman history, together with the events of his own time, namely the revolution led by Garibaldi in Italy and the American Civil War, had aroused in him such an interest in Spartacus' character that he called him "a genuine representative of the ancient proletariat."[5] This identification of the historical character was clearly rhetorical, since Marx wanted to use Spartacus as a representation of his own conception of history and ideology.

While Marx's perspective was not innovative in terms of a hermeneutical exercise, it had the effect of launching a portrayal of the ancient figure that reached its peak precisely in Fast's novel and Kubrick's film. As several authors have noted,[6] the recovery of Spartacus' image began in the second half of the eighteenth century, in the context of the Enlightenment, and within the framework of the American and French Revolutions. At the time, the figure of the slave-gladiator emerged as a projection and symbol of the struggle for human rights and freedom and resistance against oppression and tyranny: this was in fact a romantic vision of the hero that reflected the main values of a time of change. Historian Brent D. Shaw notes this particular interpretation of Spartacus was manifest in historiographical works on the Roman Republic that were published in the eighteenth century, in which the role of Spartacus as a slave is emphasized.[7] However, Shaw also notes the most significant statement of that time about the Thracian gladiator was perhaps that of Voltaire in 1769, when he referred to the rebellion of the slaves in 73–71 BC as "a just war" and "the only just war in History."[8]

This overview of the interpretation of the Spartacus figure in the second half of the eighteenth century, to which can be added a number of works of fiction, including dramatic plays and operas, shows the significance of the historical character of the Thracian slave during the period. Spartacus was used as a flag for debates about freedom, slavery, and independence, which in the eighteenth century were the order of the day. During the nineteenth century, however, Spartacus came to be understood above all as a representative of the ideals of independence, associated with the emergence of the new nations that were emancipated from European rule or those that were affirming themselves within Europe.[9] The play *The Gladiator* (1831), written by the American playwright Robert Montgomery Bird, and the novel *Spartaco* (1874), the romance of the Italian writer Raffaello Giovagnoli, are two examples of this ideological manipulation of the character, where the chief goal was to represent the armed revolutionary struggle against oppressive and colonialist states; but these two works relegate the issue of slavery to the background. Note, too, that the first film productions about Spartacus, which were made in Italy in the first decades of the twentieth century, were based on the novel by Giovagnoli.[10]

The image of Spartacus in the Marxist reading, while not losing its ideological expression, changed significantly. Within this new interpretation, the anti-slavery debate and independence ideals gave way to the ideology of class struggle and egalitarianism, especially as developed by Lenin and Stalin.[11] As Shaw observes, "Within this acceptable version of history, Spartacus suddenly assumed a new and greater importance. After all, he had actually led the final great slave war, the revolutionary armed struggle that, in Stalin's view, was the direct cause of the overthrow of the ancient slave system."[12] Soon this view would influence other models of resistance and political protest in the first half of the twentieth century, such as that led by Rosa Luxemburg and Karl Liebknecht during the First World War. The *Spartakusbund* was a political leftist movement that opposed the war and whose public protests took the form of subversive pamphlets signed with the name "Spartacus."[13] In this context, the figure of the rebel gladiator began to take shape as an icon of the so-called left wing of political thought.

These events were at the root of the increased use of Spartacus' image in the 1940s and 1950s, once again in a political context, but now within the politically dangerous America of McCarthyism: it was during this period that Fast wrote the novel *Spartacus*. Fast's socialist convictions led him to be blacklisted by the FBI, an event that constrained the publication of the novel, which was not released until 1951 and was self-published.[14] The use of the historical Thracian gladiator's character as a theme of inspiration for a fictional narrative was not, as we have seen, a novelty. Both Giovagnoli's *Spartaco* and Arthur Koestler's *The Gladiators* (1939) show how Fast's idea was far from original: his originality, however, lay in the specific rhetorical use of the image. While Giovagnoli was chiefly preoccupied with the ideas of independence and nationalism, and Koestler was building a Spartacus moved by revolutionary ideals who ended up degenerating into the abuse of power (thereby offering a critique of what European socialism had become in the third decade of the twentieth century), Fast's hero claimed to be the prototype of the socialist, if not communist, man, the heir to the view that Marx and his ideological successors had of him.[15]

After reading Fast's novel in 1957, Kirk Douglas began a process of self-identification with the historical character of Spartacus as

shaped by the American writer. In fact, although the fictional character of Spartacus was rooted in what the ancient sources report about
the hero, the novel extended far beyond that.[16] Douglas identified
mainly with the ideology that Fast had used to create his version
of the historical character, revealing the significant impact that the
rhetorical manipulation of historical images had on the construction of the myth of Spartacus. As a result, the Thracian gladiator on
film ended up being used as a metaphor for the struggle against the
modern capitalist system, represented by ancient Rome, as he became
the figure of a martyr killed in battle for his ideals.[17]

Even though Kubrick relied on Fast's *Spartacus* for his film, we must
not forget that before the American film, the Italians had released the
film *Spartaco* in 1953, directed by Riccardo Freda, and that this film
had already played an important political role in post-war Italy. As
noted by Maria Wyke, after a series of productions in which Roman
antiquity was evoked as a political model for the present, particularly
in the formulation of nationalist models for Mussolini and Italian
fascism, the first production with a classical subject in post-war Italy
was *Fabiola* (1949).[18] The novelty of this movie was the fact that it
focused on the victims of Roman imperialism, namely the Christians,
and not on the Romans' military achievements, as the earlier films
had emphasized. Freda's *Spartaco* followed *Fabiola*'s rhetoric, as the
hero regained the image of a rebel against the oppressive forces of
a totalitarian state. According to Wyke, some of the sequences of
this film even use the figure of the crucified Christ as a prototype
for the representation of the Thracian slave, which is symptomatic
of the functions the movie played in the contexts of its production
and release.[19] Thus, Freda's film was mainly exhibiting "the Thracian
gladiator as a prototype of Italy's wartime resistance heroes" and that
"Italy had more than paid for its support of Mussolini's regime with
the courage its partisans had demonstrated in resisting the German
occupation."[20] In this sense, the Italian Spartacus film from 1953
already had an ideologically marked political function, making it
the forerunner of the American film released in 1960, albeit with a
different purpose.

Although Kubrick's name ultimately became associated with the
direction of *Spartacus*, he was not the only director responsible for the
film. The circumstances surrounding its production are well known
and have been widely detailed in scholarship.[21] But it should be noted
that while Douglas was the main force in the production of the film,
the first director associated with the project was Anthony Mann, who
would later go on to direct *The Fall of the Roman Empire* (1964). As

noted above, Douglas was deeply impressed by reading Fast's novel, in which he recognized in particular the themes of the human struggle for freedom and resistance to oppression. In order to emphasize these motifs, Douglas hired screenwriter Dalton Trumbo, a left-wing sympathizer who was known as one of the infamous "Hollywood Ten" for refusing to report to the authorities the names of people involved with the socialist and communist political movements.[22] For this reason, Trumbo had been imprisoned and, even after his release, was forced to work under a pseudonym. The 1960 *Spartacus* marked Trumbo's return to authoring a screenplay under his real name.[23]

Douglas began the project with Trumbo's text and direction provided by Mann. But after shooting some of the early scenes, Douglas replaced Mann with Kubrick, who set the definitive form of the film, as exemplified by, for example, the minimalist sets and the stark realism of many of the scenes.[24] However, as noted by Monica Cyrino, the story that supports the screenplay is based on Douglas' initial idea of Spartacus. The character dialogue written by Trumbo helped accomplish this specific representation of the Thracian gladiator in the film and established the meaning of his political movement.[25]

This idealization of the political Spartacus is naturally visible over several sequences in the film, as well as through some of the marketing materials used for promotion at the time. Alison Futrell highlights how the souvenir guide cover of the premiere played with elements that were intended to suggest a clear political ideology. On a red background, pictures of the movie characters appear represented on coins, thereby becoming "money, the organizing force of a capitalist system, set against the red of Communist solidarity."[26] Another point to note is the balance achieved in the distribution of the characters, in which Spartacus takes on a paternal role, Varinia (Jean Simmons) a maternal function, and Antoninus (Tony Curtis) embodies the figure of a son. Thus, the characters refer to a sort of a "holy family" in the communist system, in which everyone has a well-defined role in the struggle for the fulfillment of utopia.[27] The use of this familial image in the film is not unique.

According to the ancient sources (Plutarch, *Life of Crassus* 11), Spartacus died in combat and his body was never found. But Kubrick's film shows the gladiator suffering crucifixion with the other rebels, an innovation that was also used in the Italian film of 1953. This cinematic option may have derived not only from the fact that death by crucifixion was usually applied to slaves as a *supplicium seruile* (and sources tell us some of the rebel slaves were indeed crucified), but also from the intention to link the rebel gladiator to the figure of Jesus of Nazareth, albeit in an agnostic and perhaps heretical fashion. Together with the familial unity, the crucifixion scene offers the "other side of the Christian message."[28] Associations with the theme of Christ's passion are clear: Spartacus is crucified, and Varinia remains at the cross holding their son; Varinia wears a blue tunic, a color that often symbolizes the Virgin Mary; the wife touches the feet of the crucified husband, now as an *uxor dolorosa*; and beside them, Batiatus (Peter Ustinov) watches the scene, as he hurries Varinia, saying to her, "Have mercy on us."[29] In this openly materialistic context, the holy family image reveals itself in an almost mystical way.

Yet there are elements in the design of the novel and the screenplay that seem clearly anachronistic and incongruent with the ancient sociohistorical realities. It seem improbable, for example, that the rebellion led by Spartacus could gather together under one ideology, uniting slaves as diverse in their origins and functions as those in Kubrick's film. Mine-slaves or gladiator-slaves, like Spartacus, would hardly have had the same interests as domestic and elite slaves, such as Antoninus (Curtis), who is identified as an educated singer. Likewise, the idea of fellowship and community among the slaves, celebrated throughout the movie, also seems forced to fit into a specific ideology and unlikely to portray historical accuracy.[30] These are ideas that seem to have more to do with nineteenth- and twentieth-century societies than with classical antiquity.

As Shaw has pointed out, the most striking representation of Spartacus in the modern world is that of Douglas on horseback, with his sword held high and a determined look on his face;[31] this is the expression of someone who is ready to die fighting for an ideal. And indeed, this image sums up the whole structure of the film. One may add also the rousing speech of unity and kinship that Spartacus delivers before the final battle to the great community of the slave army with their simple and communal life, as opposed to the brutal individualism of the Romans. The reconstruction of aristocratic and elitist Roman settings gives the film's audience a harsh contrast to the world of the slaves in the film. The sequence in which all types of slaves, varying in age, gender, and social integration, come to Spartacus ready for combat evokes the ideology of the collective utopia so dear to socialist views. The varied provenance of the gladiators, among whom we find blacks and Jews, such as Draba (Woody Strode)[32] and David (Harold J. Stone), is also symptomatic of the values at stake and the political message of the film. The attack on the patricians attending the special gladiatorial combat followed by the rebellion at the *ludus* are at the center of the film's economy, as is Draba's refusal to kill the defeated Spartacus or the forced fight between the Roman nobles, as if they were animals, for the entertainment of the rebel slaves. These are just some examples of how the creators of the 1960 film realized their particular vision of Spartacus. But perhaps the most emblematic scene is the one in which the rebel slaves cry aloud to be recognized as the leaders of the revolt, with the memorable phrase "I am Spartacus!"[33]

In this highly politicized context there is little room for eroticism and sexuality. These are not, however, totally excluded from Kubrick's perspective. But the little we find of these elements in the film is almost always associated with perversion and debauchery, relegated to a decadent Roman society whose values are determined in the first place by what money can buy – such as a deadly gladiatorial combat for the titillation of some – as befits a capitalist system,[34] a kind of "bourgeois elite" before the term was coined. Rome and the Romans clearly represent this perspective in the 1960 film. Moreover, the dialogue between Gracchus (Charles Laughton) and Batiatus on the subject of women, their beauty and sexuality, is above all a brilliant philosophical exercise with an Epicurean, even Cynical tone from which eroticism is mostly excluded. Still, Gracchus does not hesitate to confirm that he has a promiscuous nature, which has forced him to reject traditional marriage vows, as the character claims with an essentially modern irony.

One scene in particular in Kubrick's film may be seen as suggesting eroticism, but it seems to revolve chiefly around the idea of love.[35] This is the moment early in the film when Batiatus and Marcellus (Charles McGraw) select Varinia to mate with Spartacus. The two Romans display a conspicuous attitude as if they were dealing with animals, as they go so far as to take on the voyeuristic posture of those who watch cattle breeding to ensure procreation. But Spartacus' and Varinia's reactions are clearly opposed to this bureaucratic coldness that allows the distribution of the females by the males. Spartacus desires Varinia, but refuses to be watched like a beast: he shouts, "I am not an animal!" Varinia confirms this with even greater dignity, for while Spartacus is held off by Batiatus and Marcellus' voyeurism, Varinia feels offended by the way she is used, without any option, to satisfy a man, regardless of who he is. At that moment, her innocent desire for Spartacus turns into love and ultimately overcomes the simple impulses of the flesh.

Thus there is a prominent and positive place for love in Kubrick's film. This Spartacus is not a mere sex symbol, but rather someone who struggles for dignity in the act of love. His restraint is sublime and is manifested in the way he loves Varinia's body, like someone who admires a work of art. When Varinia serves a meal to Spartacus, small gestures and touches acquire strongly emotional overtones, with a mix of sensuality and affection. Henceforth, Spartacus and Varinia will always be a couple, evoking the idea of a happy family, the basis of society, but in an often nearly asexual manner.[36]

Even the scene of Varinia's bath, in which Jean Simmons' nudity is hinted at quite assertively and in which Spartacus says he wants to make love to his wife, has very little of the sensual or erotic, with a puerile, indeed almost sacred tone pervading the characterization of the young woman. Note that before they share a passionate kiss, Spartacus kisses her on the forehead, which encapsulates the overall modest tone of the film. Although the couple embrace naked under the robe of the Thracian, and Varinia confesses to being pregnant (intercourse thus being implicit), this is a "chaste" sexuality between a legitimate couple and not something promiscuous, perverse, or debauched.

Sexuality in its more carnal sense does have a role in the film, however, especially in two scenes where the theme of a depraved sexuality is shown to be associated with the Romans and their corrupt authority.[37] The first is when the special gladiatorial combat takes place between Spartacus and Draba. The scene is displayed in a double hierarchical structure, providing two parallel readings. On the one hand, down in the arena, we see the struggle for survival of two men trapped in an unfair system, men who are being used as if they were animals. Still, they do not despise their dignity as human beings, which is manifested especially when Draba refuses to kill Spartacus, an act that is an indication of solidarity among individuals, as expected in a communist and egalitarian society.[38] But while this drama takes place in the arena, up above in the balcony where the Romans are watching we see two men and two women whose emotions and feelings seem to be very far from those shared by Spartacus and Draba. The Romans are Crassus (Laurence Olivier) and Glaber (John Dall), paired with Helena (Nina Foch) and Claudia (Joanna Barnes). These four elite Romans have come to Capua to attend a gladiatorial combat simply for fun and titillation. For this purpose, the two women admire and select the combatants, as if they were choosing animals, and request that the gladiators fight half-naked, with only clothes "enough for modesty."

Clearly, the intention is to present the two Roman elite women as vicious, erotically capricious if not debauched, delighting in the sight of the half-naked bodies of the male slaves. After choosing the men who will face off in the arena to the death and approving the choice of the weapons they will use, Helena casually complains about the burning sun: the contrast with the dignified posture of Spartacus is evident. Note that the episode makes little historical sense, since we know that gladiators had their own equipment which was essential for their definition.[39] But in terms of ideology and message, the scene allows for the construction of an image through the rhetoric of the male body, eroticism, and sexual language, but one that has no place in the emerging communist utopia. Such sexuality has its place only in the decadent society the Romans typify. It is so significant that this is one of the scenes that precede and partly explain the rebellion of the slaves in the *ludus*.

The second scene in Kubrick's film is the famous "oysters and snails" sequence starring Olivier and Curtis that was censored from the original cut of the film but restored in 1991.[40] In this scene, Crassus, who has also been shown to desire Varinia, demonstrates his attraction to Antoninus, thus embodying a Roman outlook that desire and sexual attraction were fluid and could be felt toward any individual, regardless of gender: hence, as Crassus declares to his handsome slave boy, he enjoys "both oysters *and* snails." As long as the role played in the relationship was of the active male, the relationship was not considered socially or morally inappropriate.[41] Moreover, if the individual who took on the passive role was a slave, there was no reason to criticize the person who played the active role in the relationship. In Kubrick's film, this issue is portrayed in Crassus' character, albeit in a significantly subtle way. But it is most significant that this particular philosophy of sexuality, subject to unfavorable judgment and opinions by Western societies in the twentieth century (despite the way homosexuality has been understood, the objectification of passive individuals is totally repudiated), appears associated with one of the "villains" of the plot. Moreover, for Fast, Kubrick, and Douglas, Crassus personifies the oppressive establishment that must be fought, an attitude that emphasizes the negative connotations for the sexual custom or practice here suggested.

The Socratic nature of the dialogue that takes place between Crassus and Antoninus has been widely discussed,[42] just as it evokes yet another reflection of Trumbo's genius in the screenplay. With Alex North's dissonant music in the background and while he bathes with the help of his domestic slave, Crassus makes a clever apology for bisexuality using the remarkable metaphor of oysters and snails, culminating in the paradigmatic statement that "taste is not a question of morality." Crassus comes out of the bath and, after confessing his simultaneous appreciation for oysters and snails as he is being toweled off by Antoninus, faces the view of Rome outside his villa window, and proclaims, "You must serve her! You must abase yourself before her! You must grovel at her feet! You must love her!"

The words spoken by the Roman general suggest a double meaning with undertones of a sexual nature. In an ancient Roman context, Crassus' suggestion is in no way dishonorable, neither to the patrician nor to the slave; but this was not the case for the audience in 1960. Moreover, given the political ideology that sustains Kubrick's film, the fact that such feelings and attitudes toward sexuality, homosexuality in this case, are associated with the character of Crassus should not be disregarded. The meaning of this association can only be negative and clearly reflects abusive power relations.[43] It is nonetheless significant that precisely after this episode Antoninus leaves the house to which he belongs to join the rebel slaves led by Spartacus. In fact, in the censored version, the omission of the scene makes Antoninus' escape both meaningless and confusing. The fact that a domestic slave like Antoninus would carry out such an action, joining gladiators and mine-slaves in a rebellion, may be considered improbable. But by doing so, he is judging the dissolute sexual attitude of Crassus, who is thereby shown to be the debauched and immoral Roman.

THE SPARTACUS OF STARZ

When compared to the 1960 film, the television series created by Steven S. DeKnight is far from focused on the same type of political ideology; the STARZ *Spartacus* has an altogether different set of objectives. In fact, the argument of the series, which was divided into three seasons (*Blood and Sand*, *Vengeance*, and *War of the Damned*) and a prequel (*Gods of the Arena*), uses historical data from the ancient sources, but also employs some of the previously proposed fictional plots from earlier receptions. Thus, for example, from the historical sources we find "real" characters like Spartacus (Andy Whitfield and Liam McIntyre), Crixus (Manu Bennett), Oenomaus (Peter Mensah), Gannicus (Dustin Clare), Batiatus (John Hannah), Glaber (Craig Parker), Crassus (Simon Merrells), and Julius Caesar (Todd Lasance). There is a kind of realism, too, in the spoken English dialogue, which closely follows the rhythms of Latin syntax, using absolute expressions such as "Gratitude!" or "Apologies!" as well as numerous Latin terms, such as *dominus*, *medicus*, or *ludus*.

Above all, what seems to matter in this new version of Spartacus is the glorified and eroticized image of mostly the male, but also the female, bodies.[44] These visuals are heightened by the use of CGI, as in Zack Snyder's *300* (2007), which overemphasizes certain aesthetic details, such as the vivid chromatic aspects and the graphic representation of the bodies in motion. The main character retains his essential characterization as a deliverer hero who is clearly associated with positive values such as the search for justice: he is an avenger of the oppressed and the enslaved. But the nature and disposition of this new Spartacus appears to be different from the one found in Kubrick's film. While the new television series expresses contemporary social concerns and advances particular issues, especially in terms of the portrayal of same-sex relationships, it is difficult to find a purely political message, as in previous versions of the story.

To be sure, the representation of the physical body dominates this new production, as well as a heightening of the depiction of the sexuality and violence associated with it. In terms of the display of the female body, the appearance of female nudity and sexuality is ubiquitous and frequent. For example, the women who attend the shows at the amphitheater often exhibit bare breasts. There are scenes of lesbian sex, as between two female slaves in the house of the senator Albinius (Kevin J. Wilson) in episode 101; while these scenes are shown to perplex the enslaved Thracians as they are exposed to this strange new type of physicality, they also bring back to the screen a modernization of the old topic of the "Roman orgy" in ancient world movies. In episode 106, the orgy is depicted as even wilder, mixing both nudity and sexual acts, and it takes place in the *ludus* among the gladiators. Spartacus, however, remains stoic before the spectacle of male and female bodies sweaty in intercourse. Likewise, Varro (Jai Courtney) remains a restrained hero. A similar scene of group sex is shown to take place in a brothel (episode 201), but now Spartacus is already the avenging warrior: the debauched are those who must die. Here too, sexuality does not cease to represent ideas associated with corrupt authority and power.

But there is no doubt that it is the male body that is most often on display and exalted. The depiction of slaves and gladiators becomes a pretext for the exhibition of male nudity. Even the gladiatorial fights are opportunities for the exposure of the male body. Likewise, the most common way the series presents the slaves, particularly the household ones, is by displaying their bodies. In one scene during a party at the house of Batiatus (episode 103), the moments before a special gladiatorial fight are filled with shots of the elite matrons admiring the bodies of the gladiators, and the ladies do not hesitate to touch and fondle them with a heavy dose of eroticism and sensuality.

Along with the display of the objectified body, depictions of sexual intercourse are another common feature of the series. Sexual relations even take place among the audience members in the amphitheaters, for instance, as the series links together the notions of sexuality and spectatorship. In the very first episode of the series, the future slave Spartacus makes love to his wife Sura (Erin Cummings), and the bodies of both spouses are visible in full nudity. The historical sources only refer to a woman of Spartacus, without naming her, saying she was a fervent devotee of Dionysus (Plutarch, *Crassus* 8.4). In Kubrick's film, the character of Varinia is not even Thracian, but rather a slave from Britannia. In the STARZ version, however, Sura's ethnicity is consistent with Plutarch's testimony, and her mantic nature is highlighted. In episode 107, the nudity of the couple is once again the center of the sequence, filmed mostly in the shadows. This scene serves to establish a contrast with the presentation of the funeral rites of Sura that will soon follow it, leading the viewer to associate nudity and sexuality with life, in stark contrast to death and loss of love.

In the first episode of the series (101), the Roman couple Glaber and Ilithyia (Viva Bianca) also engages in a scene of vigorous sexual relations that exposes the woman's full nudity. The scene presents Ilithyia as a sexually eager woman, who demonstrates a level of sexual desire that is apparently disproportionate to the alleged restraint of Roman marriage.[45] Although this scene also presents a married couple, the behavior of Ilithyia is crucially different from that of Sura: Spartacus and Sura are shown to make love, whereas Glaber and Ilithya are having sex.

After coming home from a party at the house of Albinius (episode 102), the married couple Batiatus and Lucretia (Lucy Lawless) are casually shown to be sexually stimulated by slaves, as they discuss business and social networks, which then ends with the consummation of the sexual act between husband and wife. The couple enjoy sex in front of all the slaves, in a scene of obvious exhibitionism/voyeurism. The same type of sexual exhibitionism is presented in subsequent episodes (106 and 109). In addition, Lucretia uses the gladiator Crixus for sex (episode 103): the dialogue between the two is entirely sexualized and the images follow the tone of the words. Lucretia appears almost naked in front of Crixus and does not hesitate to be united with the gladiator (also in episode 108). The notion of relations between the two is certainly exaggerated but not totally unfounded: Roman matrons were known to seek out the sexual services of famous gladiators.[46] In fact, a gladiator's success was associated with the sexual attraction provoked in the audience.[47] It should be noted, however, that penalties for adultery were heavy and therefore the risks were great.

The overall narrative and visual purpose of these scenes seems to be to give the viewer the idea of normality regarding ancient – and more specifically Roman – sexuality.[48] But this approach also suggests a kind of "pornotopia," a term used by Gideon Nisbet in terms of the exploitation of antiquity as a setting for adult movies.[49] Thus, the series conveys the notion that in Roman times, before Christianity, morality was different, more permissive, and sexuality was understood accordingly.

After purchasing a new lot of slaves to be trained in the *ludus* (episode 108), Batiatius presents them to the members of the house. With them is the elite matron Ilithyia, whom Batiatus and Lucretia try to convince to buy a gladiator for her own enjoyment. Given her indecision, Batiatus suggests that Ilithyia look at the *virtus* of the new gladiators: on his master's suggestion, the *doctore* orders the slaves to strip their garments and to stand completely naked. The camera moves slowly behind them as each slave removes his *subligaculum* ("loin cloth"), revealing their buttocks. Finally, the camera halts at Segovax, the Gaul, who also displays an oversized penis. Delighted at the sight, Ilithyia exclaims: "He has truly been blessed by the god Priapus!" As a Roman matron, Ilithyia is used here as a symbol of the pornotopic excesses attributed to the pre-Christian ancient world. This is a markedly contemporary image of antiquity as something both good and bad, leaving it up the viewer to decide what position to take.

Three important scenes highlight the sexualized way in which the gladiators are presented in the series. The first takes place in the third episode of the first season: to capture the attention and interest of Ilithyia, Lucretia exhibits some of the best gladiators of Batiatus' house. Ilithyia is fascinated with them and so Lucretia prepares a show, in which Varro is forced to copulate with a female slave, to the delight of all the Romans who attend the event and watch the gladiator and the slave mating in full view like animals. The episode has a greater impact because Varro is a Roman and free gladiator, who has opted for life in the *ludus* to raise enough money to pay off his debts and return to his wife. Lucretia's choice aims at humiliating Varro and at the same time functions as a characterization of the elite and debauched Romans who, giving in to their most basic impulses, are gratified and titillated by such a scene. In this regard, the ethical value of the episode is functional. But at the end of the scene, what stays in the memory of the viewers is the image of the explicit sexual act between the female slave and the gladiator.

The second scene can be found in the eighth episode of the first season: it is the end of the month, and the gladiators are entitled to receive as a reward either money or a moment of sexual satisfaction. Ashur (Nick E. Tarabay), the manager of the *ludus*, parades through the gladiators' cells a group of women, most likely slaves, who will be used to reward the gladiators sexually, if they so choose. The scene clearly alludes to the one in Kubrick's film where the gladiators are rewarded with females for their sexual gratification. In the series scene, some of the gladiators accept sex as payment. Others, like Crixus, whose love is directed to one woman in particular, prefer money. Crixus only participates in sexual acts when obligated to do so. Among those who opt for pleasure is Varro, who after discovering the betrayal of the woman for whom he had fought decides to give in to debauchery. Spartacus, however, like Crixus, remains sexually restrained for now. Yet here again, sexual activity is explicit in its "pornotopic" effect on the viewers: that is, the sexuality of the ancient Roman world is depicted as random, casual, and anonymous.

In these two scenes, Spartacus is present not as the protagonist but as a witness. But it is clear that in the course of the series, the character of Spartacus earns the designation of sex symbol as suggested in the title of this chapter: this can be seen in the third scene to be discussed. In episode 108, Lucretia offers a meal to Ilithyia and some of her friends, including Licinia (Brooke Harman), all women of a higher social status; the women make fun of Lucretia and annoy her by suggesting that she introduce the famous Spartacus to them. So the gladiator is brought to the *triclinium* and is displayed to the desiring eyes of the matrons. One of them compares him to Mars, "ready for war." Quickly, the sexual tension in the scene is intensified, mingled with the women's appetite to see blood flowing from Spartacus' body, an erotic metaphor suggesting the release of fluids from his body in the sexual act. "He is a god among men!" says another of the women present. The exhibition of Spartacus in this scene conquers his audience and confirms his characterization as a sex symbol.

In the following episode (109), an aggravated Lucretia engenders a strategy to deceive Ilithyia. The plan includes Licinia, who wants to have intercourse with Spartacus. So that everything goes well and anonymously, the players must wear masks: Licinia chooses one that represents the goddess Diana. The same type of arrangement is made to please Ilithyia, but she requests to have sex with Crixus. In her jealousy over this choice of her own lover, Lucretia devises a plan to

Figure 2.1 Spartacus (Andy Whitfield) masked in episode 109 ("Whore"). STARZ.

join Spartacus with Ilithyia, although they despise each other. When Spartacus is brought almost naked to Lucretia, the *domina* gives him instructions on how to behave, including his sexual performance. She informs him that the woman who will join him is socially above him, and he must understand this and not offend her. Spartacus is anointed with a substance that makes him look golden, as though he were a statue of an Olympian god. The viewer sees the hands of the female slaves working on and touching the completely nude male body of Spartacus. A woman, almost naked, awaits him wearing the mask of Diana. But she is not Licinia, as planned: she is Ilithyia. Spartacus appears fully naked and wearing a mask that likens him to Apollo (Figure 2.1). The gladiator has been fashioned by the women to look like a Greek sculpture. The choreography of the scene suggests sexual intercourse, in a crescendo that goes from a softer tone to a wilder and more aggressive one. Though the scene ends with the revelation of the deadly trap, Spartacus emerges as the pure construction of a sex symbol.

The rampant exhibition of the male gladiator bodies is so extreme that we may think the series is catering to a specific viewership, in particular a gay audience. The considerable presence of naked men throughout the series, particularly in the first season, as well as the accentuation of male sexual imagery throughout the narrative, contributes to this perception. In several sequences, Spartacus appears wearing the clothing of some types of gladiators who had an armored covering known as a *manica* to protect the right arm, which was often held by leather straps:[50] dressed in this way, Spartacus' outfit resembles the chest harness, an iconic image in gay culture.[51] The portrayal of gay sex was also not excluded from the show, as shown in the orgy scene in the brothel (episode 201): this type of scene could have hardly occurred in the 1960 film.[52] But the series is also remarkable for its positive depiction of several loving, sexually active relationships between men, such as that between the gladiator Barca (Antonio Te Maioha) and his partner, Pietros (Eka Darville), which is congruent with its pervasive privileging of the image of pair-bonded couples.[53] These are just some elements that allow us to surmise that this production may be catering to this particular audience.

CONCLUSION

The STARZ series without a doubt highlights the significance of depictions of nudity and sexuality to meet the tastes of modern audiences of media representations of antiquity. The new Spartacus himself, especially in the first season, is ultimately presented as a sex object to be consumed by the other characters and the viewers. At first, the gladiator stands out for his stoic restraint which rejects the sexual excesses enjoyed by others, and the representation of his conjugal fidelity provides continuity with the image presented in Kubrick's film. Moreover, as in the 1960 version, incontinent sexuality among the elite Romans is associated with a sense of outrage, becoming a catalyst that triggers revolt. But once his wife is dead, the hero of the STARZ *Spartacus* series assumes the role of sex symbol, which can perhaps best be demonstrated by the scene of the masks in episode 109. Still, the character of Spartacus as loyal and just seems to emerge unscathed, as he is shown in later seasons to be able to distinguish love from pure sexuality, which only increases the audience's fascination for this character.

The elite and powerful Romans in the story, such as Batiatus, Lucretia, and Ilithyia, seem to be those most often associated with a more excessive or alternative sexuality, suggesting some negative aspects to their delineation as characters. But there is some ambiguity in this perspective, for it is clear that the constant use of nudity and the depiction of sexuality in this series have to do with attracting viewers, as it hinges on the idea of "pornotopia" in onscreen representations of ancient Rome. Moreover, this series' portrayal of sexuality is inseparable from the violence that infuses the visual narrative of the gladiators in the arena. If in the 1960 film version, the depiction of violence was at the service of a political ideal, in the twenty-first-century television version, it is mainly a way to make a show of (mostly) male bodies. As Wyke observes: "*Spartacus* even problematizes the epic genre's customary invitation to audience pleasure in the display of male bodies."[54] Thus, from political icon, representative of ideas such as freedom, equality, and independence, the new Spartacus has become the image of a hypermasculinity and hypersexuality, as appropriate for an audience of the twenty-first century.

NOTES

1. Wyke (1997: 63–72), Futrell (2001: 97–111), Cyrino (2005: 100–20), Cooper (2007a) and (2007b), Rodrigues (2010) and (2012: 187–97).
2. Winkler (2007a: 9).
3. Futrell (2001: 90).
4. Wyke (1997: 34–62), Futrell (2001: 88–90), Cyrino (2005: 101).
5. Quoted by Shaw (2001: 14–15); see also Wyke (1997: 48), Futrell (2001: 89).
6. Wyke (1997: 34–60), Futrell (2001: 83–8), Shaw (2001: 19–21), Cyrino (2005: 100–2).
7. Shaw (2001: 19).
8. Quoted in Shaw (2001: 19).
9. Wyke (1997: 34–56), Futrell (2001: 83–90), Cyrino (2005: 101).
10. Wyke (1997: 48–59), Shaw (2001: 22).
11. Wyke (1997: 63–72), Futrell (2001: 83–90), Shaw (2001: 16–17), Cyrino (2005: 101).
12. Quoted in Shaw (2001: 17).
13. Wyke (1997: 48), Futrell (2001: 89–90), Shaw (2001: 17).
14. Shaw (2001: 18), Futrell (2001: 90–7).
15. Wyke (1997: 59–61), Futrell (2001: 90–7), Shaw (2001: 18), Cooper (2007b: 59–60).
16. On the ancient sources on Spartacus, see Shaw (2001: 31–165), Winkler (2007a: 233–47), and Schiavone (2013: 151–3).
17. Futrell (2001: 77, 92).
18. Wyke (1997: 47–56).
19. Wyke (1997: 51–3).
20. Wyke (1997: 52, 54).
21. Wyke (1997: 63–72), Futrell (2001: 97–111), Cyrino (2005: 100–14), Cooper (2007b).
22. Cyrino (2005: 103).
23. Futrell (2001: 90–1, 97–8).
24. Cyrino (2005: 104).
25. Cooper (2007b).
26. Futrell (1997: 77).

27 Futrell (1997: 95–7, 108–10).
28 Alonso *et al.* (2008: 90).
29 Cyrino (2005: 113).
30 Futrell (2001: 100–1).
31 Shaw (2001: 18).
32 On Draba, see Prince in this volume.
33 Wyke (1997: 67), Futrell (2001: 109), Winkler (2007a: 6–7). A recent echo is found in the assertion "Je suis Charlie!" after the attack on the offices of the magazine *Charlie Hebdo* in Paris in January 2015.
34 Futrell (2001: 93).
35 *Pace* Futrell (2001: 104–5).
36 Futrell (2001: 90–107).
37 For the cinematic association between the Romans' deviant sexuality and their abuse of power, see Cyrino (2014).
38 See in particular Futrell (2001: 99–101).
39 Alonso *et al.* (2008: 84–5).
40 Cooper (2007a: 50–2), Alonso *et al.* (2008: 82–3).
41 Williams (2010: 132–42).
42 Alonso *et al.* (2008: 80).
43 Futrell (2001: 106).
44 On the portrayal of nudity and sexuality in the series, see Strong (2013).
45 For example, Treggiari (1991: 262–319).
46 Mañas (2013: 254–7).
47 See Petronius, *Satires* 126; Juvenal, *Satires* 6.102–12; *CIL* 4.4342, 4345, 4353, 4356.
48 For sexuality in Rome, see, for example, Treggiari (1991: 262–319) and Williams (2010).
49 Nisbet (2009: 150): "Pornotopias are the genre-specific narrative worlds into and through which mass culture figures its visions of sex-as-con-sumerism." From this we can infer an "ideal world for sexual fantasy"; see Rodrigues (2013) and (2014).
50 On the *manica*, see Mañas (2013: 64–5).
51 That Spartacus has long been considered a gay symbol is supported by the name of one of the best-known modern gay publications, the *Spartacus International Gay Guide*; the most recent issue is Bedford (2015). Note too that the city of Lisbon is home to a gay sauna called Spartacus.
52 Blanshard and Shahabudin (2011: 95–8).
53 On the positive depiction of homosexual couples in the series, see Augoustakis (2013: 160–2).
54 Wyke (1997: 70).

3 The Life and Death of Gannicus

Juliette Harrisson

The aim of this chapter is to explore the portrayal of heroism and the hero's journey in STARZ *Spartacus*, particularly in the character of Gannicus. The idea of the "hero's journey," inspired by Joseph Campbell's *The Hero With a Thousand Faces* (1968, 2nd ed.) and formalized into a root structure for screenplays in Charles Vogler's *The Writer's Journey* (1998), is a popular one among screenwriters, highlighting the need for clear character development leading to an emotionally satisfying end for the characters with whom they want their audience to identify.[1] In a series like *Spartacus*, in which the majority of the lead protagonists are doomed to die in the series finale, this means thinking long and hard about the way in which each character will be killed. With the shadow of Stanley Kubrick's 1960 *Spartacus* looming large over the production, it is particularly interesting that creator Steven S. DeKnight and his team of writers chose not to include Spartacus among the surviving rebels crucified by Crassus, as Kubrick had, but to put their second protagonist Gannicus into that position. Drawing loosely on narratological theory and approaches to screenwriting, this chapter will explore the nature of Gannicus' heroism in the series with a view to answering the question: why crucify Gannicus, rather than Spartacus?

HISTORY AND LEGEND

In retellings of mythology, both ancient and modern, there is a certain amount of leeway allowed to writers to play with the material, but this freedom only stretches so far. So, for example, the reason Medea's children die might change with each new version of the story, but they still have to end up dead.[2] Even when extremely drastic alterations are made, such as Agamemnon and Menelaus both being killed at Troy in Wolfgang Petersen's 2004 film, the Greeks must still sneak into the city in a giant horse and destroy it. Works of fiction based on Roman history usually have less leeway, because more is known about the history. However, these are still fictionalized retellings, and a certain amount of artistic license is still allowed even in the face of known historical facts. For example, the writers of the HBO-BBC series *Rome* kept Octavian's mother Atia alive far longer than was the case historically in Season Two, because the character was popular and the writers wanted to do more with her.[3]

In the case of Spartacus' story, there is even more space for artistic license than usual due to the state of the primary evidence. Of the five extant sources that describe the revolt in some detail, all written by Greco-Roman authors a substantial period of time after the revolt, the longest, most detailed, and possibly the most reliable are Plutarch's *Life of Crassus* (8–12) and Appian's *Civil Wars* (1.14.116–21).[4] These few sources are brief, mostly hostile to Spartacus – with the exception of Plutarch, who writes with admiration and describes him as "more Greek than Thracian" (*Life of Crassus* 8) – and mutually contradictory in several details.

The sources do, however, broadly agree on a few facts: between 60 and 80 gladiators escaped from a *ludus* in Capua. They were led by a Thracian gladiator called Spartacus, who was aided, according to several sources, by two other gladiators, Crixus and Oenomaus (Appian, *Civil Wars* 1.14.116; Florus, *Epitome* 2.8; Orosius, 5.24; Crixus alone is mentioned as a fellow leader by Sallust, *Histories* 3.96 and Livy, *Periochae* 96). All the sources that mention Crixus by name report that he split from Spartacus and was killed in battle at an earlier point in the war. Spartacus' own fate varies from source to source; Florus and Plutarch claim that Spartacus was killed in battle, Plutarch adding that he continued to defend himself after many others had run away, and the *Periochae* states that he was killed with 20,000 others, implying death in battle (Florus, *Epitome* 2.8.20; Plutarch, *Crassus* 11; Livy, *Periochae* 97). Appian, however, says that Spartacus was wounded but his men surrounded him and his body was not found (Appian, *Civil Wars* 1.14.120). Other sources are not specific beyond the fact that he was defeated. Afterwards, Crassus crucified 6,000 surviving rebels along the Appian Way.[5]

From these sketchy sources, a mythical story emerges with certain points hit by all adaptations. The revolt is always the story of the escape of a group of gladiators from Capua. Spartacus is the leader, but in most versions he has several lieutenants close to him, and these will usually include Crixus and often Oenomaus, Gannicus, and Castus, as well as some invented characters particular to each version.[6] Spartacus must always be defeated – he does not actually have to die, since some sources report his body was never found, though he usually does – and Crixus must always break away from Spartacus before the end and be killed. Beyond that, writers are more or less free to invent their endings, within a few clear options. Each of their rebel heroes can be killed in battle, escape, or be captured and crucified along with 6,000 others along the Appian Way.

The choice of which fate to give each heroic rebel character is determined by a number of factors, including the need to produce an ending that is not unremittingly depressing and downbeat. This is especially true of a long-running television series, in which the audience have grown attached to the characters over a long period of time and will be particularly affected if all of them are horribly killed: the tragic death of every main character is an option, but it is not one used often, and not usually without good reason.[7] In writing the finale, then, it was necessary to assign appropriate fates – crucifixion, death in battle, or escape – to the surviving rebel leaders: Spartacus, Agron, and Gannicus, together with Agron's love interest, Nasir, and Crixus' love interest, Naevia. A number of factors are at play in the decision of what fate to give which character. Aside from the available historical information and the need for satisfying drama, one significant factor is the ever-present shadow of the best-known screen version of the story of Spartacus: Stanley Kubrick's 1960 film, an adaptation of Howard Fast's novel *Spartacus* (1951), with a screenplay written by Dalton Trumbo.

INFLUENCE OF THE 1960 *SPARTACUS*

Kubrick and Trumbo's film includes two particularly significant and famous scenes. The first is, of course, the moment at which all the surviving rebels stand up and declare "I'm Spartacus!" to show their solidarity with the real Spartacus and sacrifice their lives out of loyalty to him, its "most imitated" scene.[8] This scene is so frequently referenced in other media that it is undoubtedly familiar even to those who have never seen the film. The second is the scene of the crucifixion of Spartacus along with the other captured rebels. In Howard Fast's source novel and in the 2004 television miniseries adaptation of it directed by Robert Dornhelm, it is not Spartacus who is crucified but the Jewish rebel, David, thereby emphasizing the Christ-allegory of the crucifixion scene by giving it to the character of the same race and religion as Jesus. Spartacus, following the sources, is killed in the final battle. But Kubrick and Trumbo's decision to depict Spartacus on a cross carries a clear message for a Western audience. In the ancient world, crucifixion was a humiliating punishment meted out to runaway slaves and lower-class criminals – including Galilean carpenters accused of inciting anti-Roman sentiment. When Crassus had all the survivors of the slave revolt crucified, his message was clear: this is what happens to runaway slaves. In a modern Western context, however, the image stands for willing self-sacrifice, following the Christian story of Jesus sacrificing himself to save the souls of his followers.

All Christian denominations make more or less use of the symbols of crucifix (an image of the figure of Jesus on the cross) and cross. Regardless of the personal religious beliefs (or lack thereof) of writers, producers, directors, or audience, the image of a man on a cross inevitably brings up a particular set of ideas and associations for a twentieth- or twenty-first-century Western audience. The image evokes the idea of a savior who sacrifices himself for the good of his people, regardless of whether the audience believes that to be true of Jesus of Nazareth.

It is for this reason that Trumbo and Kubrick chose to include Spartacus among those crucified at the end of the film. Monica Cyrino has discussed the several ways in which the scene references Christian imagery and the "overt religiosity" of these final images, pointing to the depiction of Varinia holding Spartacus' baby as a Nativity as well as the obvious reference to Jesus on the cross, and the Christianized dialogue given to Batiatus, "Have mercy on us."[9] Although Elena Theodorakopoulos has suggested that the line of crucifixion victims undercuts the Christ-like imagery by reminding us how common the practice was in antiquity, I would suggest that this only reinforces the secular but messianic message, referring back to the "I'm Spartacus" scene – we must all be messiahs, all fight for a just cause. The alternative cut Theodorakopoulos mentions in which only Spartacus' feet were shown further reinforces the implication that this was intended as a Christ-metaphor, as films featuring Jesus in the 1950s often chose not to show his face (for example, William Wyler's 1959 *Ben-Hur*), so a woman embracing the feet of an otherwise unseen crucifixion victim would once again bring depictions of Jesus' crucifixion to mind.[10]

STARZ *Spartacus*, unlike the 1960 film or 2004 miniseries, is not an adaptation of Fast's novel but a new version of the story. In this retelling, Spartacus is not a slave from the mines, but a former Roman auxiliary, giving him the knowledge of Roman tactics that he uses frequently. Where Fast and the adaptations of his novel provided a sense of hope in the face of the story's grim conclusion by having Spartacus' wife and baby son escape, this Spartacus loses his wife early on in the first season and never loves another woman, taking comfort in the survival of an unnamed stranger and her child: thus the motif of the baby who is born free remains to offset the downbeat nature of the finale.

However, the series is in constant dialogue with the famous Kubrick film, as it frequently references and plays with well-known themes and moments from it. Kubrick's Spartacus, for example, is taken aback by the appearance of Varinia in his cell because he has never had sex with a woman, and he ultimately refuses to have sex with her when she responds to his angry assertion on noticing Batiatus watching them that "I am not an animal!" with "Neither am I." DeKnight's Spartacus is considerably more experienced, but also refuses to have sex with Mira (episode 109); he is prepared to have sex with the presumably willing Licinia in the same episode as part of his "duties as champion" but shows no interest in a woman sent to him by others to fulfill an imagined need. The scene directly echoes the Kubrick film, albeit tweaking the meaning slightly: indeed, Spartacus in the series comes across as more uninterested than concerned for Mira's welfare, whereas Kirk Douglas' Spartacus is clearly interested but put off by the circumstances.

In some cases, scenes from the film are inverted. For example, where Kubrick's Draba refuses to kill Spartacus, a man he barely knows, and instead attacks Crassus and is killed, DeKnight's Spartacus, when ordered to kill his only friend Varro, does so at Varro's own insistence that if he does not they will both die anyway, and that he needs Spartacus to look after his family (episode 110).[11] Another echo of that scene occurs when Spartacus and Crixus are finally ordered to fight each other *sine missione* ("no quarter given") for a small crowd, and Crixus changes his mind and joins the rebellion at the last moment, allowing Spartacus to leap up and attack the Romans on the balcony above – in a manner similar to Draba in Kubrick's film – rather than killing Crixus (episode 113).

The most famous moment of Kubrick's Spartacus is referenced several times to produce several different meanings. While acknowledging that the name "Spartacus" is Thracian, the series chooses to depict it as the slave name given to the title character by Batiatus when purchasing him, not his "real" name: this draws on the use of slave names in early modern slavery in the Caribbean and the United States which would be more familiar to American audiences, as well as reflecting genuine Roman practice. For the first half of the first season, *Blood and Sand*, Spartacus is motivated by his determination to find and rescue his wife. After her death, Batiatus persuades him to leave aside his old life and embrace his new life as a gladiator, and we see him do so in episode 107 of the first season; when he sees visions of his victim in the arena as himself, he symbolically decapitates the man while embracing his new identity as a gladiator and declaring "I am Spartacus!" The captured Thracian has been killed, and only the gladiator created by Batiatus survives.

Following the discovery that Batiatus had his wife killed and his decision to reject Batiatus and the *ludus*, Spartacus displays a certain discomfort with this identity in several episodes in the later two seasons, *Vengeance* and *War of the Damned*. For example, when asked if he is Spartacus in episode 303 of the third season, Spartacus replies, "I stand so named," carefully answering the question without claiming the name as his true identity. But he never tells anyone his "real" name, because it remains associated with his wife and what he has lost; and as he dies in the finale, he talks about how he looks forward to hearing it again spoken by her in the afterlife.

In the final episode (310), however, the famous phrase is used again, and this time its use echoes the significance Trumbo originally gave it, as a statement of unity and solidarity.[12] In an attempt to throw Crassus off by having Spartacus reported to be in several different places at once, several characters, including Spartacus himself, declare "I am Spartacus!" while attacking Roman sites. Within the story, this is a tactical maneuver on Spartacus' part, but as the opening sequence to the final episode, it is a clear reference to Kubrick's film and to the rebels coming together one last time to support Spartacus and his ideals.[13]

GANNICUS AS HERO

The first of Spartacus' followers to utter the iconic line in the finale is Gannicus, on whose image this final episode opens. Gannicus is a minor character in Fast's novel, in both previous adaptations of it and, indeed, in the histories (he is mentioned briefly as a leader of Gauls and Germans, along with a man called Castus, in Livy, *Periochae* 97, and Frontinus, *Strategies* 2.4.7 and 2.5.34).[14] He does not appear in *Spartacus: Blood and Sand*, which focuses on Spartacus, Crixus, and Oenomaus (whose name is not revealed until episode 113, suggesting a desire to ensure that members of the audience familiar with the history were fully focused on Spartacus and Crixus). However, Gannicus became a particularly important character in STARZ *Spartacus* when the need arose for a prequel series not featuring the title character in between *Blood and Sand* and *Vengeance*.

Current English usage of the term "hero" when referring to a fictional or fictionalized character has broadly two different meanings: protagonist or "heroic" character. "Protagonist" and "hero" are often used interchangeably,[15] but to be a protagonist is not necessarily to be a hero; and a title character may be one, both, or neither. The protagonist of a work is the main character, whose journey the story follows, who is the main point-of-view character and with whom the audience members are expected to identify. Films will often have a clear main protagonist facing a main antagonist, with a number of supporting secondary characters; for example, the protagonist of Ridley Scott's *Gladiator* (2000) is Russell Crowe's Maximus, and the antagonist is Joaquin Phoenix's Commodus; the protagonist of William Wyler's *Ben-Hur* is Judah Ben-Hur, and the antagonist is Messala. Television series usually have a larger ensemble cast and may have several protagonists: HBO-BBC's *Rome*, for example, has two lower-class protagonists (Vorenus and Pullo) and a number of amoral anti-heroic main characters among the upper-class Romans including Julius Caesar, Mark Antony, Cicero, Atia, Servilia, and Octavian.[16] *Spartacus: Blood and Sand*, however, has one clear primary protagonist, Spartacus himself – with Batiatus and Lucretia as primary antagonists and Claudius Glaber waiting to become such in *Vengeance*.

Ideas of what it means to be heroic in the sense of having a heroic character vary widely, and were very different in the ancient world. In the ancient world a hero could mean, in literature, a man whose glorious deeds are sung by the epic poets, or in cult, a deceased person (usually a mythic hero in life) who possessed power after death and was honored accordingly.[17] Modern conceptualizations of the hero, including modern retellings of ancient stories, tend to point to a strong moral position and helping others as equally important as glorious deeds, and a major aspect of heroism is often a willingness to sacrifice oneself for the greater good. In Disney's *Hercules* (1997), for example, Hercules must prove himself to be a "true hero" in order to ascend to become a god and live with his divine birth family on Mt. Olympus. He tries to become a hero by killing monsters and rescuing damsels in distress, but eventually proves himself to be a "true hero" when he shows he is willing to give his life for Megara's. This concept of heroic self-sacrifice is perfectly expressed in more adult-oriented works by crucifixion, which, as noted above, implies martyrdom for a greater cause than oneself.[18]

The primary hero of STARZ *Spartacus*, then, is of course Spartacus himself, who is title character, protagonist, and hero all in one. Although a gladiator, so his deeds in the arena would not have been recognized as heroic or worthy of glory in the ancient world, Spartacus does carry out glorious deeds that win him eternal fame and glory in a modern context, as the subject of several film and television adaptations; the series itself repeatedly insists that prowess in the gladiatorial arena is a source of personal glory, referring to champion gladiators as "gods of the arena" on numerous occasions, not least in the subtitle of the prequel.[19] Spartacus certainly fulfills the criteria for a modern hero, as he is morally upright: he prevents Crixus from bullying new recruits to the *ludus* (episode 108); he tries to look after his friend Varro's wife, Aurelia, after Varro's death; he saves damsels in distress, rescuing Mira from an angry guard (episode 110), and telling her, "I would have done the same for any woman"; he tries to limit the violence inflicted on the Roman survivors in Sinuessa in *War of the Damned*; and he is willing to sacrifice his life for others, fighting for his fellow Thracians in *Blood and Sand* (101), and fighting for the lives of the women and children following him in *War of the Damned* (310). Moreover, Spartacus is the named title character and primary protagonist of the three main seasons.

Spartacus, however, is not the protagonist of *Spartacus: Gods of the Arena*, the six-episode prequel series aired in 2011, although his name remains in the title to identify it as part of the main series. Hoping that the star of *Blood and Sand*, Andy Whitfield, would be successfully treated for cancer and recover, the prequel series was designed to fill in the gap in time with a season that would not require the presence of the protagonist, that could take advantage of the popularity of the characters of Batiatus and Lucretia, and that would lead into and inform Season Two when it returned to the main story.

This prequel season, then, needed a new hero; a new protagonist was required, as well as a character who could take on the heroic role, since Batiatus' behavior in the first season had put him well beyond any possibility of being accepted as even an anti-hero. Oenomaus or Crixus could have become the protagonist, but both had well-defined character arcs in the existing show. There was also the acknowledged possibility that Whitfield would not be able to return and the series would need to emphasize the presence of well-known and well-liked characters to help embed a new actor in the lead role (as was eventually the case).

The prequel has a largely equal ensemble cast made up of a handful of protagonists (Gannicus, Oenomaus, Melitta, Crixus, and Naevia) and substantial focus on the series' main antagonists, especially Batiatus and Lucretia (along with Gaia, Solonius, Tullius, and, among the slaves, Ashur). Since it is a prequel series, the audience already know the ultimate fates of Oenomaus, Crixus, and Naevia, so it was necessary to introduce a central character whose fate was not known around which to build the story; DeKnight points out in the DVD commentary on Gannicus' fight in the arena in the sixth episode that the audience "could fully expect" Gannicus to die, adding tension to the sequence. Gannicus' position as central character is somewhat complicated by the fact he is also a human plot device; as DeKnight points out in the same commentary, the entire prequel and everything that happens in it is constructed around Batiatus' refusal to give up Gannicus in the first episode, resulting in an unusual lack of agency for a television leading man – this is partially reclaimed when Gannicus willingly loses to Crixus in an attempt to get himself sold to Tullius in the fifth episode. However, Gannicus is the focalizer for much of the prequel, being a much more sympathetic character for audiences to identify with than the antagonists Batiatus and Lucretia and with a much more open fate in the story than the familiar characters of Oenomaus, Crixus, and even Melitta, whose death cannot be wholly surprising to an audience well aware that Oenomaus does not have a wife in *Blood and Sand*.

When reintegrated into the main series in *Vengeance* (episode 205), Gannicus is left in an unusual position. He was the primary protagonist for *Gods of the Arena* but must necessarily play a secondary role to Spartacus in the rest of the series. The other characters in this position were written as secondary protagonists from the start; and so, Crixus is hot headed and constantly at odds with Spartacus, Agron is Spartacus' loyal right-hand man, and Oenomaus is their mentor. Their characters' journeys are predetermined by their relationship with Spartacus; Oenomaus will die first, as mentors must, Crixus will separate from Spartacus and be killed, while Agron will remain with him until the end (though this is interestingly, if temporarily, subverted in episode 308, as discussed below). Gannicus, however, is on his own hero's journey, separate from but parallel to that of Spartacus, with an entirely discrete set of motivations; unlike most other characters in the cast, he is not even fighting for his freedom, because he was already granted freedom at the conclusion of *Gods of the Arena*. He is a second protagonist, a second hero, requiring a heroic climax to his story.

Gannicus is a very different brand of hero from the series' primary protagonist, Spartacus. He is referred to as a "rock star" several times on the DVD commentaries for *Gods of the Arena*, with writer Brent Fletcher noting on the commentary for prequel episode 5 that they wanted a very different character from Spartacus, someone who loved the life of a gladiator, and women and wine as well (he is described as "Han Solo meets Achilles"). Lucy Lawless notes on the same commentary that actor Dustin Clare interpreted the character as also possessing a strong self-destructive streak, to the point of being suicidal, which is why he throws himself into battle in the arena so enthusiastically.

Despite the womanizing and the drinking, though, Gannicus is not really amoral enough to be described as an anti-hero. Despite this self-destructive streak and his lack of enthusiasm for Spartacus' cause, more often than not Gannicus is the voice of reason and morality by the time we reach *Spartacus: War of the Damned*. He points out repeatedly that their group members are becoming more and more like Romans, and he is the only lead character to acknowledge from the beginning of the final season the complete impossibility of overthrowing the Roman Republic and wiping out slavery. Paradoxically, he is also the character who misses the arena the most; but, as he explains to Sibyl (309), while he misses the thrill of the arena, he does not miss the shackles of slavery. Gannicus, with his hedonistic lifestyle fueled by alcohol and four-way sex acts, is probably the most "free" of the lead characters throughout the series in some ways, but he is also frequently the most moral, certainly in terms of the violence inflicted on "innocent" (albeit slave-owning) Romans. With Gannicus ever present as a second protagonist, Spartacus can teeter more precariously on the line between moral and amoral as regards the violence of their rebellion while Gannicus, although amoral in other ways and enthusiastically violent when he feels it is appropriate, can be the voice of morality in terms of the treatment of prisoners and methods of capturing a city.

CRUCIFIXION AND THE SERIES FINALE

When it came to the series finale, one of the main characters would inevitably need to be crucified along with the unnamed survivors of the final battle, as the crucifixion scene would not pack the right dramatic punch if it featured only minor characters and Crassus' slave Kore, who was only introduced in the final season. It could not be Crixus, who had to die earlier, so the main options were Spartacus himself, Agron, Nasir, Naevia, and Gannicus. Agron, Nasir, and Naevia had other roles to play in the finale (see below). But why crucify Gannicus rather than Spartacus, as Kubrick had?

For Spartacus himself, the writers found a fourth option – he does not die gloriously in battle, nor is he executed, nor does he escape. In any adaptation of the story of Spartacus, the idea of freedom and what it means to be free is, naturally, one of the main overarching themes of the production. Spartacus fights back against execution in the arena in the first episode and is motivated to live, first by the drive to rescue and be reunited with his wife, then by the dream of glory in the arena, then by the desire for vengeance. Finally, he reaches the first episode of *War of the Damned* and Gannicus asks what is driving him now? Bringing down the Roman Republic, as Crixus eventually tries to do, is, as Gannicus points out, impossible. In the final episode, Spartacus eventually concludes that what is most important is life for others, and dying a free man; and although Pompey massacres most of those who try to flee north, a very specific group of the two women Spartacus named (Laeta and Sibyl), the mother and child he mentioned, and Agron, the sole survivor of Batiatus' *ludus*, are shown to have survived. By dying of his wounds in the mountains, away from the battle, not only are all the historical sources more or less satisfied (as he is cut down in battle but his body is never found), but Spartacus is reunited with his wife in the afterlife and dies free, seeing visions of Sura in a clear nod to *Gladiator* – a film in which the final track on the soundtrack, played after Maximus dies, is "Now We Are Free."[20]

Being the last remaining main character for whom crucifixion is appropriate is not, however, the only reason Gannicus is given this fate (Figure 3.1). Crucifixion symbolizes self-sacrifice, but in order to sacrifice oneself, one has to have something in life to sacrifice and a desire to live that is thwarted. For the Gannicus of *Gods of the Arena* and *Vengeance*, who is self-destructive and willingly re-enters the arena as a free man, a glorious death in battle would seem the most appropriate end. However, much of *War of the Damned* undercuts the idea of any death as glorious, even while reveling in the imagery of it; and the two characters who most want a glorious death in the arena or in battle, Crixus and Gannicus, are both denied it and are executed. Sheer dramatic irony has a role to play here, too, which is partly why Naevia – who reminds the audience that when she first met Crixus in *Spartacus: Blood and Sand* (episode 102), she had no interest in gladiatorial games – is killed in battle in the finale, gaining the glorious death her lover wanted.

Gannicus' crucifixion, however, is the culmination of his character's development throughout the series, as by the final few episodes

Figure 3.1 Gannicus (Dustin Clare) on the cross in episode 310 ("Victory"). STARZ.

of *War of the Damned*, he has finally found a reason to live and no longer wishes for a glorious death. This is made clear when Crixus splits off from Spartacus with Agron and Naevia in the eighth episode (308). While Crixus seems broadly optimistic, most other characters treat the choice between whether to try to escape to the mountains with Spartacus or attack Rome itself with Crixus as a choice between going down fighting and running away from Rome and the Republic in an attempt to start a new life. While Agron, at a low point, goes with Crixus because he cannot see a life for himself beyond fighting, Gannicus stays with Spartacus, not just because he thinks Crixus' plan is even less likely to work than that of Spartacus, but because he has found something to live for beyond fighting.

What he has found is romantic love, which is depicted as redeeming and as a saving power throughout the series. In the DVD commentary on *Spartacus: Gods of the Arena* episode 4, over a scene of Gannicus and Melitta kissing, DeKnight explains that the "driving force of the show" is not sex, power, or violence but love, and "everything comes back to love." Love is the ultimate motivating force for all the protagonists, and even some of the antagonists (in particular, for Batiatus and Lucretia).

The rebellion was started because of romantic love – not just Spartacus' desire to avenge his wife, but his fondness (albeit not true love) for Mira, who points out to him that everyone in the household including her will be executed if he murders Batiatus (episode 112), and Crixus' love for Naevia, which drives him to try to escape and

rescue her. Agron wants to die fighting because he is worried Nasir
will leave him for Castus and sees no future for himself. However,
although he is the first of the lead characters to be crucified (and the
only one to be fixed to the cross through the palm of the hand, which
is even more Christ-like as Jesus films frequently, if inaccurately,
depict him crucified through the palms – everyone else in *Spartacus* is
more correctly crucified through the wrists), Agron is spared and survives, and is seen walking away with Nasir at the end. According to
Gannicus, he was "more dead than alive" as the battle approached,
but when Nasir finds a way for him to fight and reaffirms that they
will stay together no matter what, Agron is reinvigorated. The last
survivor of Batiatus' *ludus*, he is the last character we see in the main
action and speaks the last line of the series (outside of the credits),
reassuring the audience that the bloody climax of *Blood and Sand*
was not entirely in vain, because Nasir's love for him has saved him
and given him something to live for.

In Gannicus' case, romantic love has given him something to live
for, but more significantly, something to die for as well. For the
first half of the third season, Gannicus is in a fairly open relationship with the German warrior Saxa, but this appears to be based
primarily on friendship and physical attraction on his part, rather
than romantic love. When Gannicus tells Spartacus that his death
would be of "lesser concern" than that of Spartacus, so he should
stay behind in Sinuessa to create a distraction for the Romans, Saxa
tries to tell him it is "of concern to me," but she is largely ignored
(episode 306). Gannicus here is still self-destructive, perhaps suicidal.
However, after starting a relationship with Sibyl (episode 307) and
ending things with Saxa in the next episode (308), when Crixus tries
to persuade him to join his group later in the episode, Gannicus looks
toward Sibyl as he refuses. True love has given him something to live
or, if necessary, to die for.

Sibyl herself is depicted as extremely similar to Spartacus' late
wife Sura, to drive home her position as true love to the series'
second protagonist by comparison with the true love of its first. Sura,
following Plutarch's description of Spartacus' wife as a prophetess
(Plutarch, *Life of Crassus* 8), claimed that the gods came to her in
dreams and told her things, including that Spartacus would never
love another woman; likewise, Sibyl is named after one of the most
famous Roman oracles and is one of the series' most religious characters, persuading Gannicus to start believing in the gods even as her
own faith is shaken after she is nearly killed praying in a snowstorm
(307). The two women are very similar in looks (petite and pale-

skinned with long dark hair) and costume (both frequently dressed in blue, a color also associated with Christian symbolism due to its frequent use in visual depictions of the Virgin Mary).[21] These parallels between the two characters clearly indicate to the audience that Sibyl is to Gannicus as Sura was to Spartacus – but where Spartacus was unable to save Sura, Gannicus has a chance at saving Sibyl.

As this relationship starts to change Gannicus' character, the development parallels Spartacus' character development implied in his back-story, but completed before the start of the series. In a flashback in *Blood and Sand* (episode 107), it is revealed that Spartacus had something of a reputation – by implication as a ladies' man – before he fell in love with Sura. She says, "Every woman knows your name," which is partly a way to avoid revealing his name, but also indicates that he seems to have been a womanizer. Spartacus himself is shown smiling, laughing, and relaxing in a way that he never does at any other time throughout the series. So, Spartacus had moved from carefree womanizer to a man motivated solely by love for a very feminine wife (as opposed to the more masculine female characters Saxa, Mira, or Naevia) before the series began. Just so, Gannicus' journey becomes that of the pre-series Spartacus, from carefree to the point of self-destructive to someone whose life revolves around love for a small, feminine woman in need of his protection. This relationship is also depicted as better for him than his previous relationship with Saxa, as Spartacus notes in the final episode that he has also stopped drinking, functional alcoholism having been one of Gannicus' defining traits throughout the series. The love of a good woman, it seems, can cure all sorts of things.

In "Separate Paths" (308), Gannicus had expressed his desire to live for Sibyl, as Agron is eventually persuaded to live for Nasir. His crucifixion, however, shows the other side of that coin, as he dies for her and for the others escaping into the mountains. The self-destructive Gannicus of much of the series had nothing to lose and thus a glorious death would have been almost welcome for him. By the finale, however, it is his desire to live that makes his ultimate sacrifice more meaningful. To give up something you barely want anyway is not a sacrifice; to give up something you have realized you do want is. Crucifying Gannicus, rather than allowing him a death in battle, emphasizes that point.

Early on in the final episode, Gannicus insists that he still does not fully follow Spartacus' "cause" and tells Spartacus, "I am no martyr upon cross. But I would gladly give my life so that those more deserving may live," looking directly at Sibyl and at the unnamed mother and baby with her as he says it. Spartacus was a martyr from the moment he decided to incite a rebellion rather than simply murdering Batiatus and allowing everyone else (particularly Mira) to be killed in retribution. Gannicus' motivations, however, were more personal for much of the series, motivated by his desire for forgiveness from Oenomaus in *Vengeance*, and afterwards staying with Spartacus largely because he had nowhere else to go. But the anachronistic reference to the concept of martyrdom confirms that by the finale, Gannicus has found more of a purpose in life through his love for Sibyl.

Gannicus does not get the glorious death he wanted, but he does get a death that may be read in a modern Christian context as glorious, and this is emphasized in the way his final scene is constructed. As he dies, Gannicus sees visions of the long-destroyed arena, with crowds chanting his name, as he relives the heights of his fame. Gannicus had told Oenomaus and Melitta in *Gods of the Arena* (episode 2) that as slaves they were only truly free when fighting (or having sex). Spartacus is glad to die a free man in the mountains, but Gannicus is able to experience some of this feeling as he imagines his glory days of fighting as he dies. And so Gannicus dies dreaming with fondness of his time as a slave and the feeling of "freedom" he felt in the arena, while Spartacus is able to say he is victorious because he dies a free man, with friends in the mountains, far away from the Romans. The slow death of crucifixion also allows Gannicus to see Oenomaus waiting for him, just as Sura waits for Spartacus, and he is the only other character whose death is so prolonged and who sees such visions. It is, in this way, an appropriate death for the show's second protagonist.

NOTES

1 See, for example, the advice on the subject in Frensham's *Teach Yourself Screenwriting* (2003: 140–5).
2 On alternative early versions of the Medea story, see Gantz (1993: 368–9).
3 See Cyrino (2015: 5).
4 On the ancient sources on Spartacus, see Shaw (2001: 31–165), Winkler (2007a: 233–47), and Schiavone (2013: 151–3).
5 For more on the ancient background, see Cyrino (2005: 95–100).
6 In addition to Howard Fast's novel *Spartacus* (1951) and the two screen adaptations of it discussed elsewhere in this chapter (also discussed by Daugherty and Rodrigues in this volume), see for example Colleen

McCullough's *Fortune's Favourites* (1993), which features Crixus, Oenomaus, Castus, and Gannicus, as well as a female love interest for Spartacus (called Aluso) based on his wife as described by Plutarch ("a Thracian priestess," *Life of Crassus* 8).

7 Exceptions include *Das Boot* (1985), in which the bleak ending reinforces the horror of warfare and particularly submarine warfare; *The Black Adder* (1983) and *Black-Adder II* (1986), in which the ending is played for comedy, and *Blackadder Goes Forth* (1989), in which it once again reinforces the horror of twentieth-century warfare; and, more unusually, the space opera *Blake's 7* (1981). It is also worth noting that all of these examples except *Blake's 7* are much shorter series than STARZ *Spartacus*.

8 See Solomon (2001: 53), who notes that imitations appear in productions including *Monty Python's Life of Brian* (1979), *Punchline* (1988), *That Thing You Do!* (1996), *In & Out* (1997), and *The Mask of Zorro* (1998). As this list makes clear, imitations of and references to this scene are not restricted to stories set in ancient Rome, but the connection between the famous scene and its Roman setting can be played up when appropriate; for example, in the fourth season of *Doctor Who* (2007), in the episode "The Fires of Pompeii," when stuck for a name more convincing to a Roman than John Smith, the Doctor says "I'm – Spartacus," and his companion Donna, equally improvising, adds, "And so am I."

9 Cyrino (2005: 113–14).

10 Theodorakopoulos (2010: 70).

11 On Draba, see Prince in this volume.

12 As Futrell (2001: 109) puts it: "The collective identity transcends the individual."

13 The phrase is heard once more, at the very end of the finale's closing credits in a clip from "Great and Unfortunate Things," but in this case it appears more as a tribute to the late actor Andy Whitfield rather than for story reasons.

14 The character of Castus, equally thinly sketched in the source, is split between two characters in STARZ *Spartacus*: the German gladiator Agron, who supports Spartacus most wholeheartedly from the beginning of the rebellion in Batiatus' *ludus*, is Spartacus' right-hand man alongside Crixus, Oenomaus, and Gannicus, and assumes the place of fourth lieutenant to Spartacus and leader of the Germans; while the name Castus is given to a Cilician pirate who joins the rebels and is killed in the final battle. In a possible nod to the blending of the characters, Castus, who is in love with Agron's partner Nasir, tells Agron he wishes he could have been him as he dies.

15 See Frensham (2003: 72).

16 The relative position of the various characters in television is further complicated by the issue of which actors are credited as "main" characters, with their names appearing prominently in the credit sequence, an

68   *Juliette Harrisson*

issue tied in to contract negotiation that can be the source of some tension between actors and producers outside of the in-series story world.

17 On the epic hero, see Nagy (1999); on the hero in cult, see Burkert (1985: 203–8).

18 While crucifixion itself is rarely seen outside productions set in the ancient Roman world, a hero sacrificing themselves with arms outstretched in a cruciform position is extremely common, especially though not exclusively in science fiction and fantasy; see, for example, the death of messiah-figure Neo in *The Matrix Revolutions* (2003); the death of Ellen Ripley in *Alien³* (1992); or the death of Buffy Summers in *Buffy the Vampire Slayer* Season 5, episode 22 "The Gift" (2000–1). In Zack Snyder's *300*, set in the ancient world but not in Rome, King Leonidas is portrayed in cruciform position after his death.

19 In Petronius' *Satyrica*, when the protagonist Encolpius enters the house of the vulgar freedman Trimalchio, he learns that the wall frescoes include depictions of the *Iliad* and the *Odyssey* (the implausibility of fitting the whole of both these poems on a wall being part of the joke) and a gladiator show. The incongruousness of the combination and the unsuitability of gladiatorial shows for sophisticated decoration is the point of the joke, indicating that gladiatorial shows would not be considered an appropriate source of heroic *kleos* or "glory" in the ancient world (Petronius, *Satyrica* 29).

20 See Augoustakis in this volume.

21 Cyrino (2005: 113).

4 A New Crassus as Roman Villain

Gregory N. Daugherty

There were many in the late Roman Republic who, like Cicero,[1] might have had reason to fear Marcus Licinius Crassus (ca. 115–53 BC). He was born to power, amassed even more wealth first as a partisan of Sulla and then as a shrewd entrepreneur, and finally rose to authority in his own right as consul (70 and 55 BC) and a member of the First Triumvirate. He fell short in his quest for military glory when Pompey stole what credit there was to be had for the defeat of Spartacus (72–71 BC) and when he and his three legions were wiped out in the invasion of Parthia at the battle of Carrhae (53 BC). He was a player in the rough world of the final generation of the Republic and the tale of his life is as compelling as any work of fiction, ancient or modern. His immense wealth, although stigmatized for its non-agricultural sources, made his political and military career possible, as did his uneasy alliances with Caesar, Pompey, and other upstarts and malcontents. Since we are dependent largely on Plutarch's *Life of Crassus* as a source, questions about his character, motivation, and goals remain vexing for modern scholars.[2]

Before we can address the fictional receptions of this man, we should reflect on what we actually know. Our assessment of the real Crassus has evolved over the years, although according to Eric Gruen, "his image as the money-grubbing capitalist, second-rate politician, and incompetent military man still prevails in some scholarly circles."[3] While the revisionist efforts of scholars such as Theodore Cadoux, Frank Adcock, B. A. Marshall, and Allen Ward have helped to dispel this calumny,[4] we still lack a well-rounded picture beyond the "familiar Crassus: a man absorbed in gaining parity with Pompey, conspiring with Caesar, goading Catiline, exploiting Clodius, reckoning with Cicero, courting the *optimates*."[5] The real Crassus is and will always remain, in Gruen's words, "an enigma indeed: fearsome and unpredictable, greedy and beneficent, ostentatious and temperate, affable and explosive."[6]

One of the major episodes of his career was the campaign against Spartacus.[7] While this event looms large in the popular consciousness of the Roman Republic, it is in fact rather poorly documented,[8] as our principal source takes up only four out of 33 sections (or six out of 42 pages in the Penguin translation) in Plutarch's *Life of Crassus*. Thus we have a murky individual and a shadowy event of some significance, ripe for adaptation, reception, and even transvaluation by generations of writers and artists, beginning with anti-slavery activists in the late eighteenth century. For the purposes of this chapter, it is best to begin in mid-twentieth-century America.

RECEPTIONS OF CRASSUS

It is fitting that Crassus should have appeared in several works of fiction, especially when viewed through the sociopolitical sensitivities of the twentieth and twenty-first centuries. These are representative of the range: Howard Fast's *Spartacus* (1951), Alfred Duggan's *Winter Quarters* (1956), David Drake's *Ranks of Bronze* (1986), and Conn Iggulden's *The Death of Kings* (2004). Duggan presents a rather positive portrait of Crassus, but the story centers on his second consulship and the Parthian invasion, told from the point of view of two Gallic auxiliaries. Drake's story is also focused on the Parthian disaster, but in this work of science fiction, Crassus is dead thanks to his blundering tactics, and the survivors have been bought as intergalactic mercenaries to fight where technology has been banned, in the tradition of Jerry Pournelle's *Janissaries* series (1979–). Iggulden's contribution is part two of his *Emperor* series, which focuses on Julius Caesar. Not surprisingly neither Crassus nor Pompey fare very well: Iggulden's Crassus is as individual as other characters in the series (especially Brutus) and presents the reader with a more nineteenth-century version of the greedy, ambitious bumbler. It is, however, a well-written and engaging fiction.

Fast's novel has been most influential on most film versions of Spartacus, more so than Plutarch or any modern scholar. His self-published 1951 novel was well received for its leftist take on the slave rebellion, but also because it was a thoughtful, well-written, and engaging story.[9] The saga of how much the novel's story and themes changed in the process of the production of the Kubrick film has been well documented by Duncan Cooper.[10] What is of interest here is that Fast's Crassus is a complex and nuanced character as opposed to a one-dimensional villain. But he is still a villain, as W. Jeffrey Tatum noted: "Fast's Crassus combines avarice with private immorality. He seduces Caius and rapes Caius' sister; his own household is unhappy, and his son hates him. As does the film it inspired, Fast's novel relies upon an important polarity, the distinction between the patricians and Spartacus."[11] As his own biographer put it: "Fast imagines the slave uprising as a war of grossly exploited, but unfailingly heroic, 'proletarians,' against a decadent, debauched, and brutal ruling class."[12] Fast's Crassus certainly fits that profile.

Films and television productions of the story have included Stanley Kubrick's film *Spartacus* (1960), based on the Fast novel; *The Slave* (1962), Steve Reeves' final "sword and sandal" movie; the television miniseries *Spartacus* (2004) with Goran Visnjic, another Fast remake for the USA network by Robert Dornhelm; and Steven S. DeKnight's STARZ *Spartacus* series, in which Crassus features in the final season, *War of the Damned* (2013). The Kirk Douglas version has influenced all subsequent film and fiction versions, and has been the subject of extensive and excellent analysis in Martin Winkler's volume dedicated to the film.[13] Less known is the Steve Reeves contribution, originally titled "The Son of Spartacus," which in effect functions as a sequel to the Kubrick film. The USA cable miniseries starring Goran Visnjic was a weak attempt to cash in on the success of *Gladiator* (2000). The miniseries actually credits Fast as a writer but hardly varies from the plot of the 1960 version, with the notable and bizarre exception of having Crassus deliver the "I am Spartacus" line.

Crassus is not the primary focus of any of these efforts. He is usually the villain of the piece. Towering above the rest is Laurence Olivier's performance in Kubrick's version. As W. Jeffrey Tatum notes in his excellent analysis, Crassus' capitalism has been eliminated in the film in order to appeal to an American ethic: "Crassus' character, although animated by Laurence Olivier's compelling performance, is, in the end, simply Spartacus reversed: an exponent of tyranny decked out in vices so ostentatious that they could not fail to disgust middle-class American audiences."[14] In *The Slave*, Crassus becomes an archetypal sword-and-sandal dark, bearded villain. There is no effort at historicity, since the film is set in 48 BC, and he is amassing an army of mercenary soldiers and Parthians for a confrontation with Caesar. But at least he is depicted as avaricious, power-hungry, and debauched. Although the role is better acted (by Angus Macfadyen), the USA miniseries version of Crassus is essentially the same caricature, including the evil beard, and he serves as a clear counterpoint to the virtuous

Spartacus. At least he is treated as a competent military leader and a shrewd political force. Although this version does not follow Fast in every detail, the television miniseries is quite faithful to the novel, if not to actual history. One intriguing aspect is the recurring nightmare scene where Crassus meets Spartacus in the arena, in the last of which he is both the producer of the games (*munerarius*), giving the thumbs down, and shouts "I am Spartacus." Notably, Crassus as gladiator is a theme that will be repeated in the STARZ *Spartacus*.

THE NEW VILLAIN CRASSUS

It will already be apparent to readers of this volume that the STARZ series offers a new and reimagined Spartacus. A new kind of hero requires a new kind of villain. The result is a compelling characterization of Crassus that is not merely a product of its literary and cinematic predecessors, but one remarkably consistent with the ancient source material and respectful of at least some of the realities of the period. The combination of screenwriters who had read Plutarch and the other sources, a talented actor (Simon Merrells), and the requisite sex and violence have produced a novel kind of Roman villain. This chapter will examine how the historical Crassus has been reimagined through some clever adaptations of actual events, through the same process of sexualization applied to other real characters, through the addition of a tender romance with a slave turned bitter by the machinations of an invented son named Tiberius, and through his gladiator-style physical conditioning regimen which all converge in the final two episodes.

Crassus makes his first appearance in the series' third season, *Spartacus: War of the Damned*, in the midst of just such a training session with the veteran gladiator Hilarus, attended by his son Tiberius and his mistress Kore, both fictional characters (Figure 4.1). In the first episode (301), Crassus is in superb physical condition and displays considerable skill. Sweaty, shirtless, and under the adoring gaze of his lover, Crassus is placed on a par with the other sexualized characters. It is no sham exercise. Hilarus draws blood, to the alarm of the entourage. The scene is immediately preceded by the latest slave victory, which is presented as a mounted charge by Spartacus alone and his *aristeia* of single combat against a whole Roman unit, who are reduced to shrinking into a *testudo* to ward off the hero. Thus the opening of the final season sets up a juxtaposition of the two leaders that compels the viewer to compare and contrast them. Even though Crassus is not officially involved in the conflict, he is steeling himself

Figure 4.1 Crassus (Simon Merrells) training in episode 301
("Enemies of Rome"). STARZ.

by confronting a champion gladiator and learning to think like his
future adversary. Metellus arrives as the match concludes to convince
Crassus to fund a larger army in return for a subordinate command.
Tiberius is outraged that his father does not demand more men, but
Crassus proceeds to spend his wealth on the recruitment.

The next pair of scenes continues the contrast. Spartacus is "at
home" in his camp, where he and Gannicus discuss their lack of
family and their discomfort with the leadership roles pressed upon
them. The scene shifts to Crassus' home and somewhat dysfunctional
family, where he shows affection to his wife Tertulla and younger son
Publius (both historical) but refuses to grant Tiberius any real position until he has "earned it." In the process his sexual relationship
with the slave Kore becomes apparent. His tough love for Tiberius
leads to a thrashing by Hilarus, when the youngster disparages slaves
as worthy adversaries. Crassus voices some un-Roman attitudes
toward Spartacus and slaves in general, which are reinforced by
reaction shots of Kore and Hilarus. The viewer recognizes that this
Roman respects his enemy, even if he is a slave, and wishes to understand how he acts and thinks. It is also understood that Crassus
craves that this respect be reciprocated. In the meantime, Spartacus
is acting precisely the way Crassus planned, by forcibly removing
the incompetent Roman generals whom Crassus is supposed to be
serving. Although Crassus speaks humane and insightful words, the
audience knows he is advancing his own position with the sacrifice of

his superior officers. His son Tiberius cannot fathom the delay when the enemy is on the loose. Kore urges the young man to think like his father, something Spartacus is going to have to learn to do as well.

As the fighting in the south ramps up, the series begins to show a darker side to Crassus. He becomes angry with Hilarus for holding back in their contest, reflecting his frustration at not being in the field, despite his philosophizing about waiting his turn to lead the campaign. Crassus needs to be tested, because as he says, "A man's true enemy is doubt. A thing I would not carry into battle against Spartacus." To prove the point the scene shifts to Spartacus and two others taking on the two generals and their guards, as Hilarus gives Crassus everything he can. As the scenes shift back and forth, the tight editing links Crassus and Spartacus, who exchange blows with the surrogates. As Spartacus head butts the Roman in his fight, Crassus reels to the ground from the same blow in his scene. Crassus wounds Hilarus, and his next overhead slash morphs into Spartacus, both fighting with two swords. Both men slay their adversaries using signature moves – Crassus grabs the blade of his opponent and turns it on him – but there is a stark contrast between the words spoken. Crassus cradles the dying sparring partner and promises a statue in his memory, with both avowing the honor of being adversaries. Spartacus beheads the generals with two swords as they ask for terms of surrender, saying, "There are none I would trust a Roman to honor."

When Metellus arrives with the news of the Roman defeat, he almost accuses Crassus of engineering the attack and the elimination of his superior officers but backs down and offers the command to Crassus.[15] He replies, "I serve the glory of Rome." Tiberius realizes that his father had planned the whole thing and wonders how he knew what Spartacus would do; Crassus retorts, "Because that is what I would have done." This is the first major manipulation of actual events, designed to attribute this defeat to the machinations of Crassus. Instead of fate or Spartacus guiding events, the series shows us it is Crassus who gladly sacrifices Roman lives to his ambition.

The opening episode is almost entirely devoted to setting up the Spartacus/Crassus contrast and to inviting the eventual comparison. Visually and thematically the two characters and their fates are linked. They are both clever and competent leaders with a clear vision of how to achieve their goals, but they are questioned and doubted by subordinates and close allies. Both experience disappointments and conflict within the "family." But there are differences as well: Crassus does not meet all the expectations of a villain, as in previous fictionalizations, but has redeeming characteristics in addition. His wealth and ambition are not emphasized, while he is characterized by his love for his son Publius, his drive to understand his adversary Spartacus, and his humanity toward his slaves Hilarus (whose name means "Happy") and Kore ("Young Girl"). Conversely, Spartacus brutally and savagely executes suppliants. The episode alerts the viewer to a familiar trope in Spartacus fiction: these characters are two sides of the same coin and they know it, but with a reimagined scenario that neither is entirely good or bad.

The emphasis in the second episode (302) shifts back to Spartacus and a new character, Julius Caesar. Spartacus also acquires a new foil in Laeta, the Roman wife of the dead leader of Sinuessa, a town that he has sacked and occupied. This proves to be another parallel to Crassus, as Spartacus acquires his own "happy" counterpoint in the woman Laeta ("Happy"), although as we shall see it does not pay to be so named in this series. As Spartacus, together with Gannicus and Crixus, infiltrates the fictional seaside town, he becomes disgusted by the stoning of a slave. Spartacus curses the "festering disease of Rome," and right at that moment the scene shifts to the house of Crassus, who is giving detailed military instructions to Tiberius: this underscores his intimate knowledge and control of legions in combat as well as his understanding of Spartacus' predilection for nightly sneak attacks. We also witness Crassus' methodical and careful preparations, which are irritating both to the Senate and to his hotheaded but clearly unprepared son. Crassus next examines samples of the arms Tiberius has acquired, as he approves of them and the price. Despite his youth and lack of experience, Tiberius seems destined for a place of authority; but then Caesar arrives to upset everyone in the household, except for Crassus and perhaps the dogs. Caesar is also a wolf at the gate.

Caesar presents a stark contrast to both Crassus and Tiberius. He is shaggy, violently physical, and wearing a military belt and tunic. Crassus wastes no time in proposing an alliance that foreshadows the future First Triumvirate. Crassus outlines an impressively accurate, if simplified, assessment of the political and economic status of each: he is rich but from a more obscure family, while Caesar is broke but with an ancient bloodline. Crassus wants his help now to end the slave rebellion. He does not, however, go into specifics, which leads to conflict with Tiberius and further setbacks. As his character is drawn in the series, this Crassus does not reveal himself to anyone.

Conflict erupts when Caesar molests Kore, angering Crassus as he walks in on them, and Tiberius is also enraged when he hears of

Caesar's presence from the traumatized slave girl. Yet Crassus readily overlooks this behavior, and even proceeds to give Caesar some exposition on Spartacus' military background and tactics, when Caesar gives the expected Roman assessment of this mere gladiator-slave. Caesar seems to understand Crassus immediately and is on board with Crassus' strategy: this makes Caesar appear to be the ideal second in command. Tiberius overhears them doubt his abilities, and Crassus says he needs a wolf at his side.

Crassus' family situation becomes more complicated as his wife, Tertulla, gets ready to accompany him. Crassus forbids it for her safety, but she questions this just as Tiberius arrives to announce that the army marches in the morning. Both Tertulla and Tiberius – and Caesar as well – realize that Crassus loves Kore. In a display of genuine tenderness and love, Crassus in fact asks Kore to come with him of her own free will, a request that demonstrates his gentle side on the very eve of war and reinforces his claim to sexual parity with other major characters: full nudity, preferably frontal, is the mark of a major player in this series, and the scene thereby sets Crassus within this elite group. Kore agrees, addressing him as Marcus, rather than *dominus*, "master." Apparently swayed by her advice, Crassus makes Tiberius second in command and sends him to join Mummius with strict instructions to avoid battle. Caesar is not pleased by this loss of position, but he is bribed with the position of the military tribunate. The audience is quite aware that Crassus has made a terrible mistake by listening to Kore.

The third episode (303) focuses on the mostly fictional events at Sinuessa and Spartacus' need to provide for his followers. Like Crassus, Spartacus is having trouble with his "family," a situation only complicated by the arrival of the pirates who, in a jarring change to the historical narrative, propose that they fight together for a common cause. In the meantime, Tiberius has assumed command of Mummius' troops and has dismissed Caesar, preparing to march on Sinuessa. There the young man rashly attacks the rebels, and his Romans are put to flight when the pirates firebomb them. In the process Tiberius is wounded and loses his father's sword, which becomes a "MacGuffin," an object important to both the characters and the plot.

The fourth episode (304) treats the historical and fictional aftermath. Caesar arrives disguised among the rebels, unbeknownst to Tiberius. The series offers a third-party assessment of Crassus when Spartacus learns that Laeta knows the Roman general: she bears witness to his dogged determination, his massive wealth, and the keen intellect it took to gather it. This is common knowledge, but she adds an anecdote about how Crassus had sealed a business deal by sending a fake message. Spartacus quickly realizes that he had been manipulated by the same ruse, when he was forced to attack the two Roman generals. When Laeta expresses confidence that her city will be liberated by Crassus, Spartacus prophesies: "He does not stand the only one capable of the unexpected."

Crassus demonstrates his ability to do unpredictable things in the next scene, when he orders Tiberius to carry out a decimation: that is, units guilty of cowardice are forced to draw lots and the chosen ones are then beaten to death by their comrades. While this was a historical practice, with the desired effect of influencing morale in the course of the war, in this fictional version its victims include Tiberius' best friend and savior. At the end of a rather tender love scene, Kore – not knowing what brutality is at hand – urges Crassus to stop seeing Tiberius as a child and to treat his son as any other soldier. When the moment of the decimation arrives, Crassus orders his son to draw lots with the others. In this exhibition of tough love Tiberius is spared, but his best friend is not. Meanwhile, back in the rebel camp, Caesar goads the rebels into slaughtering the Roman captives, just as the Roman army bludgeon their own comrades to death. As Tiberius joins the clubbing, the scene cuts back and forth between the equally barbaric acts. Both Crassus and Caesar watch stoically, as their will is done. Only Saxa and Spartacus intervene in time to save Laeta, but it is too late to quell the discontent with his leadership: this causes Caesar to smile. Like Crassus he has willingly shed Roman blood to further his own political advancement and desire for victory.

In the fifth episode (305), while dissension grows among the rebels and Spartacus sets sail to seek grain, Crassus is visited by Metellus who is complaining about the lack of action and Mummius' loss. Crassus claims that he has paid for the entire army – an exaggeration – and asserts his own confidence in his plans. But Metellus' news that Pompey has defeated Sertorius and would return to Italy does not fall on contented ears. Even so, Crassus remarks that his adversary is intelligent and must be countered with equal cunning. Metellus accuses Crassus of admiring Spartacus, but instead of being goaded into a premature attack, Crassus challenges Metellus to attack Sinuessa with his bodyguard. Ancient and modern historians do not agree on Crassus' prowess as a military strategist and tactician, but here he is portrayed as a master of the strategy of indirect approach, accurate intelligence, and covert operations; only Caesar's black ops and Sinuessa are complete fictions. Spartacus is on an indirect approach of his own, namely to cut off Crassus' grain supply and force him to alter his strategy. Meanwhile Crassus sets in motion his personal tragedy when he visits Kore among the camp followers where he has banished Tiberius and the other shamed soldiers. Crassus actually asks her to bring comfort to his psychotic son. As they finish making love, a single tear drops from his eye to hers. Sexual displays by Crassus often yield negative results. Spartacus releases Laeta and the Roman survivors, who have been planted with misleading information about the divisions among the rebels and his plans for Sicily. Only Crassus appears skeptical: but he has already bribed the pirates and infiltrated the troops to link up with Caesar. When his fleet arrives, the rebels barely escape the town. As Caesar states, "Now would be time to run."

This is particularly good advice, since in the following episode (306) Crassus and his troops enter the city. Crassus puts his training to good use, dispatching several minor gladiators in individual combat, as his legionaries watch in the background. Gannicus has set fire to the granaries, but Crassus ignores the intended distraction and advances on the rear gate whence the rebels are making their escape. He comes face to face with Spartacus at the gate, only to watch him roll under the falling gate. As a good general would do, Crassus pauses to secure the city, looking for rebels in hiding, just as Gannicus does the same with his mystical guardian angel, named Sibyl. But when Crassus shares his good news with Kore, she is weeping and shaken by rape at the hands of Tiberius.[16] As Kore seems on the verge of revealing the truth, Tiberius pre-empts her with a sanitized account laced with double meaning and thinly veiled threats. With this sudden physical distance between Crassus and his lover, he is drawn closer to what he mistakenly sees as maturation in his son. As Tiberius hypocritically agrees to help honor Caesar for the victory, the audience sees the young man grow into a monster: "I am what you have made me." The series shows us that Crassus understands his enemy much better than his son or his lover, and so he will eventually drive the ones he loves into the camp of his enemy.

Crassus will also drive away one who had placed in him all of her hopes for deliverance. Laeta had told Spartacus and her fellow captives that Crassus would be their salvation and would drive Spartacus from the city. When she is brought to the Roman general, he is cold and suspicious of her collusion with the slaves. In their stilted conversation assessing Spartacus' character, Crassus prophetically concludes: "Then he and I stand the same, each believes himself the hero, the other, villain. It is for history to decide who is mistaken." Up to this point Crassus has been depicted in a more positive light, devoted to his family, patriotic to Rome, and loving and tender in the arms of his slave mistress. Even his wealth, political ambition, and shrewd maneuvering are not cast as moral shortcomings as in most fictional accounts (and in Plutarch to an extent). But in this scene the audience learns, together with Laeta and through her mistreatment at his hands, that Crassus' sympathetic side is only illusory. To her horror, Laeta discovers that Crassus has given her to the pirate Heracleo as part of his massive (and historically accurate) bribe to get the pirates to betray Spartacus. Even though Gannicus and Sibyl free her, Laeta bears a slave's brand: her innocence is now lost. During the brutal *carnificina* executions, the avaricious side of Crassus emerges, when he makes it clear that the liberated city is now his own, since all of the inhabitants are dead, or like Laeta, gone. Metellus is morally outraged until bought off, with Crassus' note that "Greed is but a word jealous men inflict upon the ambitious."

Throughout this episode (306) Crassus has remained confident in his grand plan to trap the rebels who have fled the city. In the final shot, we see that Crassus has built a ditch and wall to block their escape. While this feat is historically attested, its extent and location are much debated.[17] It is commendable that the series shows a modest wall in a restricted space that conforms to the more plausible explanations of the actual tactic. And Plutarch does attest that there was snow at the time, even in southern Italy. The breakout is a bit more fanciful, as we see in the seventh episode.

After an unsuccessful attempt to storm the defenses, the main Roman army approaches from the city, and the rebels are trapped. The rest of Crassus' scheme almost works when Spartacus falls for a trap involving the general's tent and standard placed too far forward as bait. In his cunning use of deception, Crassus has learned to think like Spartacus, but he is also vulnerable to such methods. This is underscored by his inability to see through his son's deceitful words and actions. Crassus foolishly restores him to command and trust, and then alienates his true love when he arranges for her to stay with Tiberius without telling her first. Crassus has begun to miscalculate. He did not count on the gladiators fighting their way out of the tent, and utters a taunting message about deceiving death: "Spartacus slips from snare." But Crassus still thinks he is the superior intellect: "Let him feel the sting of his wounds, and reflect upon the mind that inflicts them ... Time for ploy and deception draws to an end." To make matters worse, he alienates Caesar whom Kore seeks out for aid. Spartacus is in a tough spot, "bested by more devious mind," as Crixus puts it. But after a brutally cold night, Spartacus realizes that in every situation heretofore, "Nothing is ever as it appears." He concludes that the wall must be lightly defended – another deception. Spartacus breaches the wall and makes his escape, but he has suffered huge losses in the process. The two men, Spartacus and Crassus, do set eyes on one another, as they did during the fall of Sinuessa: this adds more fuel to the Roman's obsession with meeting his foe face to face.

As episode 308 begins Spartacus is harassed by advance troops, but Crassus is pushing his men to exhaustion. Metellus arrives to remind him that he has not delivered the victory promised. Crassus' violent response shocks Caesar and Tiberius, as he pummels the senator, just as Spartacus did Crixus in the previous episode. Still the latter two part amicably (the historical Crixus had split off much earlier), but Caesar and Tiberius are now sworn enemies, since Kore escapes the Roman camp to join the rebels. While Spartacus solidifies his core allies and parts honorably with the dissenters, Crassus allows Tiberius to poison his relationship with Caesar and Kore: as the young man whispers, "I believe great power is accompanied by many burdens, father, knowing whom to trust paramount among them." Crassus follows Caesar's plan to crush Crixus first, but only after Tiberius and Caesar clash in a horrific fashion. In the final fight at the gates of Rome, Crixus fights Caesar only to have Tiberius spear the gladiator in the back.

Despite his victory in episode 309, things begin to unravel for Crassus: the trickster gets tricked, and this costs him the very people the series has allowed to be close to him, while on the other side Spartacus has gained Laeta as lover and helpmate. Crassus hopes to goad Spartacus into a fight to the end by sending Naevia to him with Crixus' head; but even the unsubtle Gannicus sees through the ploy. Instead Spartacus attempts to lure Crassus into a fake meeting with Pompey, by sending some of his men wearing Pompeian emblems. Caesar clearly recognizes the men from his time among them, but he hatches his own plot of revenge on Tiberius – who had raped Caesar and murdered a witness to his rape of Kore – by convincing Crassus to send his worthy son. Yet Spartacus is clearly the more devious of the two. When Crassus learns of the deception, he dispatches Caesar to arrange a ransom for his son. In the meantime, the slaves put on gladiatorial funeral games with the captured Romans, saving the sniveling Tiberius for last. Although the young Roman was to have been spared in exchange for 500 prisoners, Kore decides to take her personal revenge. She offers to go instead of Tiberius, and Crassus honors the deal Caesar struck; but even as they embrace, he ominously tells her to call him *dominus* instead of Marcus. While the rebels celebrate their bonds of brotherhood and honor their dead heroes, Crassus' world is falling apart from within and is threatened by the historical specters of Caesar and Pompey who owe him nothing but money and, what is worse, do not fear him. While focused on the fates and story arcs of non-historical characters, this is not an inaccurate assessment of Crassus' situation at the time.

The villain's victory is further tainted in the final episode (310), which begins with a clever homage to the Kubrick film: Spartacus sows misinformation by ordering several raids on villas led by various subordinates who all shout the phrase "I am Spartacus." The ploy aims at buying time to allow noncombatants to escape into the mountains. Spartacus is as devious as Crassus but his primary motivations are humane and he is almost saintly in his self-sacrifice. Crassus, on the other hand, can only resort to standard legionary tactics and superior numbers, which Spartacus foresees, preparing snares and ruses. Spartacus is surrounded by devoted and worshipful followers and good women who have forsaken all for him and his cause. Crassus' lack of humanity and lust for revenge is exposed when he is practicing his gladiator moves with two swords in a visual recollection of his entrance scene in the first episode. But now instead of a worthy opponent he spars with sycophants, his son is represented by a death mask, and his once beloved Kore is in chains. The final clash is foreshadowed and his glory is already tainted.

When the two armies face off, Crassus calls for a parley. Spartacus agrees if only to buy time for the noncombatants to escape. Crassus is obsessed with meeting his nemesis face to face. Whatever he had hoped to learn from the meeting is swept aside when Spartacus unknowingly reveals that it was Kore who killed Tiberius. Crassus proffers a speech on freedom, choice, and the absence of justice. They clasp arms in gladiatorial fashion, with nothing of advantage learned or gained by either. But now Crassus is distracted and enraged by the news. He confronts Caesar and Kore and is devastated when he hears her defense. He appears to forgive her, but only when he has achieved victory, which he defines as the death of Spartacus. On the other side, Spartacus tells Gannicus that he defines victory as life preserved, specifically the lives of Sibyl, Laeta, and a new mother and child among them: these females taken together as one are an homage to the character of Varinia, wife of Spartacus, from the Kubrick film. Thus Spartacus can lose the battle, lose his life, and still win the title of the hero of the series. Even the typically detached Gannicus is moved to accept the task of leading a critical cavalry charge.

As the final fight begins, we see that Spartacus still has some tricks up his wrist guards. After a rousing locker room rant, a booby-trapped ditch is revealed and engaged. Once again, Crassus shows his willingness to sacrifice Roman lives to achieve his purposes. Despite the existence of prepared ramps and the cavalry charge from the rear, the end is clearly at hand as the subordinate characters each get their *Heldentod* ("heroic death"). Crassus tries to engage Spartacus in single combat, but despite his rigorous training regimen, Crassus is unhorsed and disarmed with one blow. He is rescued by his entourage and spirited to the hilltop where they had parleyed. Spartacus pursues, slaughters the bodyguards, and engages Crassus, even though he is gravely wounded and exhausted. Spartacus is spurred on by images of those whom he loved, who had all been killed by Romans. In another allusion to the opening episode, the two men fight each with two swords, culminating in Crassus attempting to use the move with which he had killed Hilarus, but Spartacus too grabs the blade with his bare hands. As Crassus falls defeated, disarmed and vulnerable, Spartacus is speared from behind by three common soldiers. Crassus tries to deliver the final blow but cannot resist an attempt to pry a compliment from his foe: "Would that you had been born a Roman ... and had stood beside me." Spartacus replies: "I bless the fates that it was not so." As Crassus raises his sword for a gladiator-style *coup de grace* (Figure 4.2), Agron and Nasir arrive to overpower him and knock him off the hilltop and spirit the still-living Spartacus away to the mountains.

Figure 4.2 Crassus (Simon Merrells) raises his sword to kill Spartacus (Liam McIntyre) in episode 310 ("Victory"). STARZ.

Along the Appian Way the crucifixions begin with the captured Gannicus, and we are shocked to see Crassus' beloved – and supposedly forgiven – Kore next to him. At this moment an arrogant Pompey rides up to steal the glory.[18] To Caesar's dismay, Crassus concedes the claim and lays the groundwork for the historical First Triumvirate: "Supporting claim, he will be made ally. We shall stand fearsome triumvirate, with means to bend the course of history. The past cannot be altered, the present holds but regret and loss. It is only in the days to come that a man may find solace, *(cut to Kore on the cross)* when memory fades." Although he won the battle, the villain gets no credit for it: Crassus is denied his personal part in the death of his foe, has lost the ones he loved, and is forced into the company of men he does not trust.

While the barbarity of the historical crucifixions is heightened by Crassus' personal cruelty to Kore, it becomes a transcendental experience for the hallucinating Gannicus as he imagines himself back in the arena, finding a Christ-like triumph on the cross.[19] Spartacus, too, is surrounded by men who love him and women he wished to save. His mystical passing and unmarked grave emphasize his status as a hero/*daimon* whose ideals will live on through an educated woman as the narrator, a Sibyl as his priestess, and a child as his legacy. Crassus has only that with which he started: wealth and power.

This Crassus is remarkable when viewed among the Roman villains that populate the sword-and-sandal and epic genres. The events and circumstances of his character line up rather well with the broad strokes of reality. If the viewer ignores the fictional associates, such as Tiberius and Kore, the anachronistic relationship with Caesar, and the obligatory STARZ-style nudity and sex, the essential arc of Crassus' historical narrative as presented in the series is quite plausible. Since he is not painted as all evil, as a military incompetent, or even as completely avaricious and power-hungry, Crassus may be reimagined as a more complex, well-rounded, and in the early episodes of the third season, even a sympathetic tragic figure. Crassus is still a villain, but a new kind for this genre. Gratitude.

NOTES

1 Cicero, *Letters to his Friends* 14.2.
2 Marshall (1976), Ward (1977), and Gruen (1977) have tackled the political issues, while Sampson (2008), Strauss (2009), and Sheldon (2010) have addressed Crassus' military prowess, but like most ancient figures, ultimately he is hard to assess.

3 Gruen (1977: 118).
4 Cadoux (1956), Adcock (1966), Marshall (1976), Ward (1977).
5 Gruen (1977: 123).
6 Gruen (1977: 117).
7 Ward (1977: 83–98).
8 See Shaw (2001) and Winkler (2007a: 233–47) for a compilation of the sources in translation.
9 Sorin (2012: 237–43).
10 Cooper (2007a).
11 Tatum (2007: 138).
12 Sorin (2012: 238).
13 Winkler (2007a).
14 Tatum (2007: 142).
15 The actual defeat that precipitated this was at Mutina and involved the two consuls, not the fictional generals named here. See Ward (1977: 83) for references.
16 On the scene, see Strong in this volume.
17 Ward (1977: 89–91).
18 The ghostly all-white armor is reminiscent of that worn by Laurence Olivier in Kubrick's film.
19 On Gannicus, see Harrisson in this volume.

PART II

Social Spaces

5 Upward Mobility in the House of Batiatus

Monica S. Cyrino

STARZ *Spartacus* offers a rousing contribution to our understanding of how specific threads of classical reception are constantly being rewoven to engage with contemporary issues, ideas, and concerns. As the publicity materials for the new series gamely promised, STARZ *Spartacus* would deliver a heady yet relevant mixture of politics, sex, and violence: "Ancient Rome is a place where the stakes couldn't be higher. The Republic's most elite citizens are thirsty for power, and they think nothing of using the gruesome entertainment of the glad-iators' arena to get what they want. Their ambition, treachery, and corruption are intimately tied to blood and death – and the fate of a gladiator."[1] The clear proposition was that *Spartacus* would cross the boundaries of time and culture from the ancient to the modern world in order to contend with issues of social status, power, and gender: "Rome burns with romance and adventure as today's actors bring epic times to life."

The first season of the series, *Spartacus: Blood and Sand* (2010), unfurls in thirteen episodes, as it tells of the capture and enslavement of Spartacus in Thrace and his subsequent training as a gladiator at the provincial *ludus* of Quintus Lentulus Batiatus on the out-skirts of Capua. Next comes *Spartacus: Gods of the Arena* (2011), a six-episode miniseries prequel to the first season, which fills in the back-story about the rise of the ruthless *lanista* Batiatus in the ultra-competitive local Campanian gladiator business. Over the course of nineteen powerful and unforgettable episodes, these two initial seasons of *Spartacus* focus on both the domestic physical set-ting and the shifting psychological contours of the House of Batiatus, as the household grows ever richer, more decadent, and more cor-rupt, and ultimately collapses. This chapter offers an exploration of the naked ambition and relentless social striving of Batiatus and his devoted wife, Lucretia, in the first two seasons of the series, and how the narrative premise of their intensely determined desire for upward mobility is woven into this particular incarnation of the Spartacus reception strand.

SPARTACUS AND CLASS

With its persistent emphasis on the rebel slaves and gladiators who rise up in resistance against the elite commanders of the invincible Roman military, the Spartacus reception tradition has often drawn extraordinary attention to the lives and experiences of the lower classes living in late Republican Rome.[2] This image of "the common people" and their struggle against oppression exercised from above emerges in several ways within the various adaptations of the Spartacus story that have been staged and screened over the years: they can be slaves fighting for emancipation, workers fighting for their rights, artists fighting for freedom of expression.[3] As Kirk Douglas, the actor and producer who starred as Spartacus in Stanley Kubrick's 1960 film, recently claimed: "*Spartacus* represents all people who work for freedom."[4] The 1960 *Spartacus* film, in particular, underscores the realistically difficult lives of the escaped slaves and their families as they follow their leader all over the south Italian countryside: at the same time, the numerous optimistic scenes of their collective utopian society and the loving relationships they share with each other somewhat mitigate the narrative, both historical and cinematic, of their final doom.[5] Yet this remarkable focus upon characters from the lower strata of society, who are mostly fictional, rather than a sole concentration upon the aristocratic Romans, who are famously historical, has remained a prevailing feature of the Spartacus reception tradition, and this perspective is also prominent in the STARZ *Spartacus* series.

While STARZ *Spartacus* inherits this un-epic tendency of drawing attention to characters from non-elite social classes, it breaks new ground by placing center stage the lives and back-stories of the two "middle-class" strivers, the *lanista* Batiatus and his wife Lucretia, and by emphasizing their inexorable drive for upward mobility, social prestige, and financial security. The first half of the *Spartacus* series – taking the first season and prequel together – effectively revolves around this ambitious, cunning, ruthless couple and their scheming aspirations to turn their *ludus* into the foremost gladiator spectacle business in all of Capua. As the story unfolds in the prequel, a young Batiatus seizes control of the *ludus* from his sanctimonious father in order to build his stable of champions, while his scrappy bride Lucretia stops at nothing to court the snobbish and sexually rapacious urban elite of Rome to advance her social rank alongside that of her husband. The first season of the series continues with the enterprising couple still working hard and struggling to secure their place among the swells of aristocratic Roman society.

The fact that Batiatus and Lucretia's plans for upper-class ascendancy utilize violence, sexual manipulation, and murder, however, does not diminish the characters' undeniable appeal to viewers, due in no small part to the robust and charismatic performances of the pair of actors playing them.[6] Moreover, the series successfully uses numerous visual and narrative strategies to do something innovative within both the tradition of epic cinema on the ancient world and the specific Spartacus reception tradition: STARZ *Spartacus* invites the television audience to transfer their allegiance away from the arrogant, but undeniably attractive Roman elite, as well as away from the noble but oftentimes boring rebel slaves, and to identify instead with the cunning *bourgeois* boot-strappers at the head of the House of Batiatus.

BATIATUS AND LUCRETIA ON THE MOVE

In the first season of the series, *Blood and Sand*, the *lanista* protagonist Batiatus is introduced as the financially strapped owner of a gladiator school vying for prominence in the cutthroat and commercially saturated human spectacle market of Campania. As one reviewer noted of Batiatus' role in the series premiere, the character of the ancient Roman entrepreneur "keeps the show grounded with a persuasive portrait of a man engaged in a stressful daily business."[7] Batiatus and his unfaltering wife Lucretia will do anything for prestige and social advancement, as they claw and scrape their way to achieve place of privilege among the more elite ranks of Roman aristocratic citizens. And yet the narrative of the first season cheerfully introduces a decidedly non-judgmental blending of their moral virtues with their less than moral vices: the couple's naked ambition is portrayed as a sort of salt-of-the-earth, dogged determination, while it is only their extreme mutual conjugal devotion that causes them to take dangerous, often criminal risks for one another.

The series' first season reveals how Batiatus stakes his future and that of his *ludus* on the raw talents of Spartacus, the fierce and brooding Thracian slave who agrees to fight and become a champion gladiator only when Batiatus promises to reunite him with his wife, Sura, who was kidnapped and sold as a slave when he was captured (episode 101). But when Sura is returned on the point of death (episode 106), Spartacus, furious, vows revenge on Batiatus and the entire *ludus*. One journalist described the foreseeable historicity of the narrative trajectory: "Spartacus must learn to persevere so that he can someday, a few seasons from now, organize the slave revolt that shakes Rome to its core."[8] As Batiatus tries to control the vengeful Spartacus and the other restless gladiators of his camp, he continues to seek political status and advantage with the local elites by scoring wins in the arena, while relying on intelligence reports from his slimy henchman-spy, Ashur, a crippled former gladiator. Batiatus viciously murders a pompous magistrate, Calavius, who disparaged the lowly businessman's interest in holding office (episode 111), and he successfully pins the crime on a rival *lanista*, Solonius (Figure 5.1). At the same time, Lucretia attempts to climb the shaky social ladder by shrewdly manipulating the sexual desires of the rich Roman noblewomen "frenemies" who visit her "to taste the wares of the *ludus*" (episode 109); and since Batiatus has been unable to give her a child, Lucretia endeavors to become pregnant by her reluctant lover, the gladiator-slave Crixus, to ensure the legacy of her husband's house and to carry on his name.

In terms of its staging of graphic sexuality, a vital aspect of the series often mentioned by pearl-clutching reviewers, STARZ *Spartacus* is conspicuously eager to demonstrate that Batiatus and Lucretia have healthy sexual appetites reserved almost exclusively for each other, and the series presents numerous scenes of their passionate lovemak-

Figure 5.1 Lucretia (Lucy Lawless) and Batiatus (John Hannah) welcome Solonius (Craig Walsh Wrightson) at the villa in episode 110 ("Party Favors"). STARZ.

ing.[9] Certainly, the couple may use their slaves as erotic "fluffers" (as in the first season) or enjoy athletic three-ways with a close friend (as in the prequel) to spice up their sexual relationship, but it is all in the cause of maintaining the intensity and intimacy of their marital bond. Even when Lucretia takes the unwilling gladiator Crixus as a lover, it is not for her sexual pleasure (at first anyway), but only to guarantee a pregnancy, so that she might give her husband Batiatus an heir to strengthen their family dynasty: in the scene where Crixus first penetrates her, Lucretia faces away from him in disgust at the action, and tells him to "get on with it" (episode 104). The series candidly portrays Lucretia's fervent objective to become a vessel for reproduction, the traditional role assigned to good Roman women, as part of her ambitious striving for class mobility for herself and her husband; she knows her son would inherit Batiatus' business, and perhaps even climb farther up the class ladder and belong to the aristocratic Roman rank that she and Batiatus struggle to achieve. In this way the series manipulates the familiar cinematic trope of explicit sexuality to make a strong statement about this deeply bonded couple in stark contrast to the more sexually depraved elite Romans:[10] the vice of lust, for Batiatus and Lucretia, is a weakness to be exploited in others in order to advance their own fortunes.

Batiatus and Lucretia cannot maintain their tenuous, temporary grip on power and position, however, as the plot moves relentlessly forward to the famous escape of the gladiators from the *ludus* in the thrilling first season finale. Several critics and reviewers remarked on the heightened narrative and visual rigor of the opening season's second half, which seemed to increase in both focus and purpose in its later episodes: "The forward movement of the story has felt inexorable; as Spartacus' rage at his master grew and as Batiatus rose in society, a wonderful sense of foreboding enveloped the proceedings."[11] The thirteen-episode arc of *Blood and Sand* ends in a brutal bloodbath in the *atrium* of their villa, where Batiatus is violently slain by an implacable Spartacus, and Lucretia is critically injured (but apparently not killed), stabbed in the stomach by Crixus, who pitilessly – but perhaps justifiably – kills their unborn child (episode 113).[12] So the next season of the wildly successful series, according to the plan of the producers and writers, was to follow the various stories of the runaway gladiators and slaves as they encamped on the slopes of Mount Vesuvius and attempted to fend off the Roman army before the final historical denouement.

But then actor Andy Whitfield, who starred so brilliantly as Spartacus in the first season, was diagnosed with non-Hodgkin's lymphoma, which delayed the filming of the series' second season. In a clever bid to keep the popular franchise going while Whitfield underwent medical treatment, the STARZ network decided to produce a six-episode prequel, *Spartacus: Gods of the Arena*. Although born of an unfortunate and painful situation,[13] the prequel season allowed the literal resurrection of the compelling character of the ambitious *lanista*. Set within a flashback as Batiatus lay bleeding in his *impluvium*, the prequel takes the audience back about five years before the action of the first season, before the arrival of Spartacus to the *ludus*. The six hours of *Gods of the Arena* explore Batiatus' difficult relationship with his conservative father, his unending struggles with the other businessmen and politicians of Capua, his interactions with his original stable of gladiators, and his deeply devoted emotional bond with his wife Lucretia in the early days of their marriage. Series creator DeKnight promised: "It's very much about Batiatus taking his first step toward becoming the man he is in season one – or, rather, how he became so ruthless."[14] *Gods of the Arena* shows us how Batiatus and Lucretia develop into the gritty, strong-willed characters they are in the first season, why the stakes are so high for them, and indeed, how they become so persistent and uncompromising in seeking to attain their goals.

The prequel action opens with the younger Batiatus in charge of the family business, since his father, Titus Lentulus Batiatus, is conveniently away in Sicilia in semi-retirement because of his poor health (episode 1). Batiatus and his wife Lucretia have the villa and *ludus* to themselves, at least for a while until the elder Batiatus returns, and their shared exhilaration about their new life together is palpable: in the opening episodes, the audience gets to see them "hopeful, idealistic, and with plans."[15] In these early days, Batiatus administers the *ludus* and supervises his gladiators in their fights staged in the rickety old wooden arena during the less prestigious morning bouts. Yet a sense of excitement and progress permeates the dusty air in Capua, as a beautiful new permanent stone arena is being built (Figure 5.2), funded by a wealthy local merchant and butcher, Tullius. Ablaze with ambition, Batiatus and Lucretia are eager to have their gladiators placed in the games that will inaugurate the new arena, especially in the privileged evening slot known as the *primus*, so they decide they must court the favor of the hard-edged but influential Tullius. Unknown to Batiatus, however, Tullius slyly advances the career interests of the juvenile Vettius, an inexperienced but arrogant rival *lanista* from the nearby town of Nola.

Figure 5.2 The inauguration of the Capua amphitheater in episode 6 ("The Bitter End"). STARZ.

Although Batiatus is advised by his close friend and fellow low-level *lanista*, Solonius, to use caution and diplomacy to further their shared business objectives, Batiatus rejects his advice since he naturally wants to seize opportunity swiftly and by force: "With great risk comes great reward," he tells his less aggressive associate. Starting from the prequel's first episode, *Gods of the Arena* vigorously draws the character of the brash and hungry Batiatus, as he tries to capitalize on his ownership of Gannicus the Celt, his most skilled gladiator and the original champion of the House of Batiatus.[16] In an effort to curry favor with Tullius, and to distract from his demand to buy the valuable but reckless Gannicus, Batiatus purchases one of Tullius' slaves, an unruly Gaul, Crixus, at an inflated price, as he assertively seeks to earn honored placement for his gladiators in the upcoming games that will celebrate the opening of the new arena. All throughout the six-hour trajectory of the prequel, numerous low-angle and point-of-view shots progressively reveal the new arena as it is being erected: these images serve as the striking visual parallel to the growing aspirations of Batiatus and Lucretia in their relentless desire to promote their gladiators, their *ludus*, and themselves.

Other episodes center on the intercession of the recently widowed social climber Gaia, a shamelessly self-promoting party girl from Rome, who arrives in Capua eager to advance the interests of her childhood friend, Lucretia, while finding a new rich husband for herself. Gaia is well acquainted with the recreational tastes of the elite

Romans who visit the backcountry boondocks of Capua for off-the-grid thrills, both gladiatorial and sexual: as she tells Lucretia with a seductive wink of self-assurance, she "knows what they want." The urban aristocrats of Rome so familiar to Gaia are depicted as jaded, voyeuristic, and sexually deviant, which is in strict accordance with the conventions of portraying elite Romans onscreen, from Crassus with his flexible sexual tastes ("oysters and snails") in the 1960 *Spartacus* to Commodus with his incestuous yearnings for his sister, Lucilla, in Ridley Scott's *Gladiator* (2000).[17] But here in the narrative of *Gods of the Arena* the entitled boredom and degenerate sexuality of the posh Romans is presented as a clear foil to the single-minded dynamism and willpower of Lucretia and Batiatus, whose virtuous vices are made to seem more dignified by comparison, or at least more relatable to contemporary viewers.

Lucretia at first willingly accedes to the twisted desires of her high-class guests, even offering up her cherished female slaves as sex objects in order to earn favor for her house: for example, Lucretia allows her young virgin slave, Diona, to be brutalized by the vile nobleman Cossutius, who is drawn to the villa in Capua by the promised pleasures of the flesh given in exchange for the chatelaine's upward social mobility (episode 3).[18] But Lucretia soon feels herself caught in a web of compulsion mediated by her own unrelenting ambition where she realizes that the sacrifices she makes are much too costly for what little advancement is attained. After Gaia is viciously murdered by Tullius as a "message" sent to Batiatus and Lucretia, a cruel but clear warning to them to temper their aspirations (episode 4), Lucretia makes sure that her husband will punish the crime and avenge the death of the only true friend she ever had. Although Batiatus is bullied by his father to bow in submission to Tullius' unrepentant arrogance, Lucretia secretly poisons Tullius' gift of wine for the elder Batiatus, who dies gruesomely as a result (episode 5). Batiatus, enraged both by the loss of his father and by his own shameful surrender to his despicable superior, ensnares Tullius in a trap and, with the help of a vengeful Gannicus, immures him in the brick foundations of the new arena, an appropriate end for the venue's erstwhile patron; while his callow protégé, Vettius, is forced to sell his *ludus* to Solonius and is run out of town on the day of the new arena's opening (episode 6).

Revenge on Tullius for the old man's death – or rather for Gaia's, as Lucretia wanted – marks the climax of the prequel season and the high point in the advancement of Batiatus and Lucretia: the way has now been entirely cleared of obstacles to their assumption of the coveted privileged position in the VIP *pulvinus*, the raised and cushioned platform reserved for the elite members of society, at the inaugural games of the new arena. By the prequel's final episode, the audience of *Gods of the Arena* can literally see how high our scrappy heroes have climbed. Yet the very moment of the ambitious couple's greatest triumph turns bitter with the conception of a new rivalry between Batiatus and a resurgent Solonius, his much put-upon colleague, who has grown weary of occupying the *lanista* second tier, who for so long has played second fiddle to Batiatus, and who now claims he learned the skill of selfish promotion from none other than Batiatus himself. This rivalry with Solonius hardens into deadly enmity, and forms the narrative backbone of the first season, *Blood and Sand*, as the prequel comes full circle in the story of the *Spartacus* series.

CONCLUSION

The first half of the STARZ *Spartacus* series creates a brand new space in the reception thread between the sand of the arena and the cushions of the *pulvinus*, between the noble yet often wearisome sufferings of the gladiator-slaves and the louche but loathsome perversions of the Roman aristocrats, and locates in that middle area a riveting new kind of character. Within that shifting interval, STARZ *Spartacus* locates the ambitious go-getters Batiatus and Lucretia, who use their honorable, pragmatic vices to make their own destiny, but who are still subject to, and often victims of, the brutal whims of the disdainful elites they seek to join. Along with their friends and rivals, including those among the status-motivated entrepreneurial class, Batiatus and Lucretia exist vibrantly in this middle zone, constantly struggling, always in motion, where their actions offer multivalent interpretations to us as viewers: we are fascinated and appalled, we cheer them on, we know quite well what it is like to be held down by those above us and to take out our frustrations on those below. So in opening up this space, STARZ *Spartacus* poses one of the principal questions of cinematic reception studies in a compelling new way, as it asks the audience to consider if we are those striving, determined Romans on screen.

NOTES

1 This and the following quote are from a four-page advertisement insert, paid for by the STARZ network, that appeared in *Entertainment Weekly* magazine in January 2010, with the bold masthead "*Spartacus Weekly*"

emblazoned on the first page and invitingly subtitled "A 21st Century Look at 73 BC."

2 See also Augoustakis in this volume.

3 On the particularly American ideologies of freedom expressed by the Spartacus reception tradition, see Winkler (2007b).

4 Quote is from the interview in McGovern (2015: 51).

5 Solomon (2001: 53), Cyrino (2005: 116).

6 The Scottish actor John Hannah, well-known for his droll performances in *The Mummy* trilogy of films (1999, 2001, and 2008), chews the scenery as Batiatus, while Lucretia is played by Lucy Lawless, the New Zealand-born actress internationally famous for her title role in the long-running hit television series *Xena: Warrior Princess* (1995–2001), and who is also the wife of *Spartacus* producer Rob Tapert; see Tucker (2010).

7 Lloyd (2010).

8 Bianco (2010).

9 See Strong (2013: 176–7) on the committed romantic and sexual relationship between Lucretia and Batiatus.

10 See Cyrino (2014) on the cinematic trope of sexual depravity as a marker of elite Roman decadence.

11 Ryan (2010).

12 On her return to the series in the second season, *Spartacus: Vengeance*, after suffering an ostensibly mortal stab wound in the bloody first season finale, actress Lawless said slyly: "It was just a little poke in the tummy. . . Being married to the producer [Rob Tapert] had nothing to do with it." See Hibberd (2011a).

13 Whitfield's cancer later returned, which forced him to leave the show altogether, and he died on 11 September 2011; see Hibberd (2011b).

14 Quoted in Stransky (2011).

15 As described by actress Lawless in the interview in Fowler (2010).

16 On the character of Gannicus, see Harrisson in this volume.

17 Cyrino (2005: 119, 250–1).

18 On the rape of Diona, see Strong in this volume.

6 Social Dynamics and Liminal Spaces

Stacie Raucci

The villa and *ludus* of Batiatus and Lucretia. The streets of Capua. The arena. The house of Crassus. The battlefields. The slopes of Mt. Vesuvius. The tents of Roman soldiers. These spaces, among others, in STARZ *Spartacus* may seem at first glance like mere background to viewers – the passive settings for the action of the series. But as film scholars have long shown, spaces are imbued with meaning and can provide a glimpse into the world of characters.[1] As Myrto Konstantarakos notes, "Space is not merely the setting of stories but actually generates the narrative both in prose and films, assuming the status of a character and becoming the fabric of the narrative itself."[2] While all the spaces in *Spartacus* hold significance, this chapter will focus on liminal spaces and argue that they make visible the power struggles of the series' main characters.[3] Concrete physical thresholds, such as cliffs, balconies, or gates, are obvious liminal spaces, but so are spaces that function as gateways to change while being physically more self-enclosed. In the *Spartacus* series, these spaces in-between and at the margins reveal and aid acts of transgression, transformation, and resistance.

SPACE IN *SPARTACUS*

In film studies, scholars have considered how space affects viewers' perceptions of what is onscreen.[4] The same cinematic action would not have the same meaning if set in a different space. Obviously, the arrangement and use of sets and space in a production can provide context, such as temporal and geographical information. Yet if we merely consider space as a "container" for information, then we are neglecting its other roles.[5] In addition to being a passive display of context, space can be the creator of mood and the set-up for

psychological and emotional moments on screen, it can provide characters with distinct opportunities, and it can suggest to the audience
the significant ideas in a scene.

The onscreen spaces may also serve as points of engagement for
the viewer. Robert Burgoyne, in his work on the epic in film, discusses
ways in which the "physicality" of a film, including "imposing sets
and the accumulations of detail," may give the audience a feeling of
"being in history."[6] While the spaces in *Spartacus* do contain much
detail, they do not have the veneer of reality of other series, as in the
case of the HBO-BBC production *Rome* (2005–7).[7] The creators
of *Spartacus* noted in interviews that they wanted the visuals to be
modeled not on recent series such as *Rome*, but on a more distinctive
model: *300* (2007), the film by Zack Snyder based on the graphic
novel by Frank Miller, in order to "tell the story in a very graphic
novel way."[8] The effect in *Spartacus* is therefore a world between
reality and animation, with exaggerated, if not downright cartoonish,
blood splatters, skies, and landscapes. While the spaces of *Rome* are
also constructed, the fabrication in *Spartacus*, with its extensive use
of CGI and green screen, is more obviously artificial, and as a result
offers viewers a different type of engagement. Instead of space engaging viewers in history, the carefully constructed space creates a world
for certain characters.[9] Series creator Steven S. DeKnight calls attention to the lack of reality in the visuals, and how the rare moments
of reality are used strategically and with effect. He notes that "there
are moments in the series where we do go realistic and we pick them
very carefully."[10] Instead of "being in history," the set designers have
created a "being in the lives" of their characters, an entrance into
a fictional space. Although likely working from basic ideas of what a
Roman villa, for example, may have looked like or at the very least
how it looks in similar cinematic set-ups, the designers have created a
fictional world that drives the storylines of the characters of Batiatus
and his wife Lucretia.

One of the ways in which the series draws attention to spaces is
by showing the same ones repeatedly. Accordingly, many scenes take
place in the main atrium of the household of Batiatus and Lucretia.
Although the same space may appear in different types of scenes,
from everyday domesticity to crowded parties to scenes of killing, the
viewer becomes familiar with this specific space and its connection to
particular characters. The space facilitates the ventures of these characters, constantly changing to move characters and narrative forward.

Whatever message a viewer may deduce from the physicality
and visuality of the series' spaces, it is clear that space is used in

Spartacus to mark social hierarchies. The poorly equipped camp of the Thracians, for instance, is contrasted with the well-stocked tents of the Romans, and the rich colors inside the house of Batiatus are particularly striking when compared with the muted sand colors of the *ludus* below. In the audio commentary to episode 104, director Jesse Warn notes that there is a contrast between "the elegance [of the villa] vs. the stripped down brutal surroundings you guys [Spartacus *et al.*] were in." As discussed in greater detail below, the superior social standing of Batiatus is often further reinforced by presenting him perched on a balcony, looking down at his gladiators. Dichotomies such as this, established in the visuals, are at the heart of the series.

The *Spartacus* series draws attention to the importance of space not just visually, but also through dialogue about the physical space. There are numerous references to the spaces of the series and their effect on the lives of the characters. For example, there is a clear mention of the physical space of the *ludus* in the second episode of the first season (102). Oenomaus, also known as Doctore, the gladiator trainer, asks the new recruits, including Spartacus, "What is beneath your feet?" When the recruits do not give the appropriate response, he turns to the gladiator legend Crixus (Manu Bennett) and asks the same question. Crixus replies that they stand on "sacred ground, Doctore, watered with the tears of blood." Oenomaus follows this reply by noting how this sacred ground "forged into something of worth" their "pathetic lives." Earlier in the same episode (102), Crixus describes the *ludus* as a "school of training where men are forged into gods." Both Oenomaus and Crixus use the word "forged" to describe the effect of the *ludus* and its "sacred ground." They show that the *ludus* is not just a space within which gladiators live; it is a space that shapes and defines them.[11]

Moving beyond the general spaces of the series, *Spartacus* makes particularly effective use of liminal spaces. Liminal spaces here provide the visual expression of the struggle to break social, political, and traditional power structures and hierarchies. For Spartacus and his companions, this means overcoming enslavement by their Roman masters and, more broadly, the power structure of Rome. For Batiatus and Lucretia, it means the desire to surpass their current economic and social station in life.[12] Liminal spaces in the series tend to act as temporary spaces for the characters, spaces in which they wait or which they pass through to reach the next stage in life. Passage through a liminal space signifies transition, but it does not always mean a positive outcome.

While it is possible to find liminal spaces represented in all seasons of the series, this chapter will focus on those in the first season and the prequel: the villa home of Batiatius, the *ludus* attached to his house, and areas of fighting, such as The Pit. These spaces are either liminal spaces themselves or contain liminal spots within them. What follows is an exploration of how specific liminal spaces function in the series and drive or reveal the struggles of the characters.

THE VILLA AND *LUDUS*

The villa and *ludus* of Batiatus acts as a focal space in the series and it also functions for the characters as a place in-between, a step on the road to the next part of life. Batiatus refers to his life and that of his men as being tied to the "walls" of the villa and *ludus*. He tells Spartacus that the fate of his wife Sura "is tied to these walls. If they collapse around me, I will be unable to find her beneath the rubble" (episode 105). Other characters also note their direct connections to this space. For example, in the final episode of Season One, Ashur notes that "every beam, every stone in this fucking house bears the mark of Ashur" (113). The series ties the lives of both elite and slaves alike to this specific place, thereby placing an emphasis on and drawing attention to the importance of the villa/*ludus* complex.

The views of the complex establish it as a place of great significance for the first season. All distant shots of it show it as a lone structure outside the city of Capua. The first daytime image of the villa/*ludus* complex appears in the second episode of Season One (102). In the distant background, there appears to be a whole city (Capua) with many structures. With the exception of the villa, the arena is the most visible structure in the shot, even though it appears rather small in the background. The appearance of the two structures in the same shot reminds the viewer that there are two spaces permitted for those who reside within the complex of Batiatus and that each space is merely a temporary stop on the way to/from the other. When the villa appears (episode 103), it is in close proximity to mountains and hills, but not populated areas. The villa and *ludus* are clear and crisp in image, while everything surrounding them is an indistinguishable mass of rocks with no identifiable structures. The perspective provided makes the villa complex appear large in comparison to the scale of the mountain behind it, emphasizing the importance of this space in the series.

As the series shows the villa as a self-contained space, it allows for those residing within it to live by their own set of rules, permitting more than is allowed in proper Roman society. In the prequel, for example, Lucretia, with the help of her friend Gaia, hosts elite men to witness and partake in sexual acts with the slaves of the villa and *ludus* (episodes 2, 3, and 4). Lucretia and Batiatus also allow elite women, such as Ilithyia (Viva Bianca), to have sex with their gladiators (episode 109).

The series also makes a distinction between life inside the villa/*ludus* complex and life outside of it. In an aerial view of the space (episode 103), people walk both inside the boundaries of the complex and outside of its walls, drawing attention to the distinction between the two worlds at play here. In the dialogue, the same distinction is made between the space of the villa and *ludus* and the world external to it. Oenomaus refers to the "walls" of the *ludus* as a distinct space, separate from the external world. He tells the recruits to "forget everything you learned outside these walls, for that is the world of men. We are more. We are gladiators." The clear boundary between the internal world of the villa and *ludus* and everything outside permits us to see more clearly the threshold spaces of the series.

The villa seems to be a temporary space to all who enter, at least in their hopes. In the prequel, the space does not belong to Batiatus, but to his father. Only after his father has died does the space truly become that of Batiatus and Lucretia. But even once it is in their possession, they still imagine it as a temporary space, a stepping-stone to a better life in a higher class of Roman society, as Batiatus dreams of and schemes his way toward a life in politics as an *aedile*. The villa eventually serves as the threshold to death for Batiatus. Prior to the escape of Spartacus and his fellow gladiators, Ilithyia commands her men to bar the door of the villa, trapping Batiatus and all his guests within where the gladiators are ready to slaughter them. More than the mere closing of a door, this action signals the end of the social climbing of Batiatus and Lucretia, who are forever entombed in their current station in life; it is here that Batiatus loses his life at the hands of Spartacus.

The space of the villa complex is transformed in relation to the changing status of the slaves and their owners. In episode 113, the once beautifully adorned villa is shown splattered with blood and everything within destroyed. The space, once designed to help Batiatus and Lucretia achieve their social-climbing goals,[13] now reflects their demise. The first season ends with the slaves exiting the once-locked gates of Batiatus' villa, signaling the end of their enslavement. The gates of the villa are rarely shown as open in the series and almost never to gladiators and slaves. The one exception is the opening of

the gate to Gannicus at the end of the prequel (episode 6), once he
has won his freedom and has received the *rudis*, the "wooden sword"
representing his release. When the villa is again shown at the beginning of the second season (episode 201), it is in the destroyed state
from the end of the first season.[14] Claudius Glaber orders his wife
Ilithyia to clean it up, an action that signals the start of a new journey
for her, as she struggles to retain her status of wife and elite Roman
matron.

The *ludus* is attached to the villa and occupies the lower parts of
the structure. Like the villa, it is separated from Roman society and
exists as a self-contained world where gladiators are trained before
entering the arena. Within the *ludus* another temporary liminal space
is established: a wooden platform on which recruits must fight a fully
fledged gladiator in order to join the gladiators' brotherhood (episode 102). The wooden platform is thin and elevated above the other
gladiators and recruits who watch the spectacle. It is a space shown
as separate from the balcony and the sands of the *ludus* itself, and it
represents the transitory nature of the gladiators being tested, since
they are not yet part of the brotherhood. This space also serves as a
turning point for Spartacus in the first season. He faces Crixus in the
"final test" and after looking at the binding cloth of his wife Sura,
the only thing of hers he has left to hold onto, he realizes the need
to survive. In order to win, Spartacus pushes Crixus off the platform
and onto the sand below, thus pushing himself symbolically out of
the transitional space and into his new status and identity. The scene
ends with Spartacus standing triumphantly over Crixus, providing
additional visual cues of the changes to occur at the *ludus*, namely
that Spartacus will stand soon as the new champion from the House
of Batiatus.

THE BALCONY

While technically part of the house of Batiatus, the balcony juts out
above the sand of the training ground of the *ludus*. It extends into the
air, acting as a space not quite part of the house proper, yet not part
of the *ludus*, existing between the two worlds. The balcony is a complex space because while it is a structure that seemingly divides two
sets of people – those upon it from those below it – the space does
not function like a door that can be completely closed to one party. It
can divide people into groups, into those who are permitted access to
it and those who are denied access, while at the same time enabling
verbal and visual exchanges between the two separate groups. The

Figure 6.1 Batiatus (John Hannah) and Lucretia (Lucy Lawless) on their balcony
in episode 102 ("Sacramentum Gladiatorum"). STARZ.

open nature of the balcony space makes it a more fluid threshold
than other spaces.

In general, the balcony serves to establish the power hierarchy
of the early seasons: Batiatus and Lucretia, as well as other elite
Romans, float above the gladiators who are at the mercy of their
whims (Figure 6.1). The balcony is perhaps the most obvious spatial
incarnation of Batiatus and Lucretia's social superiority as a couple.
It is a mark of their worth. In episode 108, Caecilia asks Lucretia if
she would not prefer to "live in the city surrounded by real people?"
Lucretia replies, "We are perfectly located. I need only step out onto
my balcony and all of Capua kneels at my feet." In a later episode (110), Ilithyia confirms Lucretia's assessment of her property by
asking guests if they have "ever witnessed a view from their balcony?
It simply overwhelms the senses."

The balcony attached to the villa may also recall for the audience
the viewing dynamics of the arena scenes, in which Romans look
down upon the spectacle of the sands below. They have proximity to the spectacle, but seeming safety from the violence. They are
not hidden from the view of those below them. Rather, the elites
on the balcony perform their own drama and are witnessed by the
gladiators. Although access to the balcony is limited and controlled
carefully, the openness of this liminal space allows for an exchange
between the two parties of elites above and gladiators below. All
participants in the space take on the "double role of observer and
actor."[15] At times, there is an exchange of words between Batiatus

and a gladiator. At other times, the exchange consists only of glances, as Lucretia looks desirously at Crixus or as Spartacus looks up at his masters, longing for vengeance. The open space of the balcony makes possible such an exchange. It is these exchanges that drive much of the narrative of the first season of the series. The balcony at the villa is indeed used much like a viewing platform at an arena. Batiatus and Lucretia stand in judgment over their gladiators on the balcony and often invite other elite Romans here to watch the men train.

The first appearance of the balcony (in episode 102) shows Lucretia and Batiatus looking out at the gladiators and depicts the complicated dynamic of such a space. The first clear view of the balcony is when Spartacus has his preliminary experiences at the *ludus* and stands outside lined up with the other recruits. The doors of the balcony are closed until Batiatus and Lucretia make a dramatic entrance followed by slaves carrying large fans. Although the initial image is a close-up of Lucretia and Batiatus, the camera quickly shifts to the viewpoint of the gladiators looking up at them. Batiatus and Lucretia are in the center of the shot, framed by the back of the heads of Spartacus and another gladiator, Marcus. The Roman couple appears small from this perspective, even though they hold the power of life and death over the men. When the camera switches to looking down on the gladiators from the perspective of Batiatus and Lucretia, it is the gladiators who appear small. The repeated alternation in perspective allows the audience to understand not only the viewpoint of each group of characters, but also the permeability of the space and the possibility for eventual change in the hierarchy.

The balcony serves as the crucial space in the series that permits the change in social dynamics, with power shifting violently from the Romans to the gladiators. Although Spartacus had been in the house on other occasions at the invitation of Batiatus,[16] it is when he enters via the liminal space of the balcony that his status changes in the final episode of Season One.[17] As he climbs onto the balcony, he breaks through the barrier set for him by the Romans.

The scene in which Spartacus attacks the Romans (episode 113) may recall the famous scene from the 1960 film *Spartacus* in which gladiators Draba and Spartacus fight to the death for the pleasure of Crassus and the elite Romans. Instead of killing Spartacus, Draba aims his trident at the elites above.[18] The trident misses them and soars through the space between the elites. Monica Cyrino aptly notes that "the trident penetrates the space between the two aristocrats, Crassus and Glabrus, effectively sundering the power of Roman male authority; as it flies into the frame towards the viewer, the camera seems to accuse the movie audience of siding with jaded Roman spectatorship."[19] This scene ends with the death of Draba at the hands of Crassus. By contrast, in the series *Spartacus* Crixus and Spartacus work together to launch Spartacus up to the balcony. Spartacus seemingly bounces off of Crixus' shield and appears to fly through the air toward the balcony. In the audio commentary to episode 113, series creator and writer Steven S. DeKnight notes that Spartacus' "leap [is] symbolic of the lower class attacking the upper class." Just as Draba's trident pierced the power hierarchy of the Romans, Spartacus' sword stabs Sextus, the Roman magistrate, directly in the center of the head, killing him instantly and gaining Spartacus entrance to the villa proper. Sextus' body falls off the balcony to the sands of the *ludus* below, representing the imminent destruction and debasement of the elite Romans present. The sword pierces the elite hierarchy even more clearly than Draba's spear did in the 1960 *Spartacus*. The audience watches the murder of Sextus from the point of view of Batiatus and experiences his fear. We eventually see that Batiatus' face is covered in Sextus' blood and the rest of the elites on the balcony flee in terror. Within the permeable space of the balcony, the worlds of the *ludus* and the villa become intermingled. Once the gladiators have entered the villa, blood covers all the spaces, marking walls, floors, and people. It is shown as flashes of red as the trapped people are killed.[20]

The space of this final slaughter is used strategically. In the audio commentary to episode 113, DeKnight notes that this final gladiatorial battle at the *ludus* is purposely placed in the twilight of sunset, rather than at night. This use of crepuscular lighting emphasizes the transitional nature of the space and of this scene. The power dynamics are about to turn on the House of Batiatus. It is as if the sun were setting on the authority and viability of this *ludus* that had belonged to multiple generations of Roman masters.

POOLS AND BATHS

Within the villa, the atrium pool and the bath also function as liminal spaces, since they are places of transformation and, ultimately, death. Water acts as the transitional element in these scenes. The atrium pool in the center of the house is a space shown in numerous scenes of the series. We first see the pool from a bird's-eye view down into the house (episode 102). At this point in the series, there is no water in the pool because of a drought. After rain comes to Capua, the pool is always full and becomes a key space for action. In the sixth episode, Batiatus kills the gladiator Barca in the pool, in the mistaken belief that he has been betrayed by him. In the ninth episode, Ilithyia kills Caecilia as punishment for mocking her for having had sex with Spartacus. In the final episode (113), many Romans are killed in this same atrium pool (in slow motion), as they flee the gladiators who are on a murderous rampage. In the second season, Ilithyia, once the esteemed wife of Glaber, now replaced in his affections, falls into the atrium pool after she returns from being a hostage of Spartacus (episode 209).

Likewise, in the baths, other transformations occur. In the tenth episode of Season One, Numerius (Lilam Powell), a young elite Roman, loses his virginity to Ilithyia, who is trying to manipulate him with sex. In that very same bath in Season Two, Seppia attempts to kill Glaber for the murder of her brother (episode 209). Instead, she is killed by Ilithyia. A vengeful Ilithyia stabs her and then slices her throat over the water of the pool, spilling blood into the pool and all over Glaber. In the scene, Seppia appears as if she were a sacrificial animal. The blood is shown in slow motion, spurting from her throat into the water, before she falls into it and dies. The water becomes a swirl of red.

THE PANTRY

In the audio commentary to episode 104, Jesse Warn marks the pantry area of the villa as a liminal space. He says, "This pantry area became quite an interesting place in the script. It was the in-between world between the *ludus* and the villa above, where the two worlds meet." The space is the driver of numerous transgressive acts in the series. Primarily, the pantry provides a space for the love of Crixus and Naevia to flourish away from the eyes of their masters. It also serves as the space in which Mira takes an active role in the demise of the House of Batiatus, as she kills a guard so she may open the gates of the villa at the end of Season One (episode 113).

THE CLIFF

Below the balcony of the villa, looking out over the city, stands a cliff at the edge of the *ludus* of Batiatus. The presence of the cliff and its danger are noted repeatedly throughout the series. The cliff is used as a threat by Batiatus, for example when Spartacus is led to the edge and made to look down upon a straight drop onto jagged rocks. Batiatus approaches and stands over him, with his foot on Spartacus' chest. In another instance, Numerius takes notice of the danger and tells Spartacus: "You have no wall over the cliff" (episode 110). As the camera shows us in multiple scenes, the cliff is extremely steep: one mere step off the edge of the *ludus* leads headlong into the void below.

On a basic level, the cliff represents the sharp division between the life of the *ludus* and that of the world of liberation beyond it. The gladiators look out over this cliff and imagine an escape from Batiatus. Spartacus discusses such an escape with Varro in episode 106, as he imagines rescuing Sura from a life in Roman servitude. Spartacus later uses the cliff as a weapon when he throws Gnaeus from it (episode 107).

On another level, the cliff serves as the mark of the end for others, a boundary between this world and the next. In the prequel, Gaia's body is thrown from the cliff after her murder (episode 4). This moment is replayed in the second season (episode 210) when Lucretia throws Gaia's red wig from the balcony down over the cliff. The descent is emphasized as the wig falls slowly through the air. The wig is in actuality a practice run for Lucretia herself, who kills herself by jumping backwards off the cliff while holding Ilithyia's baby in her arms. According to DeKnight in the audio commentary, Lucretia's jump from the cliff makes "you realize she wants to take the child to her dead husband in the afterlife." In Season Two, Lucretia's struggle with life after the death of Batiatus comes to an end with this leap from the cliff. She moves to reunite with Batiatus in the afterlife and to give him a much-desired child.

THE PIT

In "The Thing in the Pit" (episode 104), Spartacus is forced by Batiatus to fight in The Pit, or as Batiatus and others call them "the pits of the underworld."[21] The Pit is an area of ultimate fighting, where rules do not exist and where fighters die in gruesome ways. The Pit is a liminal space in that it exists as a space outside of everyday life, even beyond the order of the *ludus*. It is a space that is not a part of civilized society, but rather a shadowy place that is between life and death. Everything in the space of The Pit is covered in dirt and blood. Bodies hang upside down from the ceiling and half-naked women are chained to the walls. As director Jesse Warn says in the audio commentary, "It just feels like hell, doesn't it?" The imagery of The Pit reflects this sentiment, with large flames rising behind the announcer of the fights. The announcer, Anubis, states that there is "but a single

rule. Only one survives. Mongrel on mongrel till Charon arrives."
Anubis invokes Charon, the ferryman of the dead, as the marker of
transition between fights and the only way out of this space for the
loser. Warn further notes that this space drives Spartacus to become
the survivor and fighter that he does. He mentions that we "catch a
glimpse of Sura, mourning the loss of who you [Spartacus] were as
who you are becoming." In this episode, The Pit drives Spartacus to
the limits of his sanity. As a result of the depravity and cruelty he
endures in The Pit, he imagines Sura speaking to him and starts to
shout to his own self. Varro notices that Spartacus has been driven
to an extreme and questions how anyone could endure it "and still
count himself of this world." Spartacus uses thoughts of Sura to hold
himself in this world and keep him from "the grasp of the afterlife."

CONCLUSION

Spartacus, the titular character of the series and the face of the struggle to escape Roman servitude, exists in a liminal space for the duration of the series, since he is always shown to be in between worlds.
He moves through numerous spaces in the series, from one threshold
to the next, breaking through barriers wherever possible. As the
series progresses from Seasons One to Three, Spartacus is constantly
in search of revenge and freedom, replacing the walls of one space
(such as the villa and *ludus*) with the boundaries of another place
(such as Mt. Vesuvius, the town of Sinuessa, and the temporary tents
of the rebels). With the exception of brief moments in his homeland
of Thrace in the first season, Spartacus does not have the chance
to exist in a non-transitory space. He is not at home in the villa of
Batiatus nor even in the *ludus*, but rather stands a prisoner, no longer
with his own country or people. The space of the *ludus* constitutes
a seeming barrier between Spartacus and his wife. Once he escapes
from the walls of the *ludus*, he does not remain in one place for any
length of time.

Each space in the series that functions as a threshold, whether
physically or metaphorically, is used with particular effect by the
creators of STARZ *Spartacus*. This chapter has focused on the significance of liminal spaces in the seasons of the series that center around
the villa and *ludus* of Batiatus. While it has focused primarily on
instances in the first season and the prequel, there exist liminal spaces
in other areas of the series as well. As Spartacus moves through his
journey, he finds himself in spaces of transition and each space holds
its own challenges. Spartacus passes through each location, only to

find himself in yet another liminal space. As a further survey of liminal spaces in *Spartacus* would show, their repeated use is, perhaps paradoxically, a firm constant in this series.

NOTES

1 A look at even foundational texts on cinema can show the narrative importance of space and sets: e.g., Barsam and Monahan (2010: 164–7) and Lewis (2013: 81).
2 Konstantarakos (2000: 1).
3 For a discussion of the role of artifacts in the show, see Futrell in this volume.
4 Shiel (2001: 5) notes, "Cinema is a peculiarly spatial form of culture, of course, because (of all cultural forms) cinema operates and is best understood in terms of the organization of space."
5 Jones (2015: 2): "This [spatial] turn – in which the spaces of social life and how they are constructed, maintained and thought about become objects of study – can reveal what is lost when space is treated as just a background or a container."
6 Burgoyne (2011: 93).
7 This is not to imply that the spaces in *Rome* or other series are historically accurate, only that they have a more realistic appearance.
8 Bennett (2010). Steven S. DeKnight here also states, "*Rome* was a staggeringly brilliant piece of work, but much like the Roman Empire it collapsed under its own weight." McGrath (2010) notes that the creators wanted *Spartacus* to be "character driven like *Rome*."
9 Zoller Seitz (2012) notes, "This is all exceptionally cheesy, but it works because it pushes the franchise even further away from history and reality, to the point that you don't fixate on anachronisms."
10 Bennett (2010): "It makes me chuckle every time I read something online that says, 'Frank Miller and Zack Snyder should sue *Spartacus*!' In every interview we give we sing their praises."
11 On the *ludus* as "sacred" space, see Cornelius (2015).
12 On the social climbing of Batiatus and Lucretia, see Cyrino in this volume.
13 As the fortunes of Batiatus and Lucretia rise, so does the level of luxury in their home. For example, Ilithyia tells Lucretia (in episode 109): "I really cannot believe the difference. When I first visited your home, I felt great sorrow for the woman forced to live in such conditions. Now look at you, surrounded by opulence, rivaling families of proper heritage."
14 On Gannicus' *rudis*, see Futrell in this volume.
15 Amiel (2014).
16 At one point, Batiatus and Spartacus play a board game (*latrunculi*) in the villa.
17 There is one prior instance of Spartacus on the balcony with Batiatus,

but at this moment he has been temporarily allowed into the space only to be displayed to the other gladiators as the paradigm of the successful slave (episode 106).

18 For the significance of the Draba character, see Prince in this volume.

19 Cyrino (2005: 107). On this scene, see also Wyke (1997: 70), Fitzgerald (2001: 28), and Tatum (2007: 134).

20 In the audio commentary to this episode DeKnight says, "STARZ, rightly ... they were worried about seeing the gladiators, our heroes, slaughtering women. So we decided to do it impressionistically."

21 For Underworld imagery, see McCoppin (2015).

7 Building a New Ancient Rome

Lisa Maurice

In visual media such as film and television, the physical setting and appearance are of paramount importance both for attracting viewers and convincing them of the reality of the illusion being presented for their enjoyment. With productions set in particular periods or places, the physical set and *mise-en-scène* provide vital clues as to when and where they are conceived as taking place. Specifically in the case of ancient Rome, there is a long and rich tradition on which to draw, and incorporation of this tradition or deviation from it will signal subconscious messages to the audience and reflect the ideas and agenda of the creators of the production. This chapter demonstrates how STARZ *Spartacus* both continues and reinvents the depiction of the Roman world onscreen in accordance with twenty-first-century sensibilities.

THE LOOK OF ANCIENT ROME ON THE BIG SCREEN

The celluloid Rome of Hollywood, with its associated visual images, developed early and involved gleaming white marble columns and statues, mosaics, inlaid pools, gilded couches, togas, eagles, and scarlet cloaks. Some of these elements stem from the earliest days of the movie industry. Italian productions led the way, with *Quo Vadis* (1912), *Cabiria* (1914), and *Theodora* (1921) introducing many of the features listed by Juan Antonio Ramirez as traditionally associated with screen depictions of the ancient world.[1] The colossal sets of D. W. Griffith's *Intolerance* (1916) demonstrated that the United States did not lag behind Italy in producing spectacles set in the ancient world, and movie after movie followed throughout the silent era. Geoffrey O'Brien outlines how the reciprocal nature of filmmaking influenced the appearance of the ancient world on screen, as directors from both countries influenced each other to create what became the accepted look of the period:

> It was as close as movies got to a cultural lineage, this process of spirals within spirals by which you got the myth (the real, original Italian epics, *Cabiria* and *Quo Vadis* and *The Fall of Troy*, that took America by storm in 1914) and the myth of the myth (the improved and homogenised American epics, *Intolerance* and *Ben-Hur* and *The Queen of Sheba*, which in turn found their way back to Italian screens) and then, beyond computing, the myths of the myths of the myths, as each photographed the others' photographs.[2]

Two films in particular from this period stand out as defining moments in the representation of ancient Rome on screen. Fred Niblo's *Ben-Hur* (1925) was a vast and expensive production,[3] with filming initially taking place in Italy, where vast sets of the Circus Maximus and Jaffa Gate were constructed, but relocating to Hollywood as local strikes and weather problems delayed shooting. Despite these difficulties, the finished film "depicted a Rome of unbelievable scale and detail – complete with breathtaking chariot races in the colossal Circus Maximus, visually stunning battles at sea, and throngs of marching soldiers."[4] Likewise, Cecil B. DeMille's *Cleopatra* (1934) set the tone for colossal spectacles of the ancient world for years to come. Designed by Roland Anderson and Hans Dreier, the style of this movie was very different from earlier productions, in that its sets were more art deco than ancient Egypt or Rome, but the scenes of Cleopatra's entry into Rome were striking for their opulence and extravagance. As always DeMille devoted time and money to research in his attempt to reproduce authentic ancient artifacts, but in this case unweathered by time. Featuring enormous sets, his Rome was of awe-inspiring size, with dozens of shining white steps leading to gigantic columns, the mere bases of which were of equal height to the pristine soldiers on guard. Boasting wide, paved streets, spotless buildings, and well-fed citizens in immaculate togas and tunics, this was a city of prosperity and success that dazzled Depression-era America.

Against competition from the new medium of television in the 1950s and 1960s, Hollywood set out to provide what the small screen could not: vast color spectacles. The introduction of color provided filmmakers with an opportunity to paint Rome in even more glowing vividness. As Thomas Doherty puts it:

> The 1950s blockbusters were high profile spectacles, "twice as big and half as good," featuring casts of thousands, exotic locales and eye-popping set-designs. Rome was burned, the Red Sea parted, and the heavens stormed,

all in wide-screen movie color ... It reached its most egregious form in the so-called antiquity kick.[5]

Quo Vadis (1951) and *The Robe* (1953) began a trend for Roman-Christian epics in this style, but at the zenith were *Ben-Hur* (1959) and *Spartacus* (1960). In the words of Robert Burgoyne on *Ben-Hur*, "The hero's sojourn in Imperial Rome and in Palestine unfolds as a kaleidoscope of colours. Rugs, tapestries and costumed characters abound."[6] These movies used both color and special effects to increase the power of their spectacle, as reflected by scenes such as the vastly expensive and iconic chariot race in *Ben-Hur*.[7]

Perhaps the biggest spectacle of them all was 20th Century Fox's *Cleopatra* (1963), arguably the most opulent and grandiose Technicolor spectacular of the era. At Rome's Cinecittà studios, under the direction of production designer Johnny DeCuir, seventy enormous sets were built on such a scale that it resulted in a shortage of building materials, as thousands of artists and workmen toiled to produce ancient Rome and Egypt from scratch, with no expense spared. So striking was the physical appearance of the ancient world in this movie that it actually started a new trend in modern design and fashion, incorporating geometric shapes and richness of style.[8]

There is no doubt that a great deal of research was devoted to the look of ancient epics, which made claims as to authenticity based on this premise.[9] Thus, for William Wyler's *Ben-Hur*, the historian and movie researcher Hugh Gray was hired, and following this research, more than 15,000 drawings were made of costumes, sets, and props, and more than a million props were finally made.[10] Since Wyler knew very little about ancient Rome at the start of the project, he had large numbers of Hollywood productions about Rome flown out to Italy, which he then spent hours watching in order to provide himself with the required knowledge.[11] Clearly, a key source of reference for Wyler was not the ancient world itself, but previous screen depictions of that world. Despite the hours, money, and large numbers of personnel devoted to reproducing antiquity authentically, creating a look that was instantly recognizable as "ancient" or "Roman," and that fit in with the aesthetic and aims of the movie, was – not surprisingly – vastly more important than historical accuracy in academic terms.[12]

Inevitably, the visual Rome of the big screen was a contrived version that bore little relation to the reality of the classical world, particularly in the idealized cleanliness and sanitized appearance of screen antiquity. This aspect in turn eventually drew criticism from

both scholars and movie critics,[13] and it was in reaction to such
depictions that Richard Lester radically altered the appearance of
his Rome in *A Funny Thing Happened on the Way to the Forum*
(1966).[14] Wanting to replace these elements with authentic historical reality, Lester, together with production and costume designer
Tony Walton, produced film sets that for the first time depicted the
grime and tattiness of the ancient world, complete with peeling paint,
cracked tiles, and rotting fruit covered in flies.[15]

It was more than thirty years before Rome returned in any serious way to the big screen,[16] and when it did, that Rome was a clear
descendant of the screen city of the 1950s and 1960s, but also a new
creation. Ridley Scott had a clear conception of how he wanted his
Rome to appear, as Arthur Max, production designer for *Gladiator*,
explains.[17] Scott and Max were inspired by artists of the late eighteenth and early nineteenth centuries, such as the English painter Sir
Lawrence Alma-Tadema, whose works are "very, very vivid reconstructions of what it was like to live in the palace, and of the street
life – going shopping in downtown Rome in the second century."
The Rome they were trying to create was not, in Max's words, "the
Rome of, say, Virgil and Pliny; we were trying to do the Rome of
Byron and Keats and Shelley." Although Scott and Max went to sites
such as Rome, Pompeii, and Herculaneum, the director found the
original Colosseum too small for his vast plans, so he asked Max to
create a larger version; Max did this through a combination of set
construction and CGI, creating a Colosseum that is the centerpiece of
the movie as it epitomizes Imperial Rome in all its corrupt and bloodthirsty glory. According to Max, "Ridley had a vision of Rome that
was original to him . . . It isn't Rome as we know it from scholarship
and academic studies; it's much more grand, much more romantic, a
Rome of the imagination."

That the Rome of *Gladiator* was also that of earlier epic movies
was equally crucial, since the film not only paid homage to earlier
screen depictions of Rome, but also regarded them as fundamental for
viewer understanding. Yet despite the influence of earlier movies on
the depiction of Rome in *Gladiator*, this portrayal of the Eternal City
was also a very different product. Gone was the vibrant Technicolor
of the 1950s and 1960s, and in place of the shining marble Senate of
earlier movies there was dark granite and grey marble pillars. As one
recent work puts it:

> The film abandons the simple, clean, neoclassical aesthetic of many depic-
> tions in favour of a rich amalgam of colours, textures and materials . . . The
> audience can see the wealth and decadence of the late Roman Empire in every

piece of overblown drapery. The dim lighting tells us that we are not witnessing the founding of a glorious future but rather the last gasp of a world past its "use-by" date.[18]

The twenty-first-century Rome, then, is both grander, due to the wonders of CGI, and darker than the Rome of half a century earlier.

BUILDING ROME ON THE SMALL SCREEN

Rome has not only featured on the big screen. Britain produced the comedy television series *Up Pompeii* (1969–70), inspired by *A Funny Thing Happened on the Way to the Forum* and showing a similarly seedy side of the ancient world in this artificial-looking sitcom world. The BBC series *I, Claudius* (1976) presented a grander Rome, where the imperial palace was an elegant location in pale shades of white and blue-gray, "consistent with the popular artistic and cinematic image of the aristocratic classical world," as Alena Allen points out.[19] Filmed entirely in the studio, with mostly interior shots,[20] focusing almost completely on the elite of Roman society, this was a Rome centered on close-ups of purple-bordered, bright, white togas, elaborately furnished interiors, and with the few outdoor sets of the city of Rome dominated by shining marble pillars.

Most prominent, however, is the cable series *Rome* (2005–7), which offers a stark contrast to *I, Claudius*. If *Gladiator* showed a darker Rome than had earlier been seen on the movie screen, *Rome* showed an even grimier one still. Historical consultant Jonathan Stamp explained that one of the aims of the program was to show Rome "in a way that we haven't seen it before, a sort of down and dirty, anti-HollyRome."[21] The elaborate sets, the biggest and most expensive ever built for television, included a full-scale Roman forum, a network of working-class streets, markets, villas and gardens, a Jewish quarter, and an arena. Yet these buildings were, in the words of one review,

> dirty and multicoloured. The set is smoky and covered with Latin graffiti, much of it obscene. On street corners there are candle-strewn shrines and drawings of giant penises. In one street there's a typical Roman toilet: a latrine with planks with holes where men and women sit side by side and use the same fetid sponge as toilet paper. Grass grows between the flagstones on the Via Sacra. There's mud everywhere. Welcome to the new, realist, "authentic" Rome: feral, vivid, jumbled, irregular.[22]

Historical authenticity was very important, as chief writer and executive producer Bruno Heller stressed; this was a "third world Rome." He explained that their approach was to disregard people's preconceptions and ideas about what ancient Rome looked like, and to ask what it had actually been like. This was a natural result of the series' decision to focus not just on the Roman elite, but also on the lower classes.[23] One of the main influences in designing such a set, in which gritty realism and authenticity were paramount, was the site of Pompeii. Production designer Joseph Bennett, who built the set, says:

> People think of Rome as white and cold and beautiful, powerful but distant. But … Rome was like Pompeii, but much bigger. And Rome was so noisy it was impossible to sleep. It was like hell. Think of it as a combination of New York and Calcutta, with insane wealth and insane poverty. It was pretty extreme.[24]

This Rome, then, was a striking departure from traditional big screen depictions of the eternal city, its provinces and peoples, and its seediness owed more to *A Funny Thing* than to *Ben-Hur*. Gritty realism and dirt were the new order of the day, an approach that would continue with the STARZ *Spartacus* series.

THE LOOK OF STARZ *SPARTACUS*

Even the most casual initial glance reveals the look of the STARZ *Spartacus* series to be strikingly different from any other screen portrayal of the tale of the rebel leader. The most important influence on this production was in fact not a work set in ancient Rome, but rather Zack Snyder's film *300*, based on Frank Miller's graphic novel of the same name. Iain Aitken, production designer for the new *Spartacus* series, explained that the initial brief was indeed "graphic novel," despite the fact that the show was not based on an illustrated comic.[25] He interpreted this as latitude to create "a stylized world"; as he stated, "the Zack Snyder film *300* was the obvious initial point of reference for its graphic look and also because it was shot on a stage." This was important since *Spartacus* was also to be filmed totally on a stage, using no outside shots of sets at all. This stylization combined with the grittier elements found in the earlier series *Rome* to create a distinctive look, which is represented in three key elements of the physical settings of the series: the villas; the cities of Capua, Sinuessa, and Rome; and the costumes.

THE VILLAS

The House of Batiatus, in both the physical and the metaphorical sense, is the center of most of the action in both the first season and the prequel. The layout of the house is based on that of a typical

Figure 7.1 Interior of the villa of Batiatus in episode 105
("Shadow Games"). STARZ.

Roman villa, with rooms surrounding a central peristyle, and with
the back of the villa leading onto a balcony that overlooks the gladiator training area of the *ludus*. As seen in numerous aerial CGI shots,
the villa building is located on the edge of a cliff, and has a pitched
roof construction and overlapping roof tiles.[26] In the villa's interior
design (Figure 7.1), the peristyled courtyard has a black marble floor
patterned with lines of irregularly sized white diamond shapes, while
the pillars of the peristyle are of dark gray plaster, with the upper
halves of lighter gray fluted marble. Doors leading from one area to
another are of carved wood or lattice design. The walls of the peristyle are plastered and painted in green, while the central open area
contains four rectangular structures, possibly pools, surrounded by
low walls, and the edges of the colonnade roof are lined with carved
stone animal heads.

Apart from the courtyard, other featured areas of the house are
graphically stylized. There is an atrium, with an *impluvium* patterned
with a mosaic of dolphins and fishes, surrounded by painted plastered
walls of terracotta, red at the lower half and green above a fluted cor-
nice rail. Marble busts also line the walls of the atrium. Busts may
also be seen in Batiatus' office, which leads out onto the balcony
overlooking the exercise ground. The area between the atrium and
the courtyard includes a large pool for bathing, and the rest of the
space is divided into smaller rooms. These rooms are plainer than the
public areas of the villa, and a few of them are divided not by walls
but by curtains on rods. Some of these curtains are shades of red in

color, with the drapes around the master bed being panels of red, cream, and orange gauze; while others are pale blue with a vertical Greek-key design in gold. In some shots, the walls are shown to be decorated with painted columns and panels in mimicry of marble.

Albinius' villa, where the obligatory scene of the cinematic Roman orgy is set, continues this stylized look but exaggerates it still further. This house features a large hall whose central area is filled with a huge shallow pool in which naked women wallow surrounded by red rose petals. The *impluvium* itself is subdivided into smaller pools by a marble walkway in the shape of a cross, and this is patterned in the same colors and design as Batiatus' atrium. This entire area is surrounded by columns, the tops of which are fluted white marble and the bottoms a dark brownish color; while the walls beyond are also divided horizontally, with a pinkish red color lower down, topped with a pale blue stripe, and a mottled marbled upper half above a fluted ornamental molding. From this molding, fountains of water flow through marble animal heads.

Wall paintings appear frequently as interior decoration. Batiatus' office has brownish walls, and features a wall painting that depicts a hunt scene behind the desk. Some walls of the smaller rooms are decorated with painted birds, plants, and leaves on a green background. In the house of Ovidius (episode 105), the walls are covered by paintings, one of which seems to be an adapted copy of a painting from the House of the Chaste Lovers in Pompeii. After the redecoration of the villa carried out by Ilithyia in Season Two, the wall paintings disappear, to be replaced by plain painted walls. Her husband Glaber's office is painted in a shade of burnt orange, against which are displayed his war banners, on red leather, topped with eagles, and bearing the inscription "COH SPECVL OPTIMA FELIX." As designed by the series' props department, the banners were presumably inspired by the *cohors speculatorum*, Mark Antony's elite guard unit of scouts.[27]

Certain features are typical of depictions of ancient Rome on screen, particularly the wall painting, pillars, marble, *impluvium*, and the emphasis on the color red. Yet the overall more graphic look is in striking contrast to many earlier depictions. Perhaps the most obvious point is the darkness of these sets. The rooms are lit either by natural light or by candles or lamps on the walls, and this results in a far murkier look than viewers in the age of electricity are accustomed to seeing. In contrast to the almost dazzling hues of even the interiors of buildings in mid-century movies such as Kubrick's *Spartacus*, Wyler's *Ben-Hur*, or most outstandingly, Mankiewicz's *Cleopatra*, these rooms seem dim and shadowy. The furnishings also reflect this: in place of vivid scarlet and shining gold, the tones are of muted reds and browns, dull greens and blues, and bronze and pewter-colored vessels. Even the wall painting in Batiatus' office is faded, with the picture barely distinguishable.

One of the clearest influences for the look of these interiors is the extant site of Pompeii, as several elements seem to be direct copies of items in that city. The half-fluted pillars with a solid base, for example, can be seen in the colonnade of the Temple of Apollo.[28] Similarly, the animal-head fountain reliefs on the wall of Albinius' villa recall both the fountain at the side entrance to the Eumachia building, and the tombs outside the Nucerian Gate.[29] The hunt scene fresco in Batiatus' office echoes various wall paintings found around the city.[30] These reconstructions, however, replicate more the faded look of modern Pompeii than perhaps they do the city at its prime. This suggests that the appearance of antiquity was the most pressing concern for the series designers.

The exceptions to this are the dwellings in the city of Rome: for example, in Season Three, the house of the wealthy Crassus is notably splendid. Most commonly featured is a wide passageway, with a balcony providing spectacular views of the city, and from which other rooms – Crassus' office, the *palaestra*, and a bathroom – open. These areas are decorated in black and white marble that is cleaner and brighter than that seen in other houses, with a square pattern in white, gray, and black on the floor, and bronze reliefs on the wall panels. None of this is marked by the shabbiness and dimness that characterize the other dwellings, and this is clearly meant to reflect both Crassus' personal wealth and the status of the city of Rome itself. Even Glaber's Roman house, while less luxurious that that of Crassus, is nevertheless similar in overall look and markedly different from the villas located outside of Rome. Glaber's city house also features a wide portico with stunning views of the digitally reconstructed Rome, and the decoration in the rooms shown is far more polished, with a floor patterned with concentric squares, and smoothly painted walls: one wall is covered with precisely aligned ancestral masks.

It is striking that one thing that hardly features in the interior sets of the new *Spartacus* is perhaps the most clichéd Roman decorative art of all, namely mosaic, despite the fact that mosaics abound in Pompeii. Mosaics also featured prominently in the titles and advertising of the series *Rome*, and it is noteworthy that *Spartacus* did not attempt to link the two in the audience's minds through a visual echo. The most likely explanation for this omission is that the look created by mosaic was deemed not to lend itself to the graphic novel stylization.

A huge number of props were built on site for the four seasons of *Spartacus*, including beds, stools, chairs, tables, lamps, braziers, and marble busts scattered throughout the rooms of the various sets.[31] Many designs are based on ancient artifacts and depictions of items, in particular those from Pompeii. Overall, the furniture of Glaber and Crassus, the more elite Romans, is more elaborate than that of Batiatus, with more intricate carving and richer fabrics. Sets include a wide variety of lamps and lamp-stands – braziers, olive oil lamps of different sizes and shapes, brass free-standing lamps, and hanging lamps, all made from terracotta, metal, pewter, or glass – reflecting the diverse forms found in the ancient world.[32] Chairs are made of bronzed metal and leather or wood, and tables are of wood, bronzed metal, or marble. Chairs in the style of the backless folding metal and leather *sella* featured in the series are found across the Roman Empire; an armchair with a wood and metal finish from a Sinuessa villa appears to be modeled on a fresco from Room H of the Villa of P. Fannius Synistor at Boscoreale, now in the Metropolitan Museum of Art in New York.[33] The Roman bed in the same museum also seems to have been an inspiration for the beds and couches of Batiatus' villa.[34] A round wooden table with legs ornamented with bulls' heads is reminiscent of a marble table found in Pompeii.[35] Other items, however, are from later historical periods, such as the two corner chairs in Batiatus' villa, which are typical of Queen Anne designs of the nineteenth century. Nevertheless, efforts were clearly made to create furniture to appear as authentic as possible. Designer Iain Aitken states, "We consumed as many books as we could get our hands on for construction methods, furniture and prop reference," and he emphasizes the importance of the Naples museum specifically for the creation of props.[36] Aitken also cites *Rome* and *Gladiator* as vital influences on the art department who used these productions for reference as much as they utilized artifacts or academic works.

THE CITIES

The cities of Capua (Figure 7.2), Sinuessa en Valle (Figure 7.3), and Rome are portrayed in the series with a distinctive aesthetic as well. The city of Capua is a poor place, having dirt or badly paved and puddled streets with raised cobbled pavements and plain, unornamented buildings topped by red-tiled roofs. In contrast to many earlier por-

Figures 7.2 and 7.3 Capua in episode 2 ("Missio") and Sinuessa in episode 202 ("A Place in this World"). STARZ.

trayals of ancient cities, the most striking thing about the city is its lack of marble. Nowhere is there any gleaming white of any kind. The walls of these buildings are roughly plastered or stuccoed and a grayish beige in color, although unmarked by graffiti. Doorways open from the buildings, marked by curtains or shabby and scratched wooden doors that lead into the street, where chickens, goats, and other livestock can be seen wandering. In other scenes, half-naked prostitutes can be seen leaning against the walls, plying their trade. Laundry hangs from lines crossing the narrow streets at first-floor level, while outside staircases leading to upper stories are of rough wood. There is an arched colonnade in the market, but again it is of rough stone and plaster. A communal public toilet also appears in the prequel, based on those found throughout the Roman world.

It is the arena, however, that dominates Capua. In the prequel *Gods of the Arena*, the arena is being built, and numerous shots of the city show evidence of this ongoing construction, with scaffolding, tools, and builders at work filling the streets as background to the main characters' actions. This activity capitalizes on the importance of the arena already established by the first season, in which the digitally constructed building can be seen at the end of streets, dominating the view in many shots. Capua's extant amphitheater postdated Spartacus historically, with the modern remains dating from the Hadrianic period.[37] This was far grander than the earlier arena built in the time of Augustus, which in itself improved upon the first amphitheater built in the city sometime at the end of the second century BC. The arena in the series is clearly meant to represent the no longer extant Republican arena rather than the more familiar later remains, since it has no arches or statues of deities, and only three levels in place of four; yet it is still an imposing edifice, especially when viewed from overhead in the digital aerial shots. The construction, prime, and destruction of the arena in the prequel, first, and second seasons respectively mirror the rise and fall of the Roman oppression of the gladiators, as represented by Spartacus; the arena is, as such, an important symbol of the gladiators' struggle throughout the series. Yet it is also a visually less imposing structure than similar arenas familiar to the audience, in particular the Colosseum, and this perhaps reflects the ultimate destruction of the symbol of Roman power by the gladiators.

The city of Sinuessa en Valle is a walled city with a harbor, built on a promontory over the sea, where Spartacus and his followers take up residence in the final season, *War of the Damned*. The predominant color of the city is gray, and many of the buildings have walls of rough-hewn stone, plaster, or wood, although large red-roofed houses spread more spaciously apart can also be seen in long shots. Built along a seaside cliff, the city slopes down at different angles and is marked by streets on different levels, linked by steps and slopes. One building in the center of the town, presumably with some official function, has tall gray pillars supporting a portico before a wide public area that is the center of much activity, and where public notices (handwritten on papyrus) are pinned. There is also a harbor with a narrow jetty that leads into the main market and commerce area of the town; it contains a wall with three large arches built along the cliff, at the top of which is a wide walkway.

Despite similarities between Capua and Sinuessa in the production with regard to building styles and materials, the overall appearance of each city is quite distinctive. Sinuessa seems a brighter and more prosperous place than Capua, the yellows and tawny shades of the latter city giving way to the lighter grays of the former. Even so, all the scenes set in both cities, like the rest of the production, were shot entirely inside the studio, using green screens and visual effects to create backgrounds and environments. The differences between Capua and Sinuessa are in large part due to the different color palettes used for each, and the careful use of digital matte painting. Where the dominance of the arena in Capua gives the place a constant Roman emphasis, it is significant that there is very little that marks Sinuessa out as specifically Roman; there are no mosaics, Latin graffiti, white marble, statues, or busts. Nor is there an amphitheater, baths, or porticoed colonnades. In short there are no clues or symbols on screen to identify this as Roman city, with the possible exception of the red roofs and white walls of the buildings seen in the distance shots.

In contrast, Rome itself is depicted in a manner far more traditional for the ancient world on screen. The city is only ever seen at a distance in digital aerial long shots, but these pictures draw heavily on popularly held images of ancient Rome. Several such shots are used: one is the view from Crassus' house, which is presumably on the Capitoline Hill, showing the Basilica Aemilia, with the Curia Julia at one end, and what is perhaps the back of the Temple of Antoninus and Faustina at the other. Another shot is the view from the Palatine, showing the Temple of Vesta in the foreground, the Temple of Castor on the left, with the Basilica Sempronia stretching away into the distance. On the right-hand side, the Fornix Fabianus is under construction, with the Basilica Aemilia beyond it. The far end of the Forum is dominated by the Temples of Concord and of Saturn, with the Tabularium behind it. A third view is of the Circus Maximus, below which lies the Aventine Hill, covered with villas and other residential red-roofed buildings. Rising above the Circus Maximus is the largely still green hill of the Palatine, topped by the Temple of Cybele. One more shot is of the troops assembled on the Campus Martius with the city in the background, and the Temple of Jupiter illuminated centrally by sunlight in an otherwise shadowed city.

Certain aspects common to all of these shots are striking. Rome appears very different from both Sinuessa and Capua: white marble pillars proliferate, shining out in contrast to the bright red tiles of the roofs of the buildings, and the city appears elegant, spacious, and airy. Even though construction is going on in the Forum shot, no dirt or grime is seen anywhere, with everything clean and bright. In contrast with the crowded grubby streets of the other cities, Rome actually seems sparsely populated, partly of course since no scenes take place in the streets of the city, which appears only in these distant aerial views. Nevertheless, even apart from this practical point, the Rome of *Spartacus* is a magnificent and beautiful place.

Two other points should also be stressed. Despite the beautification of the city, it has been created with surprising accuracy and attention to detail, as is indicated by the ability to identify buildings in the shots outlined above. It is true that construction on the Temple of Antoninus and Faustina did not begin until AD 141 – although it is not certain that this is the building represented in the shot – while the Fornix Fabianus was completed some fifty years before the slave revolt; so these elements are not historically authentic. Nevertheless, there appears to have been a fair attempt to produce a Rome that was indicative of the Republican period and to reproduce some buildings as accurately as possible. But note that this representation accurately excludes some particularly evocative ancient Roman landmarks, such as the Theater of Pompey and the Colosseum, built much later; as we have seen, the vital role of amphitheater is played instead by the arena in Capua.

One area in which authenticity is not preserved, however, is in the use of white as opposed to color. As Joanna Paul has pointed out, "We've long known that sculpture and architectural detail would have been painted in bright colors, but this so offends our cherished notions of gleaming white marble temples that it's rarely depicted on screen."[38] Although the other cities depicted in *Spartacus* broke with this convention, it seems that the great city of Rome would be unrecognizable to the audience were this element changed. While other less familiar aspects or places can be depicted with more flexibility, Rome itself has too long a cinematic tradition to allow for such a radical departure from its expected appearance.

THE COSTUMES

Since the streets and buildings of the cities depicted in *Spartacus* do not proclaim their Roman-ness through typical symbols such as marble pillars and mosaics, other elements are relied upon to set the events in the appropriate period. One of the most important of these signaling devices is costume. Barbara Darragh, the series costume designer, devoted a great deal of thought and energy to clothing the

different characters, and made a clear distinction between the gladiators, whom she classifies as typifying "glory with the raw reality
of life," and the upper classes, particularly the women, whom she
wanted to portray as extravagant beauties. She carried out extensive
historical research in designing the costumes, looking at drawings,
graffiti, sculpture, and novels, as well as taking a holiday to Liberia
in order "to reference the remains of a past civilization."[39]

This attention to detail may not at first seem obvious; consultation
of reference works on the dress of Roman women tells the reader
that married women in Rome had very clear items of clothing that
marked out their status as respectable matrons. Thus Judith Lynn
Sebesta writes: "The costume of the matron signified her modesty
and chastity, her *pudicitia*. It consisted of her distinctive dress, the
woolen *stola*, which was worn over a tunic; the protective woolen
bands which dressed her hair; and the woolen *palla* or mantle which
was used to veil her head when she went out in public."[40] With
regard to materials, Eastern fabrics became extremely popular, as a
substitute for traditional homespun wool. Silk imported from China
was rewoven in Rome to create a finer, lighter fabric, while diapha-
nous Coan silk was cited frequently as a popular but often disreputable material for women's garments, so fine that it left little to the
viewer's imagination. As Raoul McLaughlin points out, "The use of
semi-translucent silks gave respectable women the opportunity to
display their figures while still wearing traditionally cut garments."[41]
Sumptuary laws reflect the fact that women rebelled against laws
and codes that restricted their dress and appearance. The ancient
Roman woman was as fashion conscious as her descendants are two
millennia later, and although they continued to dress in tunics and
stolae, these garments were brightly colored and made of fine fabrics,
and the women accessorized with make-up, jewelry, and elaborate
hairstyles.

Many of these aspects were incorporated into the costumes of the
Roman women in *Spartacus*, who are most frequently seen in floor-
length gauzy gowns of reds, greens, blues, yellows, and pinks, often
embroidered or patterned along the borders. While tunics do not
seem to appear, and there is rather more flesh on show than would
have been the case in the ancient world, the dresses do mimic the
styles of antiquity, with shoulder straps and necklines that echo those
of the ancient Greek *chiton* or Roman *stola*. In order to achieve the
draping effect reminiscent of ancient statues, the dresses were draped
and then handworked onto individually made corsets, which were
then hidden in the folds of the bodice.[42] Jewelry and hairstyles were

elaborate and carefully designed, modeled on ancient sources but also designed and made in-house according to Darragh's individual ideas, as she created back-stories for the jewelry pieces featured in each season. Garment pins, known as *fibulae*, however, a common feature of Roman dress, do not appear. Similarly, although the central Roman women featured in the *Spartacus* series are all of matron status, none of them wear woolen bands in their hair, for this would have created an alienating distance between the character and viewers unaware of the custom. Nor do the women in *Spartacus* typically veil their heads,[43] despite the fact that this was a custom that was accepted in the ancient world.

Thus, despite the historical research carried out by Darragh and her team, she made concessions under the influence of modern couture fashion and current trends, a necessary point if the costumes were to appear attractive to a contemporary audience. It is notable that these dresses are far more elaborate than those worn by Roman women on screen during the heyday of epic movies in the 1950s and 1960s, although they do resemble the costumes seen in *Gladiator* and *Rome*. Overall, however, the gowns of these elite female Romans are both more sumptuous and more revealing than any seen on the mainstream screen to date, and this reflects contemporary tastes as well as the aims and target audience of the show.

The upper-class Roman men are generally dressed in long, colored tunics with a vertical stripe, either plain or more elaborately embroidered or woven, running down on each side. Many of these garments look somewhat rough and coarse in comparison to the women's dresses; the material for the clothes was imported from India, since this handmade open-weave cloth was felt to suit the costume style required. Such tunics are longer than those shown in Roman paintings and statues, and in fact Latin literature makes reference to long tunics being effeminate;[44] but some extant decorative art, especially from Pompeii and Herculaneum, reveals a wider range of tunic length than is usually recognized. One might assume the usual color for a Roman man's tunic to be white, whereas those worn in *Spartacus* are colored, with almost no white to be seen; here again the literary evidence may present an ideal that was not followed in real life, as the mosaic from Pompeii depicting street musicians in brightly colored tunics indicates.[45] The stripe on the tunic is presumably inspired by the *tunica angusticlavia* donned by upper-class Roman men. The tunics are worn with a mantle over one shoulder, perhaps a folded *pallium* or a *chlamys*, and the whole ensemble is belted, reflecting the fact that a belted tunic was a sign of status and formality in Rome.[46]

It is most striking that gleaming white tunics almost never appear in *Spartacus*, and not even that ultimate symbol of ancient Rome, the toga. Both of these classic items of Roman dress appear only on senators such as Varinius and Metellus, emphasizing their role as members of the political elite, far removed from the ordinary Romans such as Batiatus and Solonius.

With regard to the lower classes, slave girls are dressed in shorter knee-length tunics, open from the neck down to the chest (or lower), and slit at the sides of the skirt. Rendered in single colors, they are simple garments that tie at the neck or shoulders, and are worn with no undergarments: their principal aim is to provide titillation for the audience as they are opened, exposing the naked bodies beneath. Clearly less authenticity is required or sought here, for the aim is to provide sheer entertainment. For the gladiators too, a more fictionalized approach was taken, with costumes emphasizing the masculinity and powerful physiques of the fighters, each of whom had both an individual color palette and an animal reference – such as a snake in the case of Spartacus – that recurred in identifying elements in the various costumes worn by the individual characters.

There were, however, additional considerations. Because the show was heavily focused on constant action and vigorous stunts, all costume elements needed to be suitable for such activities; helmets, for example, had to be lightweight enough to be comfortable, and stable enough to fit perfectly on the head without wobbling, as well as sturdy and durable enough to last for several seasons. The fact that repeat shots were required for both actor and his stunt double, as well as many scenes being shot with two successive film units to create different angles, made this even more essential. As so often with filmmaking, practical considerations had to be tied in with aesthetics in creating the costumes for this production.

CONCLUSION

For all its technological advances, the post-modern world of the twenty-first century is a dark and uncertain place, full of doubts and fears, and this is reflected in the depiction of ancient Rome on the modern screen. The vivid brilliant colors of the Technicolor productions of the 1950s and 1960s gave way to the muted shades of the early twenty-first century with the film *Gladiator*, and have culminated in the murky, faded tones of *Rome* and *Spartacus*. On the one hand, there is a laudable striving for realism; the ancient world can be shown in all its grubby glory as opposed to the sanitized versions of earlier years. Yet on the other hand, this more graphic look is closing the gap between the screen genres of fantasy and historical fiction, presenting scenes and costumes that would more likely have been seen only in pornographic movies, and explicit violence of an unprecedented level, that turns the realism into a voyeuristic, titillating experience. In many ways, cinematic Rome is still the Rome it has always been, with earlier screen depictions detectable in the buildings, color, furniture, and dress of this ancient world; yet it is also a dark and turbulent new Rome that owes as much to contemporary thinking as it does to its screen antecedents, or indeed, the Roman Republic itself.

NOTES

1 Ramirez (2004: 127).
2 O'Brien (1993: 158).
3 Final costs rose to $3.9 million, making it the most expensive movie of the silent era.
4 Whitlock (2010: 49).
5 Doherty (2002: 24).
6 Burgoyne (2014: 97).
7 Hall (2010: 54).
8 Whitlock (2010) 161: "Excess was the norm of the day – Cleopatra's golden armor was made from real gold and cost a reported $1 million." See also Müller (2004: 166).
9 Eldridge (2006: 128–9).
10 Eldridge (2006: 57); also Freiman (1959: 27).
11 Kaplan (1999: 442).
12 On the nature and role of studio research departments and their differences from academics, see Eldridge (2006: 127–51).
13 Thus a comment in *Variety* (17 September 1966) talked of a Rome as "too long burdened under the homogenized and idealized unreality of laundered togas and gleaming columns," as quoted in Malamud (2001: 205); while Arnott (1970: 13) wrote of "historical films, where the Rome of the Caesars is invariably presented as spotlessly clean, with houses of gleaming marble and streets where no horse, obviously, ever set hoof."
14 Malamud (2001: 203)
15 See Cyrino (2005: 170–1).
16 Elliot (2013: 1–4) rightly points out that this is a statement not without complications, raising questions about the nature and continuing presence of epic as a genre throughout the twentieth and twenty-first centuries. Nevertheless, as he agrees, "most scholars working in the field ... are broadly in agreement that there is a certain group of films with

comparable styles, settings and themes which fell out of favour in the mid-1960s, but which have regained popularity over the past decade."

17 The following quotes are from the interview in Calhoun (2000).

18 Blanshard and Shahabudin (2011: 7).

19 Allen (2008: 185).

20 See Richards (2008: 162).

21 "HBO Rome – Behind The Scenes – 360 SET TOUR," YouTube (28 March 2007).

22 Winner (2005).

23 Winner (2005). See also Cyrino (2008a: 4–7) on the originality of focusing on the non-elite Romans.

24 Quoted in Winner (2005).

25 The quotes are from an email correspondence with Iain Aitken, dated 31 March 2015.

26 For the construction style, see Mollo and Pesaresi (2010: 409).

27 Keppie (2000: 79).

28 Zanker (1998); plate 6 shows them in color.

29 Zanker (1998: 100) and plate 5.

30 For example, the House of Sallust, the miniature villa, the House of the Hunt; see Zanker (1998: 150, 167, 185, 188).

31 Many props were then sold at auction in December 2012, and some of the items may still be viewed in the online catalog of Webb's, a New Zealand auction house (webbs.co.nz).

32 See Tschen-Emmons (2014: 172).

33 The Metropolitan Museum of Art, Department of Greek and Roman Art; see the Heilbrunn Timeline of Art History, "Boscoreale: Frescoes from the Villa of P. Fannius Synistor" (metmuseum.org).

34 Accession Number: 17.190.2076. See Picón (2007: 380–1, 493, no. 446).

35 See Overbeck and Mau (1884: 428).

36 In email correspondence with the author.

37 For this building, see Futrell (1997: 278, n.56) and Bomgardner (2002: 62).

38 Paul (2014).

39 These remarks were made in email correspondence with Barbara Darragh, for whose assistance and cooperation I am grateful.

40 Sebesta and Bonfante (2001: 48).

41 McLaughlin (2010: 148).

42 This process was kindly described to me by Barbara Darragh in private email correspondence.

43 An exception is Aurelia, the wife of Varro, who is depicted as a virtuous Roman matron and therefore does cover her head with her shawl, in contrast to women such as Lucretia, Gaia, and Ilithyia, who are corrupt and unscrupulous and do not.

44 Quintilian, *The Education of an Orator* 11.3.138, says that the tunic

should fall just below the knee; for the effeminacy of the long tunic, see Cicero, *Against Catiline* 2.2.

45 This mosaic (dating from 150–125 BC) from the so-called Villa of Cicero, with the signature "Dioskourides of Samos," may be seen in the National Archaeological Museum of Naples.

46 See Sebesta and Bonfante (2001: 221).

PART III

Gender and Sexuality

8 *The Rape of Lucretia*

Anise K. Strong

When a television series set in ancient Rome chooses to name its leading female character "Lucretia," it is impossible to ignore the dual echoes of such a name. Both the legendary Lucretia, the paradigmatic virtuous matron whose rape and suicide sparked the birth of the Roman Republic, and Lucrezia Borgia, the allegedly incestuous Renaissance poisoner, have shaded the name with nearly as much baggage as "Messalina" or "Cleopatra." From the very beginning of STARZ *Spartacus*, the question sits at the back of the well-educated viewer's mind – will this Lucretia be raped? What is her connection to sexuality and to revolution? STARZ *Spartacus* does not provide us with a quick or easy answer to this question, or indeed to the issue of rape in general. The theme of Lucretia's sexual attitudes in the series and, in particular, her relationship to the act of rape reflects on the use of rape in modern historical fiction to assert power and to demean both women and men. The cinematic motif of rape is fraught with issues of power and its abuse, the major themes underlying the tragic drive of the entire *Spartacus* series. In particular, both men and women exercise their dominance over others through sexual abuse. Television critic Maureen Ryan has commented that *Spartacus* is one of the most feminist shows on television.[1] The depiction of rape is one of the most significant and feminist aspects of *Spartacus* in this regard.

RAPE ON THE HISTORICAL/FANTASY SCREEN

Before turning to a detailed discussion of *Spartacus* itself, its representation should be placed within the larger context of the current popularity of rape scenes in historically based television series and films. Once a censored or forbidden topic, rape has become a nearly commonplace feature of premium cable dramas, especially historical and fantasy dramas. In general, television and film rape scenes are highly eroticized and seem designed for both the shock and pleasure of male viewers. As *New York Times* film critic A. O. Scott commented in his review of *The Girl with the Dragon Tattoo* (2011), "It is in the nature of the moving image to give pleasure, and in the nature of film audiences – consciously or not, admittedly or not – to find pleasure in what they see. So in depicting Salander's rape in the graphic way he did, the director ran the risk of aestheticizing, glamorizing and eroticizing it."[2] Rape has become, in many cases, a means of juicing up ratings while combining both sex and violence, without much concern for the lasting impact on the characters' psyches or the narrative arc.

The cinematographic focus in most modern rape scenes is frequently on the nude body of the woman, while the man stands or kneels behind her, physically overpowering her. If we see any of his body, it is only his rear end, not his vulnerable front. Most conventional rape scenes show the woman being assaulted from behind, perhaps going back to one of the most iconic modern cinematic rapes, that of Nola Darling in Spike Lee's 1988 *She's Gotta Have It*.[3] Such a pose makes the viewer an unintentional co-conspirator in the rape scene, since we are given the perspective of the rapist while his naked body is largely hidden from our eyes. This objectifies and dehumanizes the victim even as she is assaulted physically by the rapist.[4] Lisa Cuklanz's analysis of televisual rape depictions from 1976 to 1990 suggests that, even when the rape itself is not sexualized, the emphasis is placed on the suffering of the male partner or friend of the rape victim, who avenges her (and his own honor), rather than on her own emotional trauma.[5] Men become heroic figures by punishing the rapists of "their" women. More recently, Jessica Hammer has argued that the current popularity of televisual and cinematic rape scenes represents a failure to imagine women as human beings. Instead, a woman's vagina and its use by others serve to define the female character. If women are not human, then human tragedies do not apply to women – only special "woman" tragedies. Women on television do not suffer by being simply physically assaulted, losing their jobs, or undergoing a lasting physical injury; instead, their harm comes frequently in the form of sexual violence.[6]

Perhaps the most currently controversial and popular example of this style of rape depiction is the HBO series *Game of Thrones* (2011–), a show that so far has included three major rape scenes of significant characters as well as many other sexual assaults upon unnamed women. In the very first episode, the screenwriters altered a scene from the source novel that describes a moment of sexual awakening and consensual intimacy, transforming it into a depiction of brutal, explicit rape. The camera focuses on the anguished face of a blonde, pale, young bride, Daenerys Targaryen, during her violent assault from behind, exposing her nude body fully to the camera while hiding the form of her aggressive, dark-skinned husband, Khal Drogo. This scene is not only filmed according to cinematic tropes of rape, as discussed earlier; it also echoes the racist paranoia of many earlier works on film and television which portray the white woman as the innocent victim of the large man of color.[7] Nonetheless, Daenerys later falls in love with her rapist husband; their relationship is glorified as one of the happiest and most stable romances in the series. She appears to suffer no lasting trauma as a result of this assault.

Season Four of *Game of Thrones* features a sex scene between the siblings Jaime and Cersei Lannister, in which Jaime violently assaults Cersei while she first physically turns away and then repeatedly begs him to stop, while he yells at her, "I don't care" (episode 4.3). He continues to force her down to the floor and have sex with her; the camera focuses largely on his clothed body, on top, as well as her hair and upside-down face, which appears agonized. This scene was interpreted by a large majority of viewers as a rape scene.[8] However, the writers, directors, and actors all claim that it was in fact consensual "by the end of the scene."[9] However the scene is interpreted, the sexual violence had no lasting repercussions for the plot of the show or either character, nor did it appear to be part of a larger theme or narrative; neither character ever mentions it again.

The most recent rape of a significant character in *Game of Thrones*, that of Sansa Stark by her husband Ramsay Snow on their wedding night in Season Five, similarly erases female perspective while echoing conventional tropes of cinematic rape (episode 5.6).[10] Sansa is raped from behind, with Ramsay fully clothed. However, we catch only a few seconds of her traumatized face before the scene switches to a close-up of a male observer, Theon Greyjoy, who watches the rape to the accompaniment of Sansa's screams. Theon's suffering at watching the brutalization of his foster-sister is apparently more significant to the narrative than Sansa's own emotions; Sansa remains a largely disempowered victim for the rest of the season. As in previous televisual depictions, the rape is apparently more important as an incentive for a male character to seek justice and take action than as a transformative experience for a female character. This marital rape depiction echoes a rape on Showtime's historical drama *The Tudors* (2007–10) in which Jane Rochford is similarly brutally raped from behind by her new husband George, despite her protests, for no readily apparent narrative reason (episode 2.6).

In an early episode of the HBO-BBC series *Rome* (2005–7), both the audience and the main characters casually look on as Mark Antony stops the legion's procession home to rape an anonymous random shepherdess (episode 1.1). When he is finished, he pumps his hands in the air, expecting applause and support from his comrades for his demonstration of virility. In the film *300*, set in a highly fictionalized ancient Greece, the Spartan Queen Gorgo is brutally and humiliatingly raped from behind in a scene that owes no debt to Herodotus' account of the Persian Wars. While Gorgo ultimately takes revenge upon her attacker, she also remains a traumatized victim, and her revenge requires the assistance of male allies.

Not all modern television treats sexual assault so lightly. The current STARZ series *Outlander* (2014–), created by Ronald Moore and based on the popular time-traveling eighteenth-century romance novels by Diana Gabaldon, follows in *Spartacus'* footsteps, as outlined later in this chapter; it also uses rape as a means of addressing the inherent oppression of a society. In the case of *Outlander*, the problematized system is that of colonialism as well as that of early modern patriarchy; the occupying English forces frequently use sexual violence as a means of control and intimidation over the local Scottish populace. *Outlander* depicts several explicit scenes of sexual assault, most notably an extended finale episode focusing on the male romantic hero Jamie's violent rape, torture, and psychological breaking by the English psychopath Jonathan Randall. However, like *Spartacus*, these rapes both illustrate a larger social problem and have lasting consequences for the characters involved. The focus is not on the eroticized pleasure taken by Randall but on the lingering trauma and erasure of identity suffered by Jamie. In general, STARZ seems to be deliberately seeking a female and feminist audience in its shows, in contrast perhaps to HBO; one important aspect of that agenda is its respect for the seriousness and care needed in any televisual depiction of rape. In the second episode of *Outlander*, the female protagonist Claire asks, "Is there ever a good reason for rape?" (episode 1.2). Both *Spartacus* and *Outlander* would answer that there is, potentially, a worthwhile reason to depict rape on screen, but only with the kind of care and deliberation that is rarely seen in other historical dramas.

RAPE IN *SPARTACUS*

In contrast to most other television shows, especially historical dramas, rape in STARZ *Spartacus* is not sexualized. It is never presented as morally acceptable. It is used to condemn both the Roman slave system and specific individual characters as evil. The rapists are universally satisfyingly punished by their victims themselves – not by their victims' male relatives. In other words, rape has both narrative impact and characterological consequences; it is one significant tool in Steven S. DeKnight's arsenal to depict the larger nature of Roman corruption and immorality.

Despite the enormous amount of physical violence in the series, there is no onscreen violent rape in the entire first season, *Blood and Sand*. The rapes of named characters in later seasons are key turning points and never treated casually. In the pilot episode, Spartacus' wife Sura effectively, if implausibly, defends herself against multiple rapists (episode 101). Nearly all the major sex scenes are between either married couples or couples whose deep romantic love has been well established. These interludes are frequently initiated by women and show sexual pleasure on the part of both women and men.

Before examining specific depictions of rape in *Spartacus*, it is necessary to define what counts as a rape within this series. What does it mean to sexually assault someone in a world of oppressed slaves, upwardly striving gladiatorial school-owners, and high Roman nobles? By one reasonable definition, any sexual act between a free person and a slave is rape, since the slave cannot meaningfully consent. However, such a perspective has not been the normative view in most historical slaveholding societies. Susan Brownmiller notes that an 1851 Louisiana Supreme Court definition alleged that in sexual relationships between male masters and female slaves, "it is so rare in the case of concubinage that the seduction and temptation are not mutual," although the opinion does admit that female slaves are "vulnerable to the seductions of an unprincipled master."[11] Even American abolitionists spoke of "illicit passion" rather than "sexual violence."[12]

At the same time, there is obviously a strong argument against accepting the perspective of slave-owners upon such sexual relations. What is clear is that masters' sexual abuse of their slaves has been ubiquitous in every slave society, most certainly including the ancient Romans. Brownmiller argues that rape was "part and parcel of the white man's subjugation of a people for economic and psychological gain."[13] While Roman slavery was not ethnically based, it was a dominant part of the Roman economy and society, both in history and in its depiction in mass media. We have little direct evidence of historical Roman masters' sexual abuse of their slaves, but this omission from elite male-authored texts does not mean that it was not a common occurrence. Eva Cantarella goes so far as to describe the sexual mentality of Roman males as that of a rapist, a consummate rapist.[14] Yet at the same time, both the ancient Romans themselves and STARZ *Spartacus* seem to distinguish between forcible rape and the more commonplace master–slave sexual relations in which slaves could not meaningfully consent. If we define all master–slave relations as rape, then it is constant and ubiquitous in every episode of the series, whether we consider male gladiators like Crixus who are required to serve as fertile studs for matrons like Lucretia or the activities of the anonymous masked slave girls trotted out at Batiatus' orgies.

Crixus (Manu Bennett) is perhaps the best and most intriguing example of this type of non-forcible rape, especially given his gender and his unusual role as one of only two characters who appear in every season of the series. In the prequel season, *Gods of the Arena*, Crixus is ordered by his *domina*, Lucretia, to have sex with her in order to produce a child, since she believes her beloved husband Batiatus to be infertile. Lucretia takes the position of authority, saying "You are never to speak of this – do you understand, slave? . . . I would not look at you – lest sight turn stomach. Enter me, and do not cease until you have spilled seed" (episode 5). At the same time, the scene is filmed as if it is a conventional rape; the camera focuses on Lucretia's grimacing face while Crixus, relatively expressionless, enters her from behind, concealing most of his body. Who here is the attacker, and who the victim? Despite Lucretia's expression, she is the one with the power and control, and thus, by the rules of *Spartacus*, here she is the rapist. When Crixus later falls in love with his fellow slave Naevia, his reluctance to continue to have sex with Lucretia becomes ever more obvious; nevertheless, he has no choice but to continue his sexual service.

When the gladiators at last rebel violently against the House of Batiatus at the end of *Blood and Sand*, Lucretia asks Crixus for mercy on the grounds of the fetus inside her belly, of whom he is the presumptive biological father. Crixus responds by stabbing her belly and aborting the fetus. While this act is visually horrifying, it mirrors the modern right of American rape victims to abort any offspring of an assault, a privilege that is supported by 75 percent of Americans.[15] In this case, however, the genders are unexpectedly reversed from the modern norm. This act of violence confirms that, in Crixus' mind, his intercourse with Lucretia was indeed a series of rapes, even if Lucretia colored it with false romantic overtones. Crixus perceives himself as a rape victim with no obligation or connection to any resulting fetus; he can begin to recover from his trauma by seeking revenge directly upon his attacker.

While raising intriguing questions about standard societal assumptions regarding rape and power dynamics, the creators of *Spartacus* still make a significant and meaningful distinction between this sort of implicit rape, which is depicted nonviolently and often performed silently by extras, and the violent, explicitly abusive rape of named characters. In the first season, Spartacus is told that his wife Sura has been gang-raped by Roman soldiers. He also catches a glimpse of the clearly abused, suicidal Pietros after the young man's rape by another male gladiator. However, the only sex scenes shown in the first season are, if not freely consensual, at least nonviolent. Even in the case of Ashur's sexual encounter with Naevia, which is clearly against her will, the camera cuts away at the instant that he removes her gown. This is a scene that gives us all the horror and degradation of rape, without visually objectifying the woman in question.

In contrast, *Gods in the Arena*, the prequel season, features an extended set of violent onscreen rapes of the slave woman Diona, who ultimately serves as the tragic symbol for the entire season. Diona's character arc exemplifies both the evils of slavery and the corruption of Rome's elite. Despite being named after the Roman maiden goddess, Diona is initially actively interested in sexual pleasure and romance. In the first two episodes she repeatedly stares at the gladiators' nude bodies and giggles with her fellow slave Naevia, imagining future pleasurable encounters. In the third episode, however, the Roman senator Cossutius demands that the virgin Diona be violently raped both by the ugliest, dirtiest gladiator in the barracks and, simultaneously, by Cossutius himself, who forces anal sex upon her while abusing her verbally (episode 3).[16] At the end of this encounter, Diona is visibly bruised and distraught. Lucretia sympathetically but ruthlessly comments, "It was an unfortunate thing to be so used by men for base entertainment."

Diona's tragedy is not the loss of her sexual agency but her overall powerlessness within Roman society. Having lost the extra value of her virginity, Diona becomes a regular sex slave at Lucretia's parties, until she is finally so traumatized by her repeated rapes that she attempts suicide. Her fellow slave Naevia reacts to Diona's trauma, because of which she is described as "fading each day," by helping

Diona escape the house of Batiatus. However, at the end of the season Diona is captured and executed in the gladiatorial arena. Like the male gladiator Varro in the first season, who dies at the whim of a Roman elite boy, Diona serves as the symbolic victim of the prequel season. Her degradation from lively, innocent young woman to desperate, traumatized runaway is represented as the inevitable result not of individual evil deeds but of the Roman system of slavery and the gross inequality between elites and other citizens.

Rape as a means of demonstrating the corruption of the Roman elite is not restricted solely to interactions between free people and slaves in *Spartacus*. As *Gods of the Arena*'s initially modest Lucretia gradually turns her house into a part-time brothel in an effort to gain the favor of wealthy magistrates for her husband, the audience increasingly is led to fear that she herself will become a rape victim. Such a fate seems particularly imminent in episode 4, "Beneath the Mask," when Batiatus' enemy physically threatens a vulnerable, temporarily isolated Lucretia. However, she faces him down, only to discover that he has murdered her friend Gaia in her place. Lucretia remains free of rape while she remains the *materfamilias* of the House of Batiatus; her power and marital status protect her. To be *domina* is to be free of rape; any other status renders a woman sexually vulnerable.

Rape is an act that the creators of *Spartacus* use sparingly and explicitly to signify the abuse of power; it is never glamorized or eroticized. Following standard feminist and psychological theories, rape in *Spartacus* is always about power, not sex. This model also echoes, whether deliberately or unconsciously, the ancient Roman conceptualization of rape. For ancient Romans, the right to be free of rape was one of the defining characteristics of a citizen, as demonstrated in numerous stories from Livy and other chroniclers of Rome's early history, including the tale of Lucretia herself.[17] Rape, in the Roman context, becomes a signifier of tyranny. Sandra Joshel notes that rape in the Roman imagination is also inextricably linked to imperialism and mass slavery.[18] Powerful men step outside permissible legal and social boundaries when they abuse their authority to rape fellow Romans. When such an abuse of power occurs, the inevitable response is riot and revolution.

Most moments of dramatic political change in the Roman Republic were allegedly sparked by the inappropriate rape of a citizen. Both males and females were potential victims in these origin stories, although the male rape attempts have often been ignored by modern historians who by default assume that rape is a crime committed only against women.[19] For the Romans, rape was an act committed by the powerful against the powerless regardless of gender, either legally, as in the case of master–slave relations, or illegally, in the case of the rape of a citizen like Lucretia.[20] Within the context of the show, the rapes and subsequent execution of Diona serve as an implicit spark for the rebellion of Spartacus. It is this act that helps turn Gannicus, Naevia, and Oenomaus against the House of Batiatus, while Crixus' anger is fueled by Ashur's later rape of Naevia. Rape once again leads to rebellion and an attempt to overthrow the existing social system.

In the second and third seasons, rape becomes a more prominent feature of the narrative as a symbol of oppression, perhaps because the main characters are no longer living in a unified household of master and slave where other, more subtle dynamics of hierarchy and domination are readily visible. In one of the early episodes of the *Vengeance* second season, the Spartacani storm a house and attack an anonymous *dominus* in the midst of his violent rape of one of his slave women. The master is then interrogated about his former slave Naevia, whom he has also raped multiple times, and answers defensively, "How could I know that she held meaning?" Crixus and Spartacus answer, "You just saw something to be used." From the *dominus*' perspective, Naevia is not a creature of worth, nor human, and thus definitionally available for rape. In the final season, *War of the Damned*, Julius Caesar similarly makes excuses to Crassus for having attempted to assault Crassus' slave Kore: "Apologies. I did not know the girl held meaning" (episode 302). Kore is only protected from rape because of her emotional value to her *dominus*; otherwise, she is presumed to be readily available for sexual abuse.

The idea that vulnerability to rape is the defining distinction between free and slave persists throughout the rest of the series. In the last season, *War of the Damned*, the former Roman noblewoman Laeta is sold into slavery to a vicious pirate by Marcus Crassus. It is made clear that her new owner plans to rape her as soon as possible, but he is thwarted when Laeta runs a red-hot poker through his chest, thus symbolically raping him instead. Still, Laeta cannot escape her newfound slave-like status and escapes with the rebels. Her lack of a Roman marital partner and her ambiguous status as a former prisoner of Spartacus leaves her sexually vulnerable.

The newly empowered former female slaves of Spartacus' camp, however, also demonstrate that it is wrong to reduce human sexuality to either of the two options of violent rape or loving intimate sex between a romantic couple. The former slave Mira witnesses what appears to be the violent rape of Chadara, a recently rescued slave, by another of Spartacus' rebels. Mira steps in to successfully attack the man and drive him off. Then she turns to Chadara, expecting gratitude and sisterly bonding, only to be criticized for having broken up a largely consensual sex scene. Chadara retorts, "Freedom is not without cost. I pay with the only fucking coin I have, as do you." Chadara equates her attempt to gain social status within the rebel horde through sexual favors as equivalent to Mira's loving relationship with Spartacus himself. Female sexuality in *Spartacus* is neither simple nor reductionist. While it may be a feminist show, it does not accept radical feminist views of all sexual intercourse as inherently oppressive. In this case, Chadara, whether suffering from false consciousness or not, wishes to use sexual favors as a tool in her arsenal for greater power.

RAPE, REVENGE, AND REVOLUTION

During the second season, *Vengeance*, the show arrives at the moment that the audience has been both fearing and anticipating for some time – an actual violent rape of Lucretia herself, who has mysteriously recovered from Crixus' attack. Lucretia's rapist is Ashur, the former rapist of Naevia and one of the most complicatedly liminal figures of the entire series. Ashur is neither gladiator nor free man – a former fixer slave who moves freely both within the household and in the outside world and is obsessed with his own status. Lucretia, too, in this season has become a liminal figure – neither alive nor dead, no longer the *materfamilias* but not precisely a slave either. Ashur repeatedly rapes her as a violent means of attempting to claim his freed status and dominate over his former *domina*.

This first rape of Lucretia is explicitly violent and lacking in eroticism. Ashur forces her against a wall, with both parties fully clothed and no body parts shown. Even more than usual, the focus here is entirely on the reversal of power, not the sex. The scene begins with Lucretia attempting to assert authority over Ashur, declaring, "You forget your place. You secure nothing without me." He demonstrates that she has misunderstood the new power dynamic by raping her from behind while she screams; no one comes to her aid. Later, Ashur revels in forcing Lucretia to call him "Dominus" while he calls her "my love"; he beats and rapes her again when she tries to defend herself, reminding her that "I am not your slave" (episode 208). This twisted relationship is entirely about the reversal of the previous master–slave dichotomy.

The camera then immediately cuts to a scene featuring the loving intimate relationship of Naevia and Crixus and a soft focus on their two naked bodies. Crixus gently focuses on Naevia's pleasure rather than his own. However, their sex is interrupted by Naevia's own traumatic memories of gang rape. She confesses, "They have taken everything from me – even your touch." Here the message is clear and unsubtle – rape is destructive and violent; loving sexuality is good. Indeed, after each and every scene of Ashur's violent rapes of Lucretia, there is a quick cut to a consensual loving scene of a rebel couple. These rapes are not intended as the regular appearances of nudity and sex that seem contractually required for every episode of *Spartacus*. They do not serve as erotic pleasure for the viewing audience but rather shock and remind us of the oppression of slavery. Despite her reunion with her lover Crixus, the rape survivor Naevia still contemplates suicide, declaring, "She was a different girl, young and foolish, ripped from this world by rough hands and hot breath upon neck. The things she was forced to do to survive . . . there is no place that memory would not follow. I cannot run from this" (episode 206). When Crixus asks if he is supposed to watch her fade as Diona did, Naevia responds by expressing a desire for control and agency over her life: "No, I would not have you watch! I would have you teach – how to breathe, how to live again, how to fight, so that no man will ever lay hands on me again against my will, and so the girl whose name was raped may reclaim it." Passively watching rape and the suffering of rape victims is the wrong answer, as is denying the real trauma experienced by these men and women. Crixus can teach Naevia how to survive this experience in part because he is a rape survivor himself. Naevia cannot remain the innocent romantic slave girl, but she can transform herself with Crixus' help into a fierce, proactive rebel warrior and reclaim control over her identity.

Eventually, Lucretia and Naevia indirectly unite in their mutual revenge on their rapist Ashur. Lucretia uses her skills of intrigue to cause Glaber to turn against Ashur, which in turn gives an opportunity for Naevia to confront Ashur in a duel. This scene is one of the most redemptive and unusual treatments of the standard rape-and-revenge plot in modern media. Crixus and Spartacus, extraordinarily skilled fighters, are both willing to fight Ashur and would easily kill him. However, Naevia insists on fighting him herself, and Crixus' response is not to take the Mel Gibson approach of "defending his woman," but rather to step back and support her. During the course of the duel, even when Naevia is losing, Crixus prevents others from going to her aid. Furthermore, unlike the standard trope of the woman seeking revenge for her rape, Naevia is not represented as a solitary, asexual, bitter, and ruthless warrior; instead, she is supported by her community and her lover. Ashur taunts Naevia during their duel by attempting to assert both physical and verbal power over her. He refers to her as "Crixus' bitch," denying that she has her own identity, and reminds her of his own rape of her: "You recall this – my body pressed against yours – you trembling, like you tremble now." Naevia responds by castrating Ashur, declaring that she is "far from help-less." When Ashur mocks her that his death will not heal her scars or erase the memory of her abuse, she kills him and answers, "No, it will not, but it is a fucking start" (episode 210). Crixus then envelops Naevia in a loving embrace. She has triumphed, and can now resume a happy and consensual sexual relationship with her chosen partner, scarred but facing the prospect of eventual psychological recovery. Meanwhile, Lucretia, having revenged herself on all those who hurt her, can step off a cliff and join her beloved husband in the afterlife.

The last season, *War of the Damned*, continues the themes both of rape as the signifier of oppressive tyranny and the rebellion as the source of both justice and healthy sexual relationships. We see in this season for the first time a loving consensual romance between master and slave, that of Marcus Crassus and his slave Kore, both of whom respect each other and treat each other as near equals. At the beginning of their sexual relationship, Crassus explicitly asks for her consent, and she responds that she does indeed desire him. Unfortunately, this relationship is destroyed when Crassus' son Tiberius, seeking revenge on his father, violently rapes and terror-izes Kore, telling her that "You are yet a slave and you will do as I fucking command," despite her attempt to take a pseudo-maternal role with him (episode 305). This rape is depicted conventionally, with Tiberius being shown only from behind and a focus on Kore's anguished face. Kore escapes to the rebels, with the help of Julius Caesar, whose character development in this regard will be discussed later. Eventually, the rebels capture Tiberius. First Naevia defeats him in a duel (Figure 8.1), in vengeance for the death of Crixus, and then Kore stabs Tiberius to death. She proclaims, "I have balanced fucking scale." On the most obvious level, this metaphor refers to the scales of justice – Kore has achieved vengeance upon her rapist. Yet within the context of *Spartacus*, Kore has also temporarily balanced the power relations between master and slave: Tiberius cannot use his privilege and power to escape death and imprisonment. Kore is his equal in the moment of death. Yet the price for her vengeance is a return to slave status; she is returned in chains to Crassus and is ordered to now address him as "Dominus" rather than as "Marcus." The scale has returned to its former inequity.

Figure 8.1 Naevia (Cynthia Addai-Robinson) kicks Tiberius (Christian Antidormi) in the crotch in episode 309 ("The Dead and the Dying"). STARZ.

Although Caesar hides Kore's crime from Crassus, it is eventually discovered, ironically due to Spartacus' accidental revelation. In response, Crassus and Caesar deliver fundamentally different answers about appropriate uses of power and sexuality than we have previously heard from Roman tongues:

CAESAR: You place blame upon victim. Your noble fucking son forced himself inside her, one of many acts that led to deserved fate.
CRASSUS [to Kore]: Apologies, apologies, apologies, for all that you have suffered. Know that it shall end when Spartacus falls.

These statements contrast sharply with Lucretia's earlier vague platitudes about unfortunate occurrences. Indeed, this is the first significant moment in the entire series in which a master apologizes to a slave. "Apologies" has been a catchphrase throughout the show, generally used to communicate submission by a subordinate to a superior. Thus Batiatus and Lucretia repeatedly offer apologies to their senatorial patrons, slaves constantly apologize for inadequate service, and, humiliatingly, Lucretia is forced to apologize to Ashur for resisting his rapes. Here Crassus, the most powerful Roman character in the series, thrice apologizes to his own slave woman because she has been raped, signifying a major transformation in his attitudes.

Of course, this being *Spartacus*, and Romans being Romans, Kore is still punished by crucifixion – not for the murder of her rapist but explicitly for her connection to the rebellion. In the final moments of *Spartacus*, she stands as the representation of all female victims of Roman oppression, just as Gannicus stands as the representative of all male victims, united equally in death. They join the earlier seasons' Varro and Diona, also a gladiator and female sex-slave pair, as symbols of how slavery inevitably leads to physical abuse and the objectification of humans as mere bodies. Crassus may have learned that rape is unjustified under any circumstances, but he still is responsible for upholding and restoring the Roman slave system itself.

Of all the characters in the series, it is Gaius Julius Caesar, future Dictator of Rome, who has the most significant personal character development with regard to issues of rape and sexual control. As previously mentioned, the first appearance of Caesar depicts him as a casually abusive Roman, eager to molest Kore until he discovers that this particular slave "holds meaning" for her owner Crassus. In *War of the Damned*, however, Crassus' son Tiberius, anxious to cover up his rape of Kore, also violently rapes Caesar himself, in a scene visually echoing previous male–female rapes and cinematic conventions. Caesar is forced onto a table and assaulted from behind, as Tiberius screams, "I do not take command from you! You must be taught severest lesson in who towers above you!" (episode 308). We see Tiberius' naked rear but none of the rest of his body, focusing instead on Caesar's face, which closely resembles that of Lucretia at similar moments. This is yet again a depiction of rape as an assertion of aggressive domination rather than as a sexual act. It is an actively uneroticized scene that is immediately contrasted with a montage of the rebels fighting and then making love in romantic, intimate established pairings like that of Agron and Nasir.

While Caesar's rape causes him to seek vengeance against Tiberius, it also seems to change fundamentally his attitude toward sexual violence itself. When Caesar later interviews a prostitute who has crucial evidence against Tiberius, he reassures her that he has no plans to assault her, offering instead "to take comfort" in their mutual grief and rage. He waits for the anonymous prostitute to kiss him first before engaging in what is clearly mutually consensual and desired intercourse. As discussed earlier, Caesar then exhibits profound empathy for and support toward Kore, acknowledging her victimhood and her right to justice. Through his own trauma, Caesar learns how to respect the humanity and personhood even of slaves, a small victory for the cause of Spartacus, which nevertheless costs multiple women's lives.

In the final scene of the series, the happy male–male couple of Agron and Nasir, together with several women and children, escape to freedom over the mountains. Their group of survivors includes a newborn baby boy to whom Kore, before her death, gives a blessing: "I pray he uses his cock only upon the willing." To be free, in the world of *Spartacus*, is to have both the choice and responsibility not to rape. As in the original Roman story of the rape of Lucretia, rape itself has sparked a rebellion and revolution. While Spartacus' war on the Roman slave system was fundamentally unsuccessful, the justice taken by rape survivors within the narrative and the lessons learned by Caesar and Crassus offer the hope that Rome will at least be governed by men who have sympathy for the worst oppressions of slavery. Spartacus, Sura, Naevia, Crixus, Lucretia, and Kore may all die, but the audience can envision a future in which rape is not a ubiquitous feature of human life.

NOTES

1 Ryan (2010).
2 Scott (2011).
3 Projansky (2001: 189).
4 Projansky (2001: 125–35).
5 Cuklanz (2000: 6–7).
6 Hammer (2012).
7 Projansky (2001: 6). While Jason Momoa, the male actor in question, is of mixed Hawaiian and European descent, his representation within *Game of Thrones* is as the threatening exoticized dark-skinned Other.
8 Itzkoff (2014).
9 Sepinwall (2014). Note that the creators' definition of rape here does not appear to match standard American legal or social norms of consent, raising issues about the relative importance of authorial intent.
10 The title of episode 5.6 – "Unbowed, Unbent, Unbroken" – is particularly and horrifically ironic given its depiction of forcible rape.
11 Brownmiller (1976: 153).
12 Brownmiller (1976: 154).
13 Brownmiller (1976: 147).
14 Cantarella (2002: 98).
15 Gallup Poll, 9–12 June 2011.
16 On viewer response regarding Diona's rape, see Gardner and Potter in this volume.
17 Titus Livy, *History of Rome* 1.57–60, 3.44–58, 8.28; Aulus Gellius, *Attic Nights* 4.14; Arieti (1997: 209).
18 Joshel (1992: 123).
19 Arieti (1997: 219).
20 Valerius Maximus, *Memorable Deeds and Sayings* 6.1.

9 *The Others*
Antony Augoustakis

The indisputable success of the acclaimed STARZ *Spartacus* show can be attributed to its wide appeal to twenty-first-century viewers. Certainly the show does not avoid topics that have traditionally been difficult to treat both on the big and small screens, such as rape, pornography, and homosexuality. Closely related to the show's forthright interest in bringing ancient Rome closer to modern life is its treatment of what we would call today "second-class" citizens,[1] namely the gladiators or the male and female slaves in the house and the *ludus* of Batiatus: we might call them the *others*, those figures who are normally given very little or no voice in our sources on ancient life, society, and civilization. This chapter discusses in particular how we perceive and understand the role of the non-elite women in *Spartacus*, and how much modern scholarship and criticism on gender in classical antiquity informs our understanding of gender, love, sexuality, familial relationships, and marriage in the ancient world, whether accurately or approximately depicted on the small screen.

Important studies on the role of Roman and especially non-Roman women have shed light on the fluidity of the concept of the *other* in the ancient world, but how do cinematographers and producers imagine the role of the female in the ancient world? In reconstructing the past, what are the traits with which they endow women in order to offer a final product aesthetically and commercially pleasing to modern audiences? Building on and continuing earlier discussions of the depiction of Roman and non-Roman women and ethnic minorities on the small screen,[2] this chapter examines several of the secondary female characters in *Spartacus*, such as Kore, Crassus' slave, who is endowed with Spartacus-like features in the final crucifixion scene, or Mira, Spartacus' companion, who dies in an effort to save him; but also the Amazon-type women, such as Naevia, Crixus' lover, who is a warrior and heroine to the very last battle of the rebellion. As I shall point out, the show ends with a powerful message of hope, but the carriers of this hope are not the Romans: Crassus is overshadowed by Pompey who steals Crassus' thunder at the end and claims the victory over the rebels as his own crowning achievement. It is the *others*, the survivors of the battle – such as the gay couple Agron and Nasir – who carry on Spartacus' message of freedom.

In his study, *Rethinking the Other in Antiquity*, Erich Gruen notes that the ancient Greeks, Romans, and Jews "disparage the different and abuse the alien" in order to accentuate the differences between themselves and the *others*:

> But an alternative strand exists in the ancient mentality . . . The establishment of a collective identity is an evolving process, intricate and meandering. To stress the stigmatization of the "Other" as a strategy of self-assertion and superiority dwells unduly on the negative . . . Many ancients took the affirmative route, set the alien in a softer light, found connections among peoples, appropriated the traditions of others, inserted themselves into the genealogies and legends of foreigners, and enhanced their own self-image by proclaiming their participation in a broader cultural sense.[3]

I believe this process is taking place in the representation of *otherness* in STARZ *Spartacus*: depending on their background and social status, audiences identify with the less privileged, yearn for the deserved punishment of the rich and powerful, and connect with the humane or inhumane traits of each character. Such portrayal makes it possible for us to look at the ancient world with a different eye, locating diversity in the very roots and beginnings of our civilization.

To be sure, modern television series, such as HBO *Rome* and *Spartacus*, are dominated by the Roman female figures who play a prominent and decisive role in moving the plot forward: Atia's and Servilia's feud in the first season of HBO *Rome*, for instance, sets in motion their respective sons' desire to save or destroy the Republic as Brutus and Octavian vie for power, while Antony is often used as a mere tool in the women's scheming. Likewise, in the first season and the prequel of *Spartacus* Lucretia and Ilithyia are the dominant forces in the gladiatorial *ludus* of Batiatus, as their thirst for power and social recognition propels them to act according to their own undeniably whimsical aspirations, and more often than not, contrary to their husbands' wishes.

Juxtaposed to this set of elite Roman women, there are several non-Roman women, female figures from the periphery of the empire, cast often as slaves or freedwomen.[4] Similar to the Roman perceptions of "barbarian" women in antiquity as bodily able, ruthless nomad-warriors and stout supporters of their male companions (such as the German wives and mothers portrayed by Tacitus),[5] in *Spartacus* we encounter the same type of "manly" female figure in the women of the rebel group: Mira, Saxa, and Naevia. These women are all cast in terms of masculine virtue, when they are called upon to espouse the cause of Spartacus in seeking freedom. As Anna Foka observes, "*Spartacus*, in spite of belonging to a genre comprised primarily of heteronormative and male-centered narratives about gladiators, redefines the genre's definition of heroism by depicting a wider spectrum of sexual behaviors as well as granting female characters critical, action-infused roles."[6]

In STARZ *Spartacus*, however, we encounter a type of *otherness* that is different from the expected norm of ethnic diversity, and this type of *otherness* adds considerable depth to the formation of non-Romanness as an identity. The rebels themselves are now the *other*, as male gladiators and female slaves join Spartacus' cause for one reason only: freedom. This group of *others* will eventually encompass Romans (like Laeta) and non-Romans alike, people in search of a different type of life, far from the corrupt way of Roman moral decline and dirty politics. Freedom is expressed in manifold ways that resonate with modern audiences: for instance, consider the show's unbridled sex scenes, which often fall outside our comfort zone, with many critics considering this a hybrid genre bordering pornography;[7] or the depiction of same-sex love in the show, which takes the covert "oysters and snails" scene from Stanley Kubrick's *Spartacus* (1960) and transforms it into something more meaningful and relatable, namely the powerful love stories of same-sex couples, like Agron and Nasir or Barca and Pietros.[8] The show highlights how these groups of *others*, otherwise marginalized individuals, seek freedom and are ready to die fighting as a new set of values and ideals is promoted: bravery, honesty, partnership, and love. It is this emphasis on the *others* and the promise of a "new," changed world that ultimately render this modern version of the Spartacus legend an appealing spectacle for contemporary viewers.

SURA

The plot of *Spartacus* is set in motion by the Thracian's hatred of the Romans as the direct result of his wife's unjust death. Conjugal love is exemplified in the case of Spartacus and Sura and sharply contrasted to the Romans in the series, especially Lucretia and Batiatus:

unlike the Roman couple, whose marriage, although devoted, is a social contract based on their mutual desire for power and money, Spartacus and Sura have "signed" another type of contract, love until death. Spartacus' quest for freedom from Roman rule is precisely driven by the death of his wife on the order of the cold-blooded Batiatus in the series' first season, *Blood and Sand*. The Thracian's separation from Sura turns the hero's life into a nightmare, as he constantly dreams of her, in night visions or hallucinations that turn into blood (episode 102). Sura's ghost reappears in episode 104 as an incentive for Spartacus to stay focused on his goals. In his hallucinations, Spartacus can hear Sura saying that it is the thought of their eventual reunion that keeps her alive. As he explains to Varro (episode 106), once he is reunited with Sura, he plans to escape the *ludus*. "We will have our freedom," he exclaims, thus merging love and freedom into what becomes his personal quest for the duration of the rebellion. Spartacus stresses with intensity the importance of finding his wife: she will call his real name, "not the one the Romans branded me with," a point to which I shall return in my discussion of the final episode of the show. Tragically, Spartacus' reunion is ill-fated: Sura dies in his arms (episode 106), thus fueling his hatred of Batiatus and the Romans and steeling his resolve to seek revenge, justice, and restitution.

MIRA

Mira is one of the house-servants in Batiatus' household, the first woman who tries to replace Sura in the heart of the great rebel; in this she succeeds, in that Mira is also the first to have intercourse with the protagonist in a meaningful manner that evokes a loving relationship. In episode 111, Mira tends to Spartacus' wound after his fight with Varro, his closest friend whom he is forced to kill in a spectacle arranged for the pleasure of the Roman elite. Mira is obviously attracted to the gladiator, but in the beginning she is timid: she warns Spartacus against the rebellion (episode 112) because such an act, if unsuccessful, would endanger the lives of the rest of the slaves in the *ludus*. In the final episode of the first season, however, it is Mira who is tasked with opening the gate to the villa from the training and kitchen area and thus she facilitates the final exodus.

In the opening episode of the second season, Mira questions Spartacus' obsession with vengeance; she intimates that she wishes to escape "from the name Spartacus they have branded you with." Subservient and yet assertive, Mira asks repeatedly for her feelings to be reciprocated: in episode 202, she confronts the gladiator, asking him to express his feelings toward her, and in episode 203, she is trying to make him fall in love with her. Understanding Spartacus' cause is not an easy task for Mira, but eventually she embraces his quest for freedom: by episode 204, she underscores Spartacus' accomplishment in managing to set them free from Roman oppression. In this way, Mira becomes instrumental in fighting the Romans, as she sets the arena on fire (episode 205) and is transformed into a skilled archer, killing Chadara as she tries to escape the rebels' camp (episode 206).

Mira's intense desire to have Spartacus' approval and win his love make her seek revenge as well, as she turns against Ilithyia, who is supposed to carry Spartacus' child: while she guards Ilithyia, she confronts and tries to strangle her until Spartacus intervenes and makes clear that such an act is not going to make her win his heart (episode 208). Mira's obsession puts a wedge between her and the protagonist, one that proves very difficult to overcome. After the incident with Ilithyia, Mira complains to Spartacus that they are no longer sleeping together and that he does not give her his heart, to which Spartacus replies: "I have given you all that remains" (episode 209). Mira is a powerful figure, who knows well what she wants: freedom and Spartacus. But she fully understands in this episode that the extent of Spartacus' love for her is not adequate, and her feelings are not fully reciprocated, since he is trapped in the past and the memory of Sura. In the finale of the second season, Mira dies in place of Spartacus, as she saves him from an axe aimed at him, but her death only reinforces Spartacus' thirst for vengeance. Mira is the second partner he has lost in the war against the Romans.

NAEVIA

Naevia is Lucretia's personal body-slave and eventually she becomes Crixus' partner: despite the many tribulations and separations the couple experience throughout the series, they are reunited and stay together almost to the end of the rebellion. Naevia has a dark complexion, a clear mark of her *otherness* within the society of fellow slaves, and while her origins are never clarified, it is said she was born in the household as one of Lucretia's slaves. In the series prequel, we travel back in time to when Naevia and the slave girl Diona enjoyed a close friendship: but after Diona is raped by the Romans (episode 3) and deeply traumatized, she shuns Naevia because of shame (episode 5). When Naevia tries to save her by helping her escape, Diona is caught and later executed in the arena while Naevia is watching (episode 6).[9] Naevia is acutely marked by this experience: her innocence is destroyed with the brutal death of her close friend, a hard lesson for a young slave girl that will influence her future development into a cold-blooded heroine and protagonist in the show.

Already in the third episode of the first season, we see Crixus' attraction to Naevia; their relationship is finally consummated in episode 105, and their bond grows stronger by the day (episode 108). Lucretia finds out from Ashur that Naevia is no longer a virgin, a commodity that Lucretia was hoping to exploit at some point in the future for her own advancement (episode 112): the slave's punishment is harsh, as her mistress cuts her hair violently and sends her away. Like Spartacus who is in constant search of revenge for the death of his wife, now Crixus vows to find Naevia wherever she is (episode 113): at the bloody exodus from the *ludus*, Crixus stabs Lucretia in the abdomen, thus killing their child and exacting vengeance.

In the second season, the quest for freedom and survival takes another turn: Crixus is zealously looking for Naevia, whose whereabouts are uncertain, while some of the rebels, like Agron, oppose this exercise in futility (episode 202). Information that Naevia has been sold and suffers in the deepest mines of Rome makes Crixus want to split from the rest of the group and continue his search to save her. In episode 206, the couple are finally reunited, but Naevia's treatment during her captivity has left an indelible mark: she was repeatedly raped and abused by every master she had. As Crixus and Naevia make love, she cannot reciprocate, expressing her aversion in no uncertain terms: "They took everything from me – even your touch." The trauma of rape leads Naevia to a very low point, namely contemplation of suicide with Crixus' sword. Crixus reassures her and promises they will escape one day, but Naevia emphatically expresses her agony and desire to learn to live again. Because of the couple's strong bond, Naevia slowly recovers, and by episode 209 she has become a powerful warrior; the couple finally enjoy some intimacy. In a conversation with Mira, the latter comments on Naevia's recovery thanks to Crixus' deep and true love for her. In the final episode of the season (210), Naevia's transformation into an Amazon-like, ruthless warrior, who has no difficulty defeating and killing many a Roman soldier, is complete. She fights Ashur, wanting to see him fall and with him those "memories that haunt darkest nights." Naevia fights bravely: "I will have his life for what he did to me," she says. She cuts through Ashur's loins: "My death will not heal the scars," he says; "No, but it is a fucking start," Naevia replies as she decapitates him.

Together with the other rebels, she is prominently featured in the final battle, where she dies, fighting for freedom. While Mira and Naevia, the prominent women-warriors in *Spartacus*, exemplify the quest for freedom, facilitating the long journey of their partners toward its destined end, they are also complex characters, especially as they struggle and search for an identity, intimacy in their respective relationships, and a future that is very uncertain.

However, Naevia's transformation into a capable woman-warrior comes at a steep price in the final season, *War of the Damned*.[10] In episode 303, she kills one of Gannicus' trusted friends and mutilates another, in a paranoid frenzy, as she seems capable of trusting no one: "Men like him are bad and therefore deserve punishment," she confesses. Her master would rape her constantly (even using "tools" inside her) and then show to the public the face of a family man, "the beast from the previous night transformed." In this season the audience also witnesses the many fissures in the rebels' identity as a cohesive group: Crixus and Naevia want to separate from the rest; dissension and constant fights do not bode well for the rebels' cause (episode 304). In episode 308, Crixus expresses his desire to advance to Rome, separating himself from Spartacus; accompanied by Naevia, Crixus and his group defeat the Roman army, and in a moment of hubris, Naevia proclaims that Crixus stands as a god before Rome. But just as he is about to defeat Caesar, Crixus is stabbed in the back by Crassus' son, Tiberius. "I would not have you so easily from this world, Gaius," Tiberius exclaims, scorning Caesar. Crassus orders Crixus' decapitation in front of Naevia, who is then sent to Spartacus' camp to report the news. At Spartacus' exhortation, the rebels organize games to honor the dead, as Naevia is urged to embrace the present; and Spartacus gives her the sword of Crixus (episode 309). Spartacus stops Naevia as she gets ready to behead Tiberius, and the cremation of Crixus follows, with Naevia lighting the funeral pyre. Each hero shouts the name of a beloved friend or lover to honor them, with the most prominent being Spartacus who cries, "Sura, Varro, Mira."[11] In the finale, Caesar kills Naevia by stabbing her in the neck, as the camera zooms in on Naevia's heroic death on the battlefield.

KORE

In the final season, *War of the Damned*, which narrates the conclusion of the rebellion, the series moves in a different direction with regard to the representation of elite women: with the deaths of Lucretia and Ilithyia at the end of the second season, the third season now completely focuses on the *other* women, such as Kore, Naevia, and Laeta. While the marginalization of elite women from the plot[12] allows for the rise to prominence of the Roman men, such as Crassus, Caesar, and Tiberius, it also places in higher relief the pivotal role played by the female rebels and slaves. Kore is Crassus' slave from Gaul, as well as his lover, the woman with whom he shares his most intimate thoughts and desires.[13] In episode 302, Crassus wants to take Kore with him on the campaign, even though he denies such a privilege to his own wife: the affection shared by the couple is unique, a master with a slave, to the point that Kore even calls him by his first name, Marcus.

Such scenes of intimacy are repeated in the first half of the season (as in episode 304), while Kore constantly defends Tiberius to his father, despite the obvious antagonistic feelings of Crassus toward his insubordinate son. In episode 305, Kore says she would do anything to ease the suffering of father and son, before she and Crassus make love. Kore's vulnerability lies exactly in having a soft spot for Tiberius, who exploits the slave's erotic relationship with his father to exact revenge: later in the episode, Tiberius comes into Kore's tent to find comforts, but he quickly makes a move to kiss her. As she tries to stop him, he states his intent to take something from his father to make him feel the pain: he rapes Kore and reminds her of her place as a slave who is supposed to fulfill her master's desires.[14] In episode 307, Kore faces the dilemma of allegiance: she can find no comfort in Crassus any longer, as she realizes that his son Tiberius will always be preferred to a lowly slave, while she will always be exploited by the machinations of any Roman who wants to use her against Crassus (such as Caesar). She defects to the rebel camp, where she is treated with suspicion (episode 308) at first, even confronted by Naevia for not having seized the opportunity to kill Crassus during lovemaking.

Kore's heroism is confirmed in the penultimate episode of the show, when Naevia is ready to behead Tiberius and is stopped from doing so by Spartacus: before Tiberius gets a chance to move closer to Caesar, Kore breaks away from the rest of the rebels and kills him on the spot. The deal was to have been to exchange Tiberius for 500 rebels, and now Kore offers herself as the person to be exchanged and be led back to Crassus (episode 309). Kore and Crassus no longer share the intimacy of the past: Crassus insists on being called *dominus* (episode 310). Despite the initial lies concerning the identity of Tiberius' murderer and Kore's reference to a "man," Spartacus talks of a woman, motivated by vengeance. Kore finally admits her deed and explains her rape at the hands of Tiberius: Crassus is enraged and admits that "a son is but a reflection of his father." Crassus keeps his promise that Kore's ordeal will end with the end of Spartacus: she is crucified next to Gannicus. And here is the important distinction between the old and the new Spartacus: whereas in Kubrick's film, the final scene centers around the reunion between Varinia, her newborn baby, and Spartacus under the cross, in STARZ *Spartacus*, it is not Spartacus, but the female slave who is punished by exemplary death. Kore's crucifixion represents the ultimate revenge and proof of Crassus' ruthless personality. Together with Gannicus who dies reliving his glorious moments of victory in the arena,[15] Kore dies crying on the cross, as she beholds the man she once loved. Kore's crucifixion replaces the iconic representation of Spartacus on the cross, celebrated in the 1960 film and exploited for its messianic message, especially inasmuch as the new series portrays a more historically accurate version of Spartacus dying somewhere on the battlefield.

LAETA

Among this group of the *others* is Laeta, the wife of Ennius, the *aedile* from Sinuessa.[16] Laeta is an elite Roman woman who makes the transition from wealthy aristocrat to rebel, after she joins the cause of Spartacus and embraces the revolution. From the beginning of the last season, Laeta shows humane treatment of slaves, which signals to the audience her difference from the elite Roman women of earlier seasons. Her husband's death at the hands of Spartacus and the rebels leaves her with mixed feelings, when she discovers that her husband intended to burn grain in order to help his money-laundering business and hurt the local people (episode 302). This feeling of loss connects the rebel leader and the new widow: Spartacus understands that Laeta misses her husband, and Laeta realizes that Spartacus is not a villain ("You are not the man one expects," she says in episode 303). Laeta is used by Spartacus to fool Crassus (episodes 304 and 305), and when she is brought to the Roman camp, she defends Spartacus to Crassus: "He is not the beast . . . he is a wounded heart . . . he fights for what he believes is just" (episode 306).

At this point Laeta realizes once again the dirty games played by the Roman elite, when Heracleo, the pirate, turns out to be one of Crassus' men. Laeta's worldview is upset: these lowly men have dealings with the upper-class Romans. As Heracleo whisks her away, he brings her to an abandoned place and brands her arm with a slave's mark. Heracleo has already placed Laeta in the category of inferior beings: "You are a woman, not better than a slave." Later in the episode as Gannicus comes to rescue her, Laeta, resolved to avenge her honor, kills Heracleo. In episode 307, Spartacus and Laeta grow closer, as they both deal with feelings of loss and pain, and they make love in the following episode (308), after Spartacus makes it absolutely clear that he cannot give her his heart. Laeta is finally reconciled with her transition to one of the *others* and her feelings of disgust toward the Romans: in episode 309, she says that they are no longer her people and that she has been cast from the Republic. In the final episode, Laeta is part of the second group of rebels who are supposed to wait for Spartacus in the mountains after the last battle.

THE DEATH OF SPARTACUS

One of the series' distinct features comes at the very end, in the portrayal of Spartacus' death. Unlike Kubrick's iconic death of Spartacus on the cross, heavy with religious symbolism, the creators of STARZ *Spartacus* follow the scant historical record, which breaks into two strands: one that portrays the protagonist's death surrounded by his men, after having been wounded by a javelin and continuing to fight bravely, and the second that insists on his bravery but modifies the scene by having him die while standing, encircled by enemies.[17] In the new *Spartacus*, the two strands are combined: Spartacus, severely wounded, and Crassus fight with swords, while Spartacus has flashbacks of the deaths of Mira, Varro, and Sura, which inspired him to fight the Romans. As the rebel leader disarms the Roman and is about to finish him off, Roman soldiers wound Spartacus from behind with three spears. Before Crassus can deal the final death-blow, Agron and Nasir valiantly fight him and succeed in removing Spartacus' body from the battlefield.

In this final scene, Spartacus is surrounded by his fellow rebels, especially those who hold his hand during the last moments: Laeta, Agron, and his partner, Nasir (Figure 9.1).[18] Spartacus finds out from Agron that Pompey has arrived and decimated some of the rebel army; the Thracian gladiator insists that they should continue their march through the mountains. As he hears Laeta calling his name,

Figure 9.1 Agron (Daniel Feuerriegel), Laeta (Anna Hutchison), and Nasir (Pana Hema Taylor) surround the dying Spartacus (Liam McIntyre) in episode 310 ("Victory"). STARZ.

Spartacus opens his eyes wide and says that "Spartacus" is not his name, but that he will hear his true name soon "given voice by loving wife," when she greets him again with a longed-for greeting. "There is no greater victory than to fall from this world a free man," he proclaims as he tenderly touches Agron and Nasir and asks them not to cry for him. Spartacus expires as the background darkens and the sound of thunder is heard: Spartacus, the "bringer of rain," is finally buried under the serpent shield, as the rebels march on, and Laeta glances back at the grave with a look of reassurance and hope, as well as a tinge of uncertainty about the future (Figure 9.2).

The show ends with a message of hope, but the carriers of this hope are not the Romans: Crassus is overshadowed by Pompey who appears in the finale as the savior, with a shining light surrounding him, to steal Crassus' thunder and claim victory over the rebels. It is the *others* in the show who carry forward Spartacus' message of freedom: Agron and Nasir, the same-sex couple who managed to overcome all tribulations, including crucifixion; Laeta, the Roman woman who abandoned the rotting, corrupt Republic to join the rebel cause and fight for what is right and honorable. The series portrays the many losses and sacrifices that had to be made, and the future remains unclear and ambiguous.[19] But the message of the series finale is clear: the rebel group's search for freedom extends to a sort of liberty to choose your own life, to be free from society's norms and conventions, as the show gives voice especially to those groups

Figure 9.2 Laeta (Anna Hutchison) and other survivors escape the battlefield in episode 310 ("Victory"). STARZ.

who are not usually heard in the ancient sources. As Foka has noted, "*Spartacus* becomes a platform, an arena for the discussion of social equalities once more; yet here the social justice is viewed from both a sexuality *and* gender perspective."[20]

CONCLUSION

In its representation of the *others*, STARZ *Spartacus* invites modern audiences to ponder the similarities and differences between Roman and non-Roman people in the ancient world. In its effort to maintain a veneer of authenticity about the ancient world while offering an appealing and aesthetically pleasing product for the modern viewer, however, the series takes a lot of liberties. And yet we cannot readily reject this freedom in depicting antiquity on screen, precisely because we do not have enough information, for example about non-elite women or the daily life of slaves, as amply documented in the *Spartacus* series. In addition, gender and sexual identity were perceived differently in the ancient world, and it is often an impossible task to peel off the several layers of our own (post-Victorian) prejudices and misconceptions. By blending the ancient and the modern, therefore, the series invites twenty-first-century audiences to make connections with our own times and sociopolitical and cultural problems. If confrontation with the *other* was often a gray area in antiquity, then what is the lesson we can take from many centuries back?

Viewers of *Spartacus* will appreciate that the ancient and modern worlds are not as far apart as they seem: people in the ancient world struggled with societal issues as much as we do today; and freedom can be broadly construed to encompass the multifaceted human condition. Thus *Spartacus* emerges as the champion of a message, inspiring and unfading for millennia.

NOTES

1 Foka (2015b: 186) calls them the "lesser classes," such as gladiators, entertainers, and other Romans of lower status.
2 Augoustakis (2008, 2013, and 2015).
3 Gruen (2011: 356–7).
4 For recent work on slavery in the Roman world, including material evidence, see Joshel (2010) and Joshel and Petersen (2014).
5 Tacitus, *Germania* 7–8 and 18. As Gruen (2011: 168) notes, the Germans' "marital and familial morality serves to throw an indirect and not very flattering light on contrasting Roman practices."
6 Foka (2015b: 189). On the perception and imagination of non-Roman women in antiquity, see, for example, Joshel (1997) and Augoustakis (2010).
7 As Lesley-Ann Brandt (who plays Naevia in the prequel and first season) comments in the special features of the first season DVD, the sex scenes in *Spartacus* are produced in such a way that "a woman can appreciate" them. See Strong (2013) and in this volume; in particular, Strong (2013: 181) observes that the show "uses traditionally misogynistic modes of discourse like pornography and rape to reflect on class inequality and its dangerous consequences."
8 On the scene, see Cyrino (2014: 617–19) and Rodrigues in this volume.
9 On Diona as a symbolic victim, see Strong in this volume.
10 On Naevia and Mira as female gladiators, see Foka (2015b: 199–200).
11 On the funeral games, see McAuley in this volume.
12 With the exception of a brief appearance by Crassus' wife, Tertulla, who is quickly overshadowed by the prominent role given to his mistress, Kore.
13 On Crassus, see Daugherty in this volume.
14 For the rape scene, see Strong in this volume.
15 See Harrisson in this volume.
16 On the city of Sinuessa, see Maurice in this volume.
17 Schiavone (2013: 142–3).
18 On the same-sex couple Agron and Nasir, see Potter in this volume.
19 According to Suetonius, for many years afterward there were residues of the armies of Spartacus, who even joined forces with the remainder of Catiline's forces (*Life of Augustus* 3); see Schiavone (2011: 144–5).
20 Foka (2015b: 202).

10 Fan Reactions to Nagron as One True Pairing

Amanda Potter

Two of the rebel slaves, Agron and Nasir, who form a lasting relationship in the series STARZ *Spartacus*, were – and continue to be – extremely popular among fans of the show. An internet search provides numerous videos and pictures of the couple, including fan "vids," videos featuring clips of Nasir and Agron together set to music,[1] and original artworks on the fan art website *deviantart.com*. The relationship between Agron and Nasir, or "Nagron," has also proved to be a favorite topic for fan fiction writers, who appropriate the characters to expand on their onscreen story, and also to tell new stories.

A NEW RELATIONSHIP

The second season, *Vengeance*, introduced the openly gay relationship between Agron and Nasir. Agron, a Germanic warrior sold into slavery, had been purchased together with his brother Duro to train as a gladiator at the *ludus* of Batiatus in the first season, *Blood and Sand*. The brothers become successful gladiators and are among the first to join Spartacus in the slave revolt, but Duro is killed by a Roman guard before he can escape the *ludus* at the end of the season. Nasir, initially known by his slave name Tiberius, is a Syrian body-slave who is freed by the rebels when they capture the villa of his *dominus*. He had held a position of respect in the household and is initially unwilling to join the rebellion, even attempting to kill Spartacus. Agron wants Nasir to be killed for his actions, but instead Spartacus trains Nasir to be a fighter. When Agron and Nasir speak of the brothers that they have lost (Nasir was parted from his brother at a young age), a bond begins to form between them. After proving his loyalty by later saving Spartacus' life, Nasir joins Spartacus and

Figure 10.1 Agron's (Daniel Feuerriegel) and Nasir's (Pana Hema Taylor) first kiss in episode 5 ("Reckoning"). STARZ.

Crixus on their mission to rescue Crixus' lover, Naevia, from slavery in the mines. He returns injured, to be cared for by Agron, and they share their first kiss (episode 205, Figure 10.1).

What is remarkable about the onscreen relationship between Agron and Nasir is that this same-sex relationship progresses unremarked upon in the series. It is seen as completely natural by the other characters, and Agron and Nasir are treated as a couple in the same way that Crixus and Naevia are in their heterosexual relationship. This acceptance of an open homosexual relationship between two equals contrasts with an earlier exploration of homoeroticism and bisexuality in the 1960 *Spartacus*: the provocative "oysters and snails" scene that was famously cut from the original print by the censors. In this scene the amoral Crassus (Laurence Olivier) attempts to seduce his attractive young slave Antoninus (Tony Curtis). The advances of Crassus are declined by Antoninus, and Crassus does not resort to rape, but as Monica Cyrino has found, this hint of bisexuality marks Crassus out as "sexually 'deviant'" and casts aspersions on his morality more broadly.[2] This potential sexual relationship between the older Crassus and the handsome younger slave Antoninus foreshadows the sexual relationship between Nasir and his older Roman *dominus* before he is liberated by Spartacus and the rebels. This relationship, based on power and possession, was not unusual in ancient Rome, where male and female slaves were available as sexual partners, and attractive boys were a potential option for penetration by the Roman man displaying *virtus* ("manliness").[3] The acceptance of the relationship of equals between Agron and Nasir by their fellow rebels is perhaps an indication of the egalitarian nature of the society espoused by Spartacus, as opposed to the Roman Republic. The loving and tender sex scenes between Agron and Nasir also contrast directly with the only sex scene between two Roman elite men in the series: the brutal rape of Julius Caesar by Tiberius in the final season (episode 308).

The blossoming relationship between Agron and Nasir is encouraged, not only by the dishonorable Chadara, who had been a fellow house-slave with Nasir and advises Nasir to "pursue desire" for Agron (episode 203), but also by Naevia, who helps tend to Nasir's wounds and chides Agron for letting Nasir come to the mines to help to rescue her (episode 205). Naevia appears to be drawing parallels between her love for Crixus and Agron's love for Nasir. Their relationship grows, and after the first kiss the viewer is treated to steamy sex scenes, the potential for jealous rivalry when pirate Castus joins the rebels and has eyes for Nasir, and finally a happy ending as Agron and Nasir leave together after burying Spartacus following the final battle. Of all the couples in the series it is only Agron and Nasir who are allowed to walk off into the sunset, rewarded for their loyal and open relationship.[4] This is at odds, however, with the story of another gay couple earlier in the series, the older experienced gladiator Barca and the boy Pietros.[5] Like Agron and Nasir, Barca and Pietros are in a loving relationship, but they do not survive beyond the first season. Although not explicit in the screen text, this couple may be seen by viewers as being punished for their relationship, when Barca is killed by Batiatus' men rather than being freed as he is promised, and the young Pietros kills himself after being abused by another gladiator, without Barca's protection. To Tim O'Leary, writer for LGBT media site *backlot.com*, the loss of Barca and Pietros was a missed opportunity, and their deaths hardly unusual when "a high death toll for queer characters is nothing new for American audiences."[6] Thus the survival of Agron and Nasir is a pleasing reversal of this trend.

Anna Foka has argued that the *Spartacus* series has expanded on the types of female characters usually portrayed in "sword-and-sandal" films, including characters such as Naevia and Mira who "prove themselves as capable warriors" after acquiring "skills in battle with the help of their male counterparts."[7] I tend to agree with Foka that *Spartacus* does offer strong female characters, both among the elite Romans and among the slaves. However, it is significant that all the transgressive women, whether they transgress gender norms by political scheming or by taking up arms, are killed by the end of the series.

The only women who survive are Laeta and Sibyl, women who do not choose to become warriors. Indeed, Nasir could be compared with the female characters Naevia and Mira as a former house-slave who is taught to fight when he joins the rebellion, and who loves one of the ex-gladiators. Yet he and Agron are allowed to live, when Naevia and Mira are not. Therefore, while reading the gay relationship between Nasir and Agron as a progressive element of the series, the ending is less progressive from a feminist perspective. If female characters are scheming (like Lucretia, Ilithyia, and Gaia), choose to fight like men (like Naevia, Mira, and Saxa), or choose to avenge their own rape (like Kore), they are punished for their transgression and are not allowed to survive. Such punishment is not meted out to Agron and Nasir.

When I screened "Libertus" (episode 205), together with an episode of *Xena: Warrior Princess*, as part of LGBT History Month at University College London in 2014,[8] to an audience that was mixed in terms of gender and sexual orientation, the depiction of the relationship between Agron and Nasir was received well. Although it was a small part of the overall episode, viewers thought that the relationship between Agron and Nasir was portrayed as "sweet and intimate," "loving and tender," "touchingly dealt with and very sensitively too." Viewers particularly liked the way that this openly gay relationship was seen as "a natural part of the drama," "explicitly stated and accepted without question," and "the honest declaration of affection and a loving kiss was very welcome." It was felt that "there is not enough of this in the media/fiction."

Agron and Nasir are popular characters among LGBT fans: in 2013, Agron was rated as number 5 in the top 50 gay television characters on *thebacklot.com*, with Nasir coming in at number 14.[9] The relationship between Agron and Nasir is lauded as "a beautifully presented and much beloved gay love story,"[10] for the same reasons that it was enjoyed by the viewers in the UCL audience. According to Jim Halterman, writing for *thebacklot.com*:

> What is most remarkable about the great love of Agron and Nasir is how unremarked upon it is in the series. There is no agonizing coming out story; there is no "Is he?" or "Are they?" questions asked by other characters. There is no angst. There is simply, and quite profoundly, the scene of two men, unabashedly in love . . . Amazingly, Nasir and Agron get their happy ending, and so do we; two men, loving each other fiercely and proudly, somewhere just beyond the reach of mighty Rome, two characters fading into legend, and each an important part of our own history now.[11]

It is extremely unusual for a gay relationship to be portrayed in such an open way on television, unremarked upon by other characters.

The presentation of this couple is one of the elements that makes the new *Spartacus* seem so fresh when compared with other shows, along with the clever plot twists and the extreme violence and sexual content. Like the writer for *thebacklot.com*, I personally loved the finale when Agron and Nasir got their happy ending, while the historical characters Spartacus, Crixus, and Oenomaus died in battle and the seemingly amoral Gannicus became an unlikely martyr on the cross.

NAGRON IN FAN FICTION

The portrayal of male gay relationships on television should not necessarily be directly linked with the appearance of such relationships in fan fiction. The writing of slash fiction, a creative practice engaged in by primarily female writers for a primarily female readership, came out of the frustration of viewers at the lack of interesting female characters on television in series such as *Star Trek* (1966–69) and their wish to focus on ongoing relationships between characters rather than the adventure plot of the week.[12] However, the relationship between Agron and Nasir as portrayed in the main text of *Spartacus* is presented in the same way that a fan fiction writer might present a slashed relationship between male characters who might otherwise only have a homosocial relationship on screen, like Kirk and Spock. Many slash stories revolve around hurt/comfort, where one partner is hurt and the other partner provides the comfort, often – but not always – resulting in sex. In the violent world of STARZ *Spartacus*, the story of Agron and Nasir is filled with opportunities for hurt/comfort, and they take turns to help nurse each other back to health. Their romance starts after Nasir has been hurt helping to save Naevia from the mines (episode 204) and Agron provides the comfort. Finally, Agron is crucified (episode 309) but is returned to Spartacus and Nasir, and then it is Nasir's turn to comfort Agron. With this story as part of the main text, there appears to be little need for fan fiction writers to invent new slashed relationships and hurt/comfort plotlines in their fiction.

Fan fiction writers tend to have a preferred pairing or "ship" (relationship), which they will often write about exclusively.[13] Where there is a strong homosocial relationship between protagonists in the main text (for example, Vorenus and Pullo in the HBO-BBC series *Rome*), then fan fiction writers often choose to make this into a romantic/sexual relationship in their stories. However, even though one pairing might be preferred among many fan writers, fan writers tend to be inventive, and in the case of *Rome* fan fiction, in addition to Vorenus/Pullo, pairings are many and varied.[14] With *Spartacus* fan fiction this is not the case, with Agron/Nasir not only preferred above all other pairings, whether male/female, male/male, or female/female, but also existing when other non-main text male/male pairings appear extremely infrequently. In my sample, only one story features a potential slash pairing, "Spartacus Gets Jealous" by Brid LaCroix, where Crixus notices that Spartacus is jealous of Agron as he has a secret interest in Nasir, but the true lovers continue in their relationship, oblivious to this, and Spartacus' interest in Nasir remains unknown and unrequited. This lack of slash pairings exists despite *Spartacus* being a show in which a great number of male characters live together at close quarters, first in the *ludus* and later in a Roman villa and then encamped on Mount Vesuvius, providing many possibilities for slash fiction. As there is a sizeable and growing body of fan fiction based on *Spartacus* I decided to look at a relatively large sample, comprising all the stories written in English and posted to *fanfiction.net* between 26 February 2012, when the first Agron/Nasir fan fiction story appeared – this was very soon after "Empty Hands" (episode 204) first aired in the United States on 17 February 2012, when the relationship between Agron and Nasir began on screen – and December 2013, eight months after the final episode was aired in April 2013.

My sample included 144 stories, ranging from short stories of less than a thousand words, sometimes referred to by the authors as "drabbles" or "one shots," to much longer works of fiction of over ten thousand words with multiple chapters. Ninety-eight of these stories feature Agron and Nasir as main protagonists – far more than half of all the stories posted. This for a series with an ensemble cast led by Andy Whitfield as Spartacus in the first season and Liam McIntyre in the title role in two more subsequent seasons. From the airing of the first kiss of Agron and Nasir on 17 February 2012, these characters immediately became the pairing of choice for writers, with the first Agron/Nasir story published just nine days later on 26 February 2012.

Around half of the stories featuring Agron and Nasir are set within the timescale of the series. Many of these feature the beginning of their relationship, when the characters tentatively express their feelings for each other. These "first time" stories are prevalent in slash fiction generally.[15] Many writers classify their Agron/Nasir stories as hurt/comfort or hurt/comfort/romance. Most frequently writers draw on the main text to write about Agron tending to Nasir's wounds when Nasir returns from the mines, and Nasir tending to Agron's wounds when Agron returns from his crucifixion. Alternatively, the deaths of Chadara and Mira cause Nasir to grieve, and Agron provides comfort, and Nasir comforts Agron when Agron dreams of the death of his brother Duro. New hurt/comfort situations are also created within the overall series timescale: in rubblerousing's long work of fiction "Always and Forevermore," Nasir hits Agron publicly as part of a plot to gain the respect of the other rebels, and in SuperAwsomePandaKitty's "Peace in a Bad Situation," Agron is captured and tortured before he returns to his lover. Some of these hurt/comfort stories end with sex, but this tends not to be explicit; stories are rated by the writers as K (suitable for children), K+ (suitable for older children of nine years of age and above), and T (suitable for teens, aged thirteen or over). Of all the stories in my sample, not one was rated by its writer as M or MA (for adults only). This may seem surprising when the series on which the stories are based is rated 18 in the UK and TV-MA in the US for graphic violence and sex scenes. However, writers of Agron/Nasir stories, and also stories based on other relationships from the series, for example Gannicus/Sibyl, appear to be more interested in writing romance than writing about sex. The main text provides the viewer with sufficient graphic sex scenes, and so writers prefer to concentrate on tender, loving scenes between the characters, who embrace and kiss tenderly, and speak about their love for one another.[16]

One of the impulses of the fan fiction writer is to ask "what if," and this question is often asked about what has happened before the main text starts, what could have happened after it finished, or what would have happened if key decisions by the series writers had not been made.[17] As STARZ continued to air episodes of *Spartacus*, some writers speculated on what might happen to Agron and Nasir after the series ended. In moriya's story "Sweet Relief," Nasir is killed on the battlefield, and after he dies in Agron's arms, Agron waits for his own death. Moriya's story was inspired by "watching a sneak peak [*sic*] to episode eight," and was posted before the series ended in April 2013. Jaded79, meanwhile, has Agron die on the cross, happy that Nasir will survive after he has gone, in her story "Hearts Entwined," posted in March 2013 before she watched the last episode. In her note to readers, she states: "I love the story of Agron and Nasir, and while I would hope it has a happy ending, I fear that it won't."

IndigoNightandRayneStorm's story "I Will Follow You Into the Dark," also published in March 2013, sees both Agron and Nasir captured and crucified. The writer speculates in her "End Note" that this might be what will happen to them at the end of the series, knowing that "historically this is how the rebellion ends," with the captured rebels "crucified along the road from Capua to Rome." She thinks that there is only a "slim chance" that Agron and Nasir will be allowed to survive to retire to a "quiet farm where they hunt and raise sheep and have lots of sex" in a series where writers have often killed off main characters, and so she advises viewers to "get out your tissues."

Other writers, who published their stories after the series ended, imagine Agron and Nasir traveling to Germania, to Agron's village, where they do indeed settle down together on a "quiet farm." In the comic story "Live Long and Goat Farm" by Evergreene, we see Agron and Nasir as a happy farming couple who have named their goats after their old comrades in the rebellion. In all these Germania stories, the lovers are accepted as partners by Agron's friends and family in the same way that they had been accepted as a gay couple by the rebels. These happy ending stories are an extension of the main text, where Agron and Nasir are among the few principal characters to escape, unlike alternative happy ending stories for Pullo and Vorenus in *Rome* fan fiction, where fan fiction writers rewrite the ending of the story to have Vorenus survive to retire to a farm with Pullo, although he dies in the main text.[18] This imperative for characters who have led a violent life in the main text to find an idyllic agrarian lifestyle after the text ends is perhaps inspired by the film *Gladiator* (2000), in which Maximus' wish to return to his farm in Spain is only achieved in the afterlife. Germania offers lovers Agron and Nasir a simple lifestyle among friends and family, where the presence of Rome is not felt.

Agron's dead brother Duro is an important presence in some Agron/Nasir stories. In the main text, Agron and Nasir first become close when they talk of their brothers (episode 202), and in fan fiction Nasir specifically fills the void left by Duro. For example, in "To Live Again" by PhoenSims, set between episodes 202 and 203, Agron admits to Nasir that he wished he had died and Duro had lived, and the sharing of this confidence brings the pair closer together. In "Pain" by yetanotherside, it is the ghost of Duro, seen both as a boy and as a man, who helps Agron to survive on the cross. In "Free to Paint the Wind Crimson" by aeternium, after Agron and Nasir settle down in Germania, Agron's nightmares do not subside until he tells his family the truth about Duro's death. Other stories featuring Duro that are less poignant but still use his character effectively include "Drinks" by FlyingNymphLady, where Agron shares a drink and jokes with his dead brother; and "The Next Life" by SisiDraig-2, where Agron and

Nasir are met by Duro in the afterlife and are introduced to a world of drinking and sex, although Duro is not yet ready to trust Nasir. In alternative universe (AU) stories set within the timeline of the main text, Funky in Fishnet imagines that Duro was not killed and that he and Agron both become Nasir's lovers in the "threesome fic" or "OT3" (One True Threesome) stories, "The Pursuit of Desire" and "Tooth and Nail."

Other AU stories set both within the timeline of the original series and outside it can include complex alternative plots. Survivah's story "The Paths Chosen" reimagines Nasir as a rich Syrian boy running away with his bodyguard Agron to Agron's home in Germania. This develops popular themes from other Spartacus-inspired stories set in the ancient world, of a slave's freedom to find his own partner, and the happy ending for the lovers in escaping to an agrarian life away from Rome. Funky in Fishnet's stories "The Ghosts that Talk" and "Where the Moonflowers Grow" find Nasir becoming a body-guard at a temple where Sibyl and Sura are prophetesses, and where he meets and falls in love with fellow bodyguard Agron. Funky in Fishnet is a prolific Agron/Nasir fan fiction writer, publishing twenty-two of the stories within my sample, and her stories are set both within and outside of the timeline of the series.

An insightful story written by Funky in Fishnet, "Thieves and Beggars," transposes the story of Spartacus, Agron, and Nasir to a pirate ship in the era of the African slave trade. Spartacus captures a slave ship, and Nasir is a mixed-race house-slave on board, who has been sent to be sold in order to pay his master's debts. The story charts Nasir's emotional journey from slave to free man. He is a slave who held a privileged position within a household, and initially wishes only to be dropped off at the next port in order to obtain a similar position, with no ambitions for freedom. But at the end of the story he decides to join the pirates as a free man. Spartacus' magnanimous attitude toward him and his growing admiration for Spartacus' fellow pirate, Agron, change Nasir's mind, and make him realize that there can be benefits to being free from slavery. This echoes Nasir's emotional journey within the series and comments on slavery in our more recent history in a striking parallel with slavery in ancient Rome. Funky in Fishnet also experiments with other histor-ical periods and genres. In "Two Hearts with Accurate Devotions," Nasir is a Guide to Agron's Sentinel; he is Agron's one true partner who can keep him calm through bonding, but is given a choice by Agron, unlike the bonding enforced at government training houses. In "Hear Us Roar" and "Tell the Rain not to Drop," set in 1920s

America, Agron is part of Spartacus' gang and meets barman Nasir, with whom he first shares a kiss in an alley, and then a bath when Nasir turns up at his apartment. Funky in Fishnet has also written modern comic AU stories, where for example Agron and Nasir work in a bakery, or are professional dancers on the television program *Dancing with the Stars*.

Thirty-one AU stories featuring Agron and Nasir posted by a number of writers are set in the modern world, which is a surprisingly large percentage of my sample. A gang of rebels outside authority translates well into a group of moonshiners opposing a corrupt police force in Prohibition-era America in "Sweeter than a Georgia Peach" by dresswithoutsleeves. In "Remain Nameless" by WaldenPond313, Agron and Nasir are lovers on opposing sides of the law: an assassin and an Interpol agent. However, most writers of modern AU Agron/Nasir fan fiction choose to set their stories closer to home, in an American college or in the modern everyday world of work, where the characters are variously model and designer, novelist and fan, and a personal trainer and a lawyer, among other pairings. They take part in mundane tasks, baking cupcakes, having migraines, getting jealous about workmates and going out for dinner. In some stories they are the original Agron and Nasir reincarnated, such as "In a Whole Other Life" by Natchou, where two strangers meet in a nightclub; "The Orpheus Cycle," by SisiDraig-2, where high school students researching the Spartacus rebellion have the feeling that they know about this already; and "Never Letting Go," by twiinklestar, where Agron dreams of Nasir dying in the rebellion then meets him again on a train. In these stories the true lovers meet again, since they are destined to be together. In other stories the intensity of the attraction between the two characters is strong, although not always easy to express. Nasir needs the support of his friends and a college charity kissing booth to bring him together with Agron in "The Kissing Booth" by Mistressjinxy. In "Will You Be My Heart," by Waiting to be Broken, Agron and Nasir are friends for fifteen years before Agron can find the courage, and the right words, to tell Nasir how he really feels about him.

Some of the modern AU stories are about marriage proposals and the wedding of Agron and Nasir. This is a feature missing from the stories set in the ancient world, and so same-sex marriage appears to fan fiction writers to be a modern concept.[19] From June 2015 a Supreme Court ruling has permitted same-sex marriage across the United States, but the debate continues, particularly among some religious groups.[20] Barack Obama was the first US president to openly support same-sex marriage in an interview with ABC News in May 2012, at the time when Dark Alice Lilith Strife published her proposal and wedding stories "Surprises" and "Nerves." Writers of fan fiction are using the fictional ancient world characters of Agron and Nasir to comment on the modern issue of legalizing same-sex marriage.[21]

CONCLUSION

The decision of writers and producers to include the open gay relationship between Agron and Nasir in *Spartacus: Vengeance* and *Spartacus: War of the Damned* should be welcomed by viewers. The portrayal of this relationship in a positive light helps to provide onscreen role models for gay viewers and to break down barriers in the often conservative medium that is television. However, since this relationship is foregrounded in the main screen text, it could be argued that there is no longer a need for writers to create slash fiction. This might have stifled the creativity of fan writers, as they tend to look to the main text for the relationships in their stories, rather than inventing new ones. Instead, I found that writers have harnessed their creativity in new ways, choosing to place these favored characters in new situations, from a modern American high school to a seventeenth-century pirate ship. The relationship between Agron and Nasir has resonated with fans to such an extent that it has become a catalyst, allowing them to explore the issues of coming to terms with the death of a brother, falling in love, and the difficulty in finding the courage to express your feelings, as well as the importance of friendship, the complex ideas of freedom and slavery, and the debate surrounding same-sex marriage.

NOTES

1 See, for example, on YouTube: "Agron/Nasir (Nagron) Nirvana" (21 April 2013) and "Agron and Nasir – 3x05 – "As I would believe you . . . in all things" (1 April 2013).

2 Cyrino (2014: 617–18). On this scene and its relationship to the character of Crassus more broadly, see Tatum (2007).

3 For appropriate sexual partners for a man displaying *virtus*, see Masterson (2014: 22–8) and Williams (2010: 145–76). For sex with male slaves, see Williams (2010: 31–40) and Lear (2014: 117).

4 See Augoustakis in this volume.

5 On Barca and Pietros, see Augoustakis (2013: 160–2).

6 O'Leary (2010).

7 Foka (2015a: 43–7).
8 A number of museums in the United Kingdom, including the Petrie Museum at UCL, support LGBT History Month in February each year. Details of the event ("Subtext or main text? Same sex relationships in Xena and Spartacus") are available at events.ucl.ac.uk.
9 See www.newnownext.com.
10 Halterman (2013).
11 Halterman (2013).
12 See Jenkins (1992: 185–222), Penley (1992), and Bacon-Smith (1992: 228–54) for early discussions of slash fiction. See also Pugh (2004) on fans wanting more from characters, and Jenkins (2006: 61–88) for a discussion with fan writers. A number of essays in Hellekson and Busse (2006) also address slash fiction from a writer's perspective.
13 On preferred pairings, see Driscoll (2006: 84–5).
14 See Potter (2015).
15 Bacon-Smith (1992: 229).
16 See Driscoll (2006) on fan fiction as romance and pornography.
17 On the "what if" mode, see Stasi (2006: 126).
18 On Pullo/Vorenus "farm" fiction, see Potter (2015: 225).
19 There is some evidence of marriage between males in ancient Rome; see Williams (2010: 279–86).
20 See, for example, Schwartz (2015).
21 Fan fiction writers are following in the footsteps of commercial writers in highlighting contemporary issues, just as the 1960 *Spartacus* comments on anti-Communism in the McCarthy era in the United States; see Wyke (1997: 60–72) and Rodrigues in this volume.

PART IV

Spectacle and Violence

11 *Base Pleasures, Spectacle, and Society*

Alex McAuley

Spartacus has long been a name that is synonymous with spectacle. Regardless of the specific hue in which the dimly attested historical figure has been cast by those who have (re)interpreted his myth over the course of centuries, Spartacus and his world remain, as they have always been, a *spectaculum* in all of the word's Latin nuance: something to be seen, witnessed, and experienced in public which casts an alluring spell over an engaged audience.[1] Precisely what was spectacular about the man and his saga, of course, have varied with time and context. To Florus (*Epitome of Roman History* 2.8) and other Imperial Romans it was a spectacle of defeat; to playwrights such as Bernard-Joseph Saurin (*Spartacus*, 1760) and Robert Montgomery Bird (*The Gladiator*, 1831) it was a triumph of freedom over servitude; while to the Italian author Rafaello Giovagnoli and Giovanni Enrico Vidali, the filmmaker he inspired, it was a resounding appeal for Italian nationalism (*Spartaco*, 1874 and 1913, respectively). With the adaptation of Howard Fast's novel (1951) into Stanley Kubrick's iconic film *Spartacus* (1960) much of the story's valence remained the same, but its visual exposition became something marvelous.[2] Not only the communist-tinged narrative of social revolution, but the film's scope, its opulence, and the sheer scale of the production were spectacular in and of themselves. The sight of Rome in all of its sprawling glory, the gilded decadence of Crassus' villa, the masses of thousands-strong armies clashing, all shot in the dazzling Super 70 Technirama format, made the film along with its narrative into *miranda*, things which ought to inspire amazement.[3] Yet in all of these depictions of Spartacus, the real spectacle, as it were, only begins once the slave and his followers have escaped the *ludus* of Batiatus. The Thracian's brutal training and his experience in the arena were only necessary prequels to his more glorious revolt which formed the core of his saga and its meaning.

Such had always been the case until the STARZ network produced its controversial hit series *Spartacus* in 2010. Whatever the series may have represented to the dozens of critics who expressed opinions ranging from righteous religious condemnation to adolescent fan-boy praise, *Spartacus: Blood and Sand* and its subsequent seasons had struck a chord. Reuters called the show "a bloody spectacle,"[4] while the *Los Angeles Times* described it as "a gore-and-sex spectacle ... part 300, part Harlequin bodice-ripper and part soft-core porn."[5] The *New York Daily News* branded it an "orgy of sex, violence, and swearing,"[6] which the *San Francisco Chronicle* hailed as a "candidate for the worst series of the decade."[7] The language varied, but the indictments remained the same – in no small part because the series did not emphasize what many had expected. In place of Kirk Douglas' noble quest for freedom, this production instead devoted an entire prequel, first season, and parts of a second season to Spartacus and his companions' time in the licentious *ludus* of Batiatus and the arena of Capua. It was in this setting that *Spartacus* and its host network felt the true spectacle lay.

But the blood, violence, nudity, and sex – seemingly so gratuitous – are prefaced by the network's warning that the show provides a "historical portrayal of ancient Roman society that contains graphic violence and adult content." Many have focused on the latter, the graphic violence and adult content, but fewer have considered the former, the series' claim to some form of historical authenticity, or the notion that many of the show's principal elements are geared toward realism. This chapter addresses part of this question of "historicity" by comparing the spectacle of the arena as depicted by *Spartacus* against its ancient Roman counterpart; that is, the spectacle of spectacle itself as it appears in Rome and on the *STARZ* network. Looking beyond – or more accurately, through – the gore and sex, I argue that *Spartacus* offers a remarkably apt representation of the culture of Roman spectacle in all of its social, spatial, and moral nuance. We shall briefly review ancient Roman spectacle through pertinent primary and secondary material, before turning to the series' *ludus*, arena, and society, and the blurred intersection of all three. By means of conclusion we shall return to the contemporary critics of *Spartacus* and ponder what their objections reveal about our modern culture of spectacle and how it relates to its ancient counterpart. What they found objectionable, and what they passed over without comment, echo the pagan and Christian critics of the ancient arena.

The rift between popular entertainment in Rome and this century is not as vast as we may think, and the boastful words of Crixus in the *ludus* of Batiatus that "the world is my arena" prove equally apt in the Roman world as in our own.

SATISFYING SPECTACLE: THE WORLD OF THE ROMAN ARENA

In one of his *Moral Epistles*, Seneca disparagingly writes that, to the Romans, "it is a satisfying spectacle to see a man made into a corpse."[8] Precisely why they had such an enduring and prevalent fascination with public spectacles of violence is a question that has puzzled subsequent commentators for centuries – not least among them many of the Romans who took part themselves. Rome is far from being the only society in human history to have cherished the violent clash of competitors in a public setting, but there is something particular in the degree to which Rome "reveled in killing as in the thrills and the reassurance, the self-validation, of a love affair."[9] In the eyes of many subsequent commentators this almost amorous relationship between the Romans and their spectacles has been cause for condemnation, alienation, or both. Writing in 1967, Michael Grant described gladiatorial contests as "bloodthirsty human holocausts . . . by far the nastiest bloodsport ever invented," elsewhere going on to place the human toll of Roman spectacle on the same plane as that of Nazi Germany.[10] He was neither the first nor the last to focus on the violence itself rather than its place in Roman society, both of which were long considered to be inevitable victims of the social triumph of Christianity. As Otto Kiefer wrote, "The whole of Roman sadism is a necessary step towards a new, truly noble state of humanity."[11] It is only in recent decades that contemporary researchers have discarded such evolutionary moralizing in favor of examining Roman spectacle on its own terms in order to understand its distinct culture, function, and context – as we too will do with *Spartacus*.

Spectacula in the Roman world consisted of far more than fights to the death among trained gladiators, extending to include chariot races (*ludi circenses*), the execution of prisoners of war or politics, contests between men and wild beasts (*venationes*), and naval battles (*naumachiae*). All of these, of course, were decidedly worth seeing – hence the ambiguity inherent in the Latin term. In the interest of brevity and pertinence, however, we must focus on what was admittedly only one part of a much broader public display: the *munus* (plural *munera*), or competition between teams of trained gladiators. Before passing on to their social function a few comments on their oft-over-looked origins ought to be made. *Ludi* – games or competitions in general – are first attested in a religious context, as the fulfillment of a vow to a god or goddess by an eager magistrate or successful commander to present games on the state's behalf.[12] The desired end result on the part of the sponsor was to win over the favor of the gods and the crowd simultaneously, and their apparent effectiveness at doing both made them a regular feature in the Roman religious cycle throughout the Republic. From 366 BC until the dawn of the Empire various *ludi* were added to the calendar for various occasions – starting with the *Ludi Romani* in honor of Jupiter in 366 BC, and the *Plebeii* and *Apollinares* at the close of the third century BC, along with the *Megalenses* in honor of the Great Mother. From the Early to Middle Republic, these spectacles were at their core religious and public.

Gladiatorial combat (*munus, munera*) entered the spectacular rep-ertoire in 264 BC at the games in honor of Junius Pera, sponsored and presented by his sons. The funerary function of the gladiatorial *munera* persisted throughout the Republic, although over time their popularity led them to be included in *ludi* by magistrates who were eager to bolster their own games. Then, as now, blood drew attention and spectators; if it bled, it led, to borrow the trope of the modern news media.[13] Rivers of scholarly and non-scholarly ink have been spilled over the particularities of the *munera*: which types of glad-iators wore what equipment, how they were trained and paired, strategy and tactics, and the like. We need not resurrect these details here, save to make a few observations on the culture of gladiatorial combat to which we shall return with *Spartacus*.

Fighters were bought by a particular *ludus* and taught by a *doctor*. When it came time to compete, they were paired with other gladia-tors of comparable skill by those tasked with the management of the particular games. They were then classified according to their success and experience, creating a hierarchy that only became more elabo-rate over time.[14] Although gladiators constituted what was in effect a parallel society to Rome, the popularity of the games and their social import naturally led to intense competition among trainers and owners. Dozens of inscriptions survive from Pompeii and elsewhere that boast of upcoming events, glorifying at once the combatants along with those who provided and trained them. Today these read like sports advertising posters, and even in these public notices poli-tics are never out of sight: "The gladiatorial *familia* of Aulus Suettius Certus will fight at Pompeii on May 31. There will be a hunt and also awnings. May Nero delight in all his *munera*."[15] The patrons of organizers, along with the fighters themselves, had a great deal at stake on the sands: reputations could be made or broken, careers advanced or stalled, and their fate was implicitly tied to those whom they had purchased.

It comes as little surprise that the line between the arena and "reality," as it were, was often blurred. A variety of theories have been proposed describing the relationship between Roman society and its spectacles, and perhaps there is a kernel of truth to be found in each without the dominance of any. The tie that binds these interpretations, however, is that what happens in the arena never stays in the arena. The spectacle of gladiatorial combat, Kyle notes, created a dialogue "between the provider and the consumers of games . . . that unfolded publicly within a threefold interactive dynamic involving the crowd and the authority figure(s) as well as the direct participants or victims."[16] Various interest groups collided in the arena, a liminal space seemingly set apart from society, yet where many of its tensions played out. To Thomas Wiedemann, the killing of beasts and humans in the arena symbolized the defense of Roman society against criminals, outsiders, and the natural world.[17] The common interest of otherwise disparate parts of Roman society in the games provided a unifying strand that bound them together in the shared ideal of Romanness.

Martial noted precisely this affirming function of the games, which he viewed as a potent exhibition of imperial majesty and power (*On the Spectacles* 6). Others have taken more of a sociological perspective: Paul Plass describes the arena as something of a social relief valve, a state-sanctioned spectacle of violence that dissipated latent tension through the controlled environment of the arena. Watching gladiators allowed Romans to "get it out of their system," in the process restoring them to a reinforced social routine and security.[18] In a society that was becoming ever more hierarchical and less socially mobile throughout the course of its transition from Republic to Empire, such a relief valve was increasingly necessary. In the process, different social classes were brought into contact with one another by common interest in the spectacle: plebs shared the same stadium as senators and magistrates, all of them united in their competitive gaze.

Garrett Fagan delved into the realm of social psychology in order to find the answer to why the Romans were so fascinated by bloody spectacle, and emerged to conclude that perhaps we would be no different from them, were we to find ourselves in the stands of the

Colosseum.[19] Affective dispositions, he elaborates, produced powerful emotional responses in the Roman spectator: euphoria or pleasure were felt when a favored competitor performed well, distress when he failed; the inverse is also true, as the crowd delighted in the fall of someone they loathed. The separation of the games from the rhythm of everyday life only served to heighten these reactions: spectacles opened with an elaborate procession, clearly marking them as events separated from the normal routine. The skill and care involved in the preparation, organization, and execution of gladiatorial matches made them something approaching an art form; no expense was spared in hosting or displaying them.

The arena thus became the "people's palace," as Jerry Toner aptly puts it.[20] The prudent frugality of the Roman elite had no place here; instead the crowd's thirst for excess of all sorts was sated by the blood spilled on the sands and the wine circulated through the arena. The disorder of the games could naturally splash into the streets, and indeed often did: riots at the *ludi Augustales* of AD 14, 15, and 23 followed as a result of disagreements among actors who were performing as part of the spectacles; while in AD 59 insults thrown among inhabitants of rival towns soon gave way to stones and unrest.[21] There was such bloodshed in Pompeii that the city was forbidden from hosting gladiatorial games for the next ten years; here again, the arena and "society" were hardly distinct and isolated realms.

Where excess and inebriation tread, lust generally follows – and this sexual aspect of the arena is far too often overlooked, but will necessarily figure prominently in our subsequent discussion. Muscular paragons of martial virtue in the arena wielding swords in passionate combat unsurprisingly become sex symbols, and the trend is well attested in both elite and vulgar contexts. Pompeiian graffiti broadcast the sexual prowess of gladiators,[22] while Juvenal's *Satires* mention that Eppia, the wife of a senator, scandalously ran off with a scarred gladiator named Sergius (6.82–113). "Gladius," not unexpectedly, was slang for "penis," and the nicknames of many gladiators were similarly unsubtle; their potent masculinity was so renowned that it was customary for the hair of a new bride to be parted with a spear, ideally one dipped in the blood of a slain gladiator.[23] All of this popular renown in turn fed back into the lure of the arena: it was there that slaves were forged into objects of forbidden erotic desire for noble women, as yet again the walls between the worlds of spectacle and society were breached. Base entertainments such as these, several ancient commentators note, both breed and encourage base desires.

The best testament to the allure of the arena, in addition to its religious, political, social, psychological, and sexual appeal that we have just discussed, comes from the Roman poet Ovid, who in the first book of his *Ars Amatoria* (*The Art of Love*) offers a treasury of practical advice for the young man wishing to seduce the apple of his eye: what better setting in which to do so, he argues, than chariot races and gladiatorial combats:

> The circus offers the possibility of new love, as does the scattered sand in the thrilling and grim arena. The son of Venus often fought on those sands; whoever watches wounds being given is wounded himself. While he talks, touches hands, checks the program, and asks which of them will win as the bet is placed, he too is wounded, groans, and feels the flying arrow. He himself is a part of the fight that he is watching.[24]

While many have been quick to point to the spatial liminality, the temporal distinctness, and the general separation of Roman entertainment from everyday life, Ovid here reminds us that the lines between spectator and participant, between entertainer and entertained, and ultimately between spectacle and reality are far less clear and unyielding than some theorists may lead us to believe. The two worlds inevitably collapse into one another in antiquity as they do on television; with all of this in mind we must turn to the mirror with which STARZ *Spartacus* reflects this Roman culture of spectacle.

A BLOODY STAGE: SPECTACLE IN *SPARTACUS*

The prequel season *Gods of the Arena* (episode 4) depicts a party thrown at the villa of Batiatus at which no appetite seems beyond satisfaction, and no taste neglected by the hosts' repertoire. Rivers of wine flow amid delicacies of all kinds arrayed on tables, while in the background slaves dressed in golden masks and chains take part in pleasures of such a variety that they can only, with any sort of accuracy, be called pansexual. Beholding all of this, particularly the enthusiasm of two slaves locked in passion under the entranced eyes of the Romans, Solonius remarks to Lucretia that her offerings "are well received, as are all things born of base desire." Batiatus, some time later, addresses the crowd and thunderously proclaims to his guests:

> You have shared drink, food, distractions of the eye and ear, yet these are common things, enjoyed by men bound by accusing morality of their deeds. I would see you freed from such human constraints ... Sever all ties from the mortal world, and arise as gods in the house of Batiatus.

This orgy of excess and consumption was arranged by Batiatus and Lucretia with the help of Gaia in order to entice the elite of Capua to show favor for his *ludus*, and grant him prime placement in the games of the new arena. Strings pulled in private, it was hoped, would control movements in public. The entire domestic event is a performance, a foretaste of what might come: if such things are to be admired and enjoyed in exclusion by Capua's well-to-do, then so much more will the public offerings of Batiatus resound on the sands of the arena in front of the adoring commoners. This scene is only one of dozens in the series that aptly demonstrate the fluid barrier between society and spectacle, and the reciprocal effect of one upon the other in the Roman context.

The quest of Batiatus and Lucretia to satisfy their ambitions in the arena is one and the same as their quest to satisfy their ambitions in society: primacy at the games, they believe, will provide them with the key to unlocking the doors of Rome's elite. Throughout the series, however, they must overcome the typical contempt of the aristocracy toward the base profession of *lanista* by a combination of favor, manipulation, intimidation, and conspiracy. Private machinations win them visibility in public, which then grants them prestige among the elite, and the cycle, they hope, will continue until they find themselves at the steps of the Senate. Batiatus' desire for upward mobility forms the core of the narrative of *Spartacus'* first season, *Blood and Sand*, and its prequel *Gods of the Arena*. In the prequel, he and Lucretia outwit and, in the end, murder Tullius to secure their *primus* in the new arena of Capua; and in the first season, their political and social ambition burns to consume the magistrate Calavius, their rival Solonius, the noblewoman Licinia, the Roman citizen bond-slave Varro, and, ultimately, themselves along with dozens of others.

In this narrative that ties together the first season and prequel of *Spartacus* we find an apt representation of the tangled interaction between public and private competition that girded Roman spectacle as a whole. Though the arena was isolated, it was never completely removed from the concerns of politics or society, an element that STARZ captures masterfully. The two worlds collide when Spartacus and Varro fight (episode 110) – unknowingly to the death – to entertain Numerius at his birthday party, or later when the murder and capture of Calavius are shown interlaced with shots of the games occurring simultaneously. Solonius' wrongful execution in the arena for Calavius' murder is the clearest point of intersection between politics and spectacle. In the weeks preceding this, we can easily envision a poster praising the upcoming pairings of the gladiators of Batiatus at games in honor of a magistrate adorning an alleyway in Capua, much like the example from Pompeii we encountered earlier. Even Glaber is aware of the resonance of the arena; as he claims, "win the hearts of the crowd, and the Senate will follow" (episode 113). The culture as well as the *realia* of Roman spectacle are aptly depicted: the hierarchy among gladiators the show depicts in the *ludus*, the fickle favor of the crowd, the booming voice of Oenomaus as *doctor*, along with the brand of Batiatus and the gladiatorial *sacramentum* it signifies, are remarkably faithful to their Roman inspiration.

Other vectors of fidelity are easily overlooked in favor of the blood and breasts that typically dominate the gaze of many viewers. The religious aspect of Roman *ludi*, so typically absent from modern depictions of ancient games, are frequently highlighted in *Spartacus*. The very first competitions depicted on screen (episode 101) are the funeral games sponsored by Ilithyia's father Albinius in honor of his noble family. Magistrate Calavius hosts lavish games (episode 105) meant to appease the gods and end the drought that plagues Capua. Batiatus, for his part, is only too happy to provide the gladiators that Calavius says are meant to be a sacrifice to Ceres. Spartacus, after his victory, is referred to as "the bringer of rain," thanks to the role he played in regaining divine favor. Many if not most scenes that take place in the arena are preceded by a shot of an image of a goddess being carried around the arena on a litter, again reflecting the religious character of the Roman games. Later, in *Vengeance*, Glaber and Varinius almost exactly echo Plass' (and Martial's) argument that the games were meant to reinforce a sense of security, stability, and continuity in Roman society. Varinius hosts games in Capua both to drum up public support against Spartacus' rebellion, and to provide the populace with a comforting reminder that Rome was still Rome and life would go on as usual (episodes 202, 203, 204). The sight of Glaber's men, with their armor and eagles, is meant to be particularly reassuring to the anxious citizenry. All of this is juxtaposed against scenes depicting the slaves' incursion into the mines in order to liberate Naevia, capturing both sides of the social coin.

Even the show's rampant sexuality seems less overtly gratuitous when viewed through the lens of the arena's eroticism described above. Noble Roman women – Ilithyia first, and then Licinia and her friends – are drawn to the scandalous allure of the gladiators throughout *Blood and Sand*. Varro is made to have sex with another slave in front of Ilithyia and Lucretia (episode 103); the former is particularly appreciative of his vigor. Ilithyia's appetite swells over the next episodes as she gazes on Crixus training, and in particular his bare midsection. In "Whore" (episode 109), we see precisely this gladiatorial eroticism at its core, as the drama revolves around Lucretia's designs to satisfy the desires of Licinia, Crassus' cousin, and Ilithyia in order to gain favor and patronage for the *ludus*. The arranged rendezvous is equally elaborate and spectacular: Spartacus is painted in gold and dressed as a god, as are Licinia and Ilithyia, and the whole evening is staged as an encounter between divinities. Lucretia's long-lasting affair with Crixus begins as lust but is transformed into something approaching love through time and repetition. Any and all of the above events read as the sort of titillating tales of the forbidden lusts of elite Roman women that grace the pages of Tacitus, Livy, or Cassius Dio.

Finally we come to the crowd itself. Every beheading, dismemberment, or spray of blood in the arena is followed by a quick shot of the crowd's visceral reaction to the spectacular violence. The crowd, perhaps unsurprisingly, does not present particularly well: they wear threadbare clothes, are generally unwashed and have unkempt hair, appear inebriated, and female spectators constantly (and somewhat inexplicably) expose their breasts while jumping around. The exaggeratedly "plebeian" character of the crowd seems to echo the distaste of Cicero or Pliny, as we shall see. Yet they are engaged with the action of the arena in precisely the all-consuming manner described by Ovid and Fagan: they grimace in pain in response to a deep wound, they seethe in anticipation during lulls in the action, they celebrate the success of those they favor, and the failure of those they disparage. Even the elite cannot resist the magnetism of spectatorship, vulgar though it may be: Numerius' mother chidingly notes that her son is as taken by sport as is Ilithyia, and while not reputable among upstanding Romans, the proclivity is certainly understandable. Elsewhere there are moments in which the crowd's passion for the current bout borders on the sexual: as Spartacus and Crixus face Theokoles and the contest becomes more frenzied, the background music pounds faster, and the crowd draws its shallow breaths with growing enthusiasm. The defeat of the legend by Spartacus comes as a climax: backs arch, shouts are raised, and then everyone settles back in ecstatic exhaustion.

The series' commentary on Roman spectacle far outlasts the *ludus* of Batiatus. One of its most dramatic moments comes during the penultimate episode (309), when the rebellious slaves organize games featuring captured Roman soldiers as a tribute to their fallen comrade Crixus (Figure 11.1). This event represents the ultimate inversion of the Roman social order: now the braying crowd is comprised

Figure 11.1 Spartacus (Liam McIntyre) opens the funeral games in episode 309 ("The Dead and the Dying"). STARZ.

of slaves, not Romans, and the competitors are free citizens of Rome who have been captured and are now exhibited for the amusement of those they once owned. The episode is seemingly drawn directly from the Roman historian Florus, who claims that Spartacus sought to "wash away all his preceding shame by having gone from being a gladiator to one who instead puts on the games."[25] With this the series' creative staff seem to be making a point: the crowd of slaves watching the dismemberment of Roman captives is depicted in precisely the same manner as the Roman crowd who once enjoyed their own performances; all would behave the same way were the roles reversed. Depending on one's point of view, this inverted contest is either the moment of Spartacus' ultimate triumph as the slave has now become the master, or of his greatest depravity, as he has proven himself no better than his former captors. Regardless, the role, function, and power of the spectacle remain.

There is a rather more abstract level on which *Spartacus*' reflection of Roman spectacle operates. There are precious few moments that do not take place before some kind of audience. Whether it is the exhibition of gladiators staged for Ilithyia's purchase, or the demonstration of Batiatus' wares before Albinius, or contests among the gladiators themselves, someone is always watching. The same is true outside the walls of the *ludus*: Batiatus makes a show of displaying his wealth in public with the purchase of Crixus, Glaber crucifies seditious slaves in the marketplace, Lucretia parades herself around Capua and blesses her newfound faithful. These, along with countless other moments of great and small import, make for a culture of spectacle that is as ubiquitous and multifaceted in the series as it was in ancient Rome. Not all viewers, however, approved of this.

US AND THEM: ANCIENT AND MODERN CRITICS

The roar of the crowd in favor of what we might consider to be popular culture or mass entertainment is offset by a small but vocal chorus of critics who take less delight in such common pleasures. In ancient Rome, this chorus was composed of elite writers and commentators who objected to certain aspects of the games, and the precise character of what they found repulsive is strikingly symmetrical with the published lamentations of contemporary detractors of *Spartacus*. Roman society, particularly in the Republic but also to some degree in the Empire, was driven by competition for distinction in which status held the keys to power, wealth, and opportunity. In such an environment, several members of the elite – particularly the *nouveau riche* or those in the lower echelons of the hierarchy – voiced their opposition to the spectacles as a means of distinguishing themselves from the *vulgus*, the common mob who so dearly enjoyed them.[26]

If they did not share in the tastes of the rabble, the logic went, then they certainly stood far above them; a sentiment expressed by Rome's literary elite in a variety of formulations. Cicero, in one of his *Letters*, his pen dripping with *ennui*, consoled one of his friends who had missed the games by writing, "I am glad that you had the good spirit to neglect those things which others adore for no reason." These contests in the arena were "things which, after all, if they are worth seeing, you have seen already many times; and neither did I, who was at the games, see anything at all that was new."[27] Elsewhere in the same letter, Cicero explains that an educated man should have better things to do with his time, and he should be above such simple pleasures: "But how could this be pleasing to a refined man, when either a feeble man is torn apart by an extremely powerful animal, or a wonderful animal is pierced by a spear?"

Pliny the Younger echoes Cicero's complaint about the game's repetition, but with rather more indignant bluster: "The games were on, but I could not care less. There is nothing new, no variation, nothing at all which would not only be worth seeing once." His comments a few lines later perfectly capture the notion that some of the Roman elite criticized the games as a means of social differentiation:

When I think about those men who sit so long and idly, so insatiably fond of such an inane, indolent, and common thing, I take pleasure in the fact that I am not entranced by this entertainment and am glad to devote my leisure to literature on those days when others are wasting time on the most idle pursuits.[28]

Tacitus, ever the bitter commentator on the decline of each generation, shares Pliny's criticism while also decrying the sheer popularity of the games. The passion of young Romans for chariot races and gladiator fights, what he calls the "particular and peculiar vices of the city," is so ardent that he asks indignantly, "How many people can you find who talk about anything else at home? And what other topic of conversation among the youth will we find when we go into a classroom?"[29] Juvenal and Martial follow this thread in deploring a society that idolizes the masters of such vain pursuits while ignoring the value and skill of its poets, orators, and rhetoricians (that is, men like themselves).[30] In this vein of ancient criticism, the games represent a popular culture that is distracted from better, nobler pursuits of the mind, delighting instead in what is derided as an idle, repetitive, and uncreative pastime.

Those who do dare to mingle with the common crowd and partake of their vulgar passions do so at their own risk, according to other ancient critics. Years of education, refinement, and discipline could be compromised as one is carried away by the enthusiasm of the crowd and enamored of their base pleasures; according to Seneca, "Never do I bring back home the same customs of character with which I left."[31] Seneca goes on to put it quite bluntly: "Associating with the crowd is hurtful; there is no person who does not recommend some vice to us, or imprint it on us, or smear it over those of us who do not know any better."[32] The greater the crowd, the more popular the attraction, and thus the greater the danger to one's character. Simple exposure to such vices makes Seneca "return from them more greedy, more ambitious, more luxuriant, and even more cruel and inhuman because I was among the people."[33] Tacitus explains that mere attendance at the games was equally perilous for men and women of good repute: "Many prominent women and senators were corrupted and polluted through going to the arena."[34] Later Christian commentators, particularly Augustine, Tatian, and Novatian, adapted the language of the Stoics with the addition of charges of idolatry and impiety leveled at the games and their enthusiasts. To all three, Roman spectacle presented a lesson in sin, disrepute, and disturbance, running contrary to the inner tranquility, grace, and devotion they sought to cultivate. The good Christian, like the good Roman, ought to avoid such entertainments at all costs lest their character and soul be put in dire jeopardy.

How then does the rhetoric of the ancients compare to the modern critics of this controversial series? The critical reaction to *Spartacus*, as we have seen above, was decidedly mixed: none of the individual seasons garnered anything more than a rating in the mid-50 percent range on *Metacritic*, though it did gain increasingly favorable numbers from the site *Rotten Tomatoes*. The disconnect between the comments of professional television critics and the audience reviews of the show's gratuitous spectacle, however, is fascinating: regular users of *Metacritic*, IMDb, and *Rotten Tomatoes* all adored *Spartacus*, with over 80 percent giving favorable opinions across all three platforms. Perhaps in this we already catch some reflection of the division between the tastes of Rome's literary elite and its more common consumers of mass culture. Precisely how the series was lambasted by its detractors causes this reflection to snap into clearer focus.

The lamentations of Tacitus about the declining tastes of Rome's youth find an unlikely echo in the words of Tim Goodman of the *San Francisco Chronicle*, the critic who branded the show a leading candidate for the worst series of the decade. The show, to him, was woefully uncreative to the point that it spoiled an otherwise sure-fire combination of gladiators, violence, and nudity: "*Spartacus* even makes the vapid but visually intriguing *300* look like Shakespeare ... [it] might appeal to teenage boys strangely attracted to Venice Beach, steroids, and blood porn, but anyone past the sophomore year of high school should steer clear."[35] The tedium of the acting and dialogue, the poor scripting and uncreative violence are to him as objectionable as the bland repetition of the Roman games was to Cicero. This was precisely what Matthew Gilbert of the *Boston Globe* found most repugnant about the series. The "amateur line delivery" by "shockingly wooden thespians," scenes that are "as emotionally inert as a video game," and a story that "has no layers" lead him to conclude that "it all blurs into a dull steroid rush."[36] A lack of originality is a common refrain in reviews of the first season, *Blood and Sand*, in particular, set against the renown of the HBO series *Rome* and Ridley Scott's award-winning film *Gladiator*: "There is ... considerable irritation over such a brazen, at times laughable attempt to piggyback on their success."[37] Contemporary audiences, the reviews suggest, have come to expect better from spectacles of blood and violence such as this.

Many critics do leave room for the entertainment value of *Spartacus*, as long as one admits without a shred of self-deception that it is fundamentally base entertainment. The *New York Daily News* warned: "The P-word, porn, is worth keeping in mind for viewers who get any fool notions about this orgiastic celebration being anything other than what it is."[38] The same review goes on to admonish the reader that "to say you watch *Spartacus* to see a contemporary reworking of a cinema classic is like saying you go to Hooters for the food." *TV Guide* put it rather more bluntly: "*Spartacus* is derivative as entertainment and primitively pandering as a diverting spectacle of campy, historical fiction."[39] The viewer who enjoys such a spectacle, according to the *Dallas Morning News*, "perhaps like some [Romans] who enjoyed those games but had second thoughts once the bloodlust was sated, might feel just a little bit guilty afterward."[40] All of these taken together provide an apt modern manifestation of the invective of Cicero and Pliny the Younger against the tedium and base commonality of the games they loathed.

What is perhaps most striking, however, is that which neither ancient nor modern critics find objectionable in their respective spectacles. The common thread that runs through the otherwise idiosyncratic complaints of the ancients about Roman spectacle is that none take issue with the games themselves: they might bemoan the lack of creativity, or the excessive passion of the common crowd for the blood sport, but with the exception of the Christians they found nothing inherently reprehensible in the act of watching violent competition for entertainment. Even the Christians who objected did so in no small part because their adherents featured so prominently in many hunting games and executions. Many of these Roman commentators were either patrons or spectators of the games: a series of Cicero's letters narrate his struggles to obtain exotic panthers for Marcus Caelius Rufus, who was then running for *curule aedile*.[41] The complaints of Tacitus, Pliny, and Seneca are all born of repeat attendance at the games; thus even they could be accused of having partaken of the same vulgar pleasures with which they took such issue. Again, none attacked the fabric or principle of Roman spectacle, only certain aspects of its presentation and popularity.

The same, I argue, can be said of the modern detractors of STARZ *Spartacus*. It is fascinating that in the context of the surging popularity of television shows on network airwaves that center on crime and brutality – *CSI, Bones, Dexter, Criminal Minds*, the numerous spin-offs of *Law & Order* – to say nothing about the proliferation of such series on cable networks as *Breaking Bad, The Sopranos, True Detective, Sons of Anarchy*, or *The Walking Dead*[42] – so many critics objected not to the violence of *Spartacus*, but to its particular brand of violence. The critics seem to have no inherent qualms about the depiction of murder, dismemberment, or bloodshed, provided it is done in an engaging and unique manner. What is apparently objectionable in *Spartacus* is not the presence of sex and violence, but its bluntness, the alleged lack of creativity in its depiction or exposition. It is in this that we find the greatest parallel between the ancient and modern cultures of spectacle that we have outlined here: all partook, some questioned, but in the end the penchant for such amusements endured as they were so deeply woven into the fabric of popular entertainment as to be inextricable. Perhaps, then, in the popularity of series like *Spartacus* among the ranks of its violent contemporaries like *Cops, Lockdown, Ultimate Fighting Championship*, and dozens of others, we find the twenty-first-century manifestation of a decidedly ancient culture of spectacle. The medium, the dissemination, and the mechanics of such spectacle may have changed drastically over the centuries, but its place in society has remained eerily similar.

NOTES

1 I would like to thank Monica Cyrino and Antony Augoustakis for their friendship, support, and unfailing editorial insight – not to mention their kind inspiration for this chapter. Discussions with Toph Marshall greatly speeded its germination, and contributed immensely to its organization.
2 On Fast's novel and Kubrick's film, see Daugherty and Rodrigues in this volume.
3 This review of Spartacus in contemporary film and media is drawn from Dunkle (2014: 30–6).
4 Garron (2010).
5 Lloyd (2010).
6 Hinckley (2010).
7 Goodman (2010).
8 Seneca, *Moral Epistles* 95.33. All translations of ancient texts are my own.
9 Kyle (1998: 2); see also his introduction for the general place of the games in Roman society. On the question of the reception of the games by modern commentators, see Mammel (2014: 603–4), Kyle (1998: nn. 19–22), and Fagan (2014: 465–6) for various other perspectives.
10 Quoted in Toner (2014: 451), from Grant (1967: 124).
11 Quoted in Kyle (1998: 29), from Kiefer (1934: 106), who elsewhere (99–106) argues that the Romans were fundamentally sadistic in their pleasures and cruel in their spectacles. His Christian perspective is difficult to overlook.
12 Dunkle (2014: 382–5) provides a thorough and succinct overview of *spectacula*, as does Kyle (1998: 43–55).

13 See Kerbel (2000) on blood and violence in contemporary television media.

14 Dunkle (2014: 388) and Potter (2010: 341–5)

15 *CIL* 4.1189; see also 4.1190, 4.3881 for other such public advertisements.

16 Kyle (1998: 9).

17 Wiedemann (1992: 46–7, 179). See Kyle (1998: 1–31) for an overview of the modern schools of thought relating to the games, and Toner (2014).

18 Plass (1995: 56–8); see also Futrell (1997).

19 Fagan (2011: 230–1) and (2014). On affective disposition, see Zillmann (1991) and (2000) and Zillmann and Cantor (1977).

20 Toner (2014: 456).

21 On the games of AD 14, see Tacitus, *Annals* 1.54; Cassius Dio, *Roman History* 56.47.2; on AD 15: Suetonius, *Life of Tiberius* 34.1; Cassius Dio 57.14.9–10; Tacitus, *Annals* 1.77; on AD 23: Tacitus, *Annals* 4.14; Suetonius, *Life of Tiberius* 37.2; on AD 59 in Pompeii: Tacitus, *Annals* 14.17.

22 *CIL* 4.4289, 4342, 4345.

23 See Hopkins (1983: 22) and Kyle (1998: 65–6 and nn. 62–3) for other ancient references to the eroticism of gladiators.

24 Ovid, *Ars Amatoria* 1.163–70.

25 Florus, *Epitome of Roman History* 2.8.9.

26 Wiedemann (1992: 141–4), Wistrand (1992: 62), Mammel (2014).

27 Cicero, *Letters to Friends* 7.1.

28 Pliny the Younger, *Epistles* 9.6.4.

29 Tacitus, *Dialogue on Orators* 29.

30 Juvenal, *Satires* 7.106–14; Martial, *Epigrams* 10.74.

31 Seneca, *Moral Epistles* 7.1.

32 Seneca, *Moral Epistles* 7.2.

33 Seneca, *Moral Epistles* 7.3.

34 Tacitus, *Annals* 15.32.

35 Goodman (2010).

36 Gilbert (2010).

37 Lowry (2010).

38 Hinckley (2010).

39 Roush (2010).

40 Darling (2010).

41 Cicero, *Letters to Friends* 8.1, 8.4, 8.9.

42 On the impact of violence in entertainment, see Grimes, Anderson, and Bergen (2008), Haugen (2007), Gunter, Harrison, and Wykes (2013), as well as Potter (1999) and Signorielli (2005).

12 *Draba's Legacy and the Spectacle of Sacrifice*

Meredith D. Prince

The character Draba from the 1960 film *Spartacus*, the black gladiator who spares Spartacus and sacrifices himself, is minor, yet of major importance, as he inspires the slave rebellion.[1] Read against the social and political context of the film's release, namely the burgeoning Civil Rights movement, Draba and his actions have been viewed as a commentary on contemporary race relations in America. Although the STARZ *Spartacus* series omits Draba, his impact emerges in several key scenes from the first season, *Blood and Sand*. The twenty-first-century version replaces his blackness with ethnicity and displaces it onto other characters in positions of greater power. This erasure or shifting of race is not only appropriate for more progressive times and reflective of the un-racialized nature of Roman slavery, it also highlights the series' subordination of race and focus on the dichotomy of master and slave. Retention and reconfiguration of other elements of the scene, such as issues of choice and sacrifice, condemn the Romans and reveal the slaves' moral superiority and potential for agency and for inverting the spectacle. The dehumanizing spectacle of slaves fighting for the Romans' entertainment has been transformed as slave-gladiators fight and kill each other to advance the Romans' aspirations or fulfill their personal motivations and vendettas.

In this chapter, I explore how the STARZ series reworks this pivotal scene from the 1960 film, the private fight of Spartacus and Draba before Crassus and Draba's refusal to kill Spartacus. I examine two scenes from *Blood and Sand*, both private fights between Spartacus and a brother gladiator for the entertainment of the elite: Spartacus' fight against Varro, an exhibition turned deadly (episode 110), and Spartacus' fight against Crixus, a match to the death transformed into rebellion (episode 113). These scenes emphasize Batiatus' aspirations for social mobility and political advancement and Lucretia's and Ilithyia's desires for vengeance against former sexual partners, reveal that these Romans are baser in their scheming and desires, and lead to revolt. I then consider a variation on this scene, Naevia's fight against Crassus' son Tiberius in the last season, *War of the Damned* (episode 309). As the rebels honor the fallen with a spectacle of blood, the series presents a black woman, transformed from meek house-slave to fierce warrior and fury personified, about to avenge her lover's death. As Naevia bests Tiberius and hears of a potential trade, the scene reworks the Draba and Varro scenes and interrogates issues of spectacle, choice, sacrifice, and race.

DRABA VERSUS SPARTACUS: *SPARTACUS* (1960)

Thirty-plus minutes into Stanley Kubrick's *Spartacus*, Crassus arrives at Batiatus' gladiatorial school, a visit in honor of the marriage of Helena's brother Glabrus and Claudia. Crassus notes they "desire a private showing of two pairs," and Helena adds "to the death." Batiatus protests, but Helena appeals to Crassus, who claims, "today is an exception." Batiatus still hesitates; this never happens and would cause "ill-feeling" and be a "cost." But Crassus asks him for his price (25,000 sesterces), to which he agrees.

The women themselves leisurely select, and objectify, the gladiators. Helena chooses Crixus and Spartacus, while Claudia selects Galino and Draba, whom she calls "the most beautiful" and "the big black one." Crixus is to fight Galino, Spartacus Draba, to the relief of the friends Crixus and Spartacus.

Crixus wins his match, which we see through the slats of the box where Draba and Spartacus wait. While Spartacus anxiously peers out at the fight and occasionally glances at Draba, Draba refuses to watch, barely acknowledges Spartacus, and smiles knowingly. Neither speaks as they sit opposite each other for several tense moments.

As Draba and Spartacus fight, the Romans talk among themselves, the women paying greater attention. Draba gains the upper hand and pins a sitting Spartacus against the fence with his trident. The camera offers several close-ups of Draba, breathing heavily; he turns to look up at the Romans, and Helena gives the thumbs down. Draba, however, hesitates; more close-ups of him, as Spartacus awaits the blow. We hear Claudia ask, "Why doesn't he kill him?," then Helena, "Kill him. What's the matter now?" As Draba moves away from Spartacus, the Romans yell, "Kill him, you imbecile, kill him." But Draba turns

Meredith D. Prince

Figure 12.1 Draba (Woody Strode) challenges the Romans and viewers in *Spartacus* (1960). Bryna Productions/Universal Pictures.

and throws his trident at the Romans and the camera, as it looks out and down toward him. Draba climbs up, but a guard spears him in the back. Crassus cuts Draba's throat, and his blood spurts onto Crassus. The scene ends with a close-up of Spartacus' face as he slumps against the fence and absorbs what has happened.

Monica Cyrino describes the Romans as "consumed by their desire for power and pleasure," with "no consideration for the gladiators, whose worthless lives they demand for their amusement."[2] The placement of slaves below and Romans above presents "a visible hierarchy of power," and "the vertical axis" highlights their dominance. Yet Draba, especially with his trident (Figure 12.1), breaks this "hierarchy . . . on both the narrative and visual levels."[3] The camera position also implicates us, the audience, with the Romans in their viewing pleasure.[4] The audience in the film, however, is small and not fully engaged in the violent spectacle they demand. Their lack of interest only disappears when blood is to be shed and Draba refuses to act.

Spartacus had attempted to strike up a friendship by asking Draba his name. Draba declined, responding, "You don't want to know my name. I don't want to know your name." He explains, "Gladiators don't make friends. If we're ever matched in the arena together I'll have to kill you." Draba's refusal points to the realities of a gladiator's life. Upon hearing of the upcoming match, Crixus questioned Spartacus about what would happen if they were paired:

CRIXUS: Would you fight?
SPARTACUS: I'd have to. So would you.
CRIXUS: Would you try to kill me?
SPARTACUS: Yes, I'd kill. I'd try to stay alive, and so would you.

Draba indicates the impracticality and risk of friendship under such conditions.[5] Although Spartacus suggests a lack of choice in fighting his friend, his overtures to Draba illustrate that "slaves can be agents within a social nexus of their own creation."[6] Yet Draba also exercises choice by rebuffing Spartacus.

But when placed into the position of killing Spartacus, the aloof Draba refuses. He opts to die instead. Although Draba isolates himself, and his race singles him out, as Martin Winkler notes the two gladiators are "not really enemies" but are "victims of an entrenched system that is degrading to both and has to be overcome."[7] Draba chooses not to cooperate with the Romans' demands and denies them the pleasure of violent spectacle; instead he offers a "subversion of spectacle."[8] As Robert Burgoyne argues, "Sacrifice becomes a form of self-authorship, the slave asserting mastery over his own body."[9] Draba exerts the ultimate power by choosing to act of his own will rather than to follow another's commands.

Draba proves superior to the Romans since his "bravery shows up the cowardice of Batiatus, his silent modesty stands as an accusation against the garrulous depravity of the Roman women, and his death at the hands of Crassus introduces the audience to the Roman's cruelty."[10] Soon after this, Spartacus begins his revolt, as Draba's death and his displayed corpse, hanging upside down as a warning, set things in motion. The defiance and action associated with the only black gladiator of any prominence contributes to pro-Civil Rights readings of the scene.[11] Others, however, stress that, while Draba's actions are significant and he is an object of emulation, he dies for the white man and cannot participate in the rebellion.[12] Nevertheless, Draba's choices and the unexpected spectacle of his sacrifice impact Spartacus and contribute to his decision to rebel.

The film briefly offers glimpses of other black slaves, and Batiatus encourages Claudia and Helena to select the Ethiopian (who is not shown) before Claudia chooses Draba. Granted both something to say and do, Draba appears in several scenes before the fight with Spartacus and is invoked by Crixus and Spartacus when they return to the school after their escape. Singled out for his race, Draba notably exercises agency over himself in choosing to defy the Romans and deny them their desires.

RACE IN STARZ *SPARTACUS*

In STARZ *Spartacus*, race, along with gender and sexuality, is subordinated to the master–slave power relation. Black characters are more visible, including slaves, gladiators, and spectators at matches. Some of Batiatus and Lucretia's household slaves, including Lucretia's personal slave Naevia, are black, as are those who attend to the gladiators, such as Pietros. Although often silent or in the background, they offer a less one-dimensional portrayal of color. Steven S. DeKnight, creator and producer of the show, remarks in an interview, "I am a firm believer in promoting a world where race, gender, and sexual orientation play absolutely no part in how people interact with each other."[13]

The gladiators themselves come from a wide geographic area, reflecting the reality of Roman slavery.[14] Several black gladiators reappear, of unspecified origins, and others come from Gaul, Syria, Germany, Carthage, and Thrace. Many of the actors playing these roles are from Australia or New Zealand, including several of Maori descent (Manu Bennett as Crixus, Antonio Te Maioha as Barca), both of whom appear racially ambiguous. The cast includes people of Lebanese (Nick E. Tarabay as Ashur), South African (Lesley-Ann Brandt as the first Naevia), and Ghanaian descent (Peter Mensah as Doctore, Cynthia Addai-Robinson as the second Naevia). As Denise McCoskey emphasizes, "Ancient slavery in no way derived from a single geographic source nor corresponded categorically with any physical trait, such as skin colour."[15] The multiracial actors and characters reflect the un-racialized nature of Roman slavery and increasingly more diverse casting on television.

Romans such as Glaber and Batiatus call the gladiators animals, while Glaber labels Spartacus and his countrymen "Thracian jackals" (episode 101). The gladiators' status as non-Romans and especially as slaves matters most to the Romans. The gladiators themselves are harshest regarding each other's ethnicities. They disparage Spartacus' Thracian origins, but he reciprocates with ethnic slurs (he and Crixus, a Gaul, exchange a heated "smells like" series of insults during Spartacus' hazing in episode 102), while others cast aspersions on Syrians and Germans. Even their trainer Doctore calls the undisciplined Spartacus an "animal" and Thrace "a swamp of piss." Yet he reminds the gladiators that their origins do not matter, "the only thing that does is the sound of my voice, and the sand beneath your feet" (episode 103), emphasizing that they are all the same.

Doctore (Oenomaus) stands at the top of the hierarchy, straddling slave and Roman. In contrast to Draba in the earlier film, no one points out that Doctore is black or darker than fairer Pietros.[16] Although primarily black slaves perform the lowliest tasks within the villa and the *ludus*, Doctore, the strict and imposing trainer, the highly skilled former gladiator who dispenses both advice and discipline, exercises the most power among the gladiators and subverts audience expectations. As DeKnight emphasizes in an interview:

> The fact that we have a man of color in charge of the gladiators – including their often brutal punishment at the end of his whip – immediately and quite visually sets up the dynamic that a man's race is meaningless in this world of gladiators. The only thing that matters is your skill, cunning, and strength.[17]

Doctore's power, represented by his whip, his closeness to Batiatus, and his strict code of honor differentiate him from the other gladiators, not his race. Peter Mensah as Doctore physically resembles Woody Strode as Draba; both are tall, physically imposing, and bald. Although Doctore stands closer to the Romans than the slaves, he also ultimately must choose between the two sides.

SPARTACUS VERSUS VARRO: *BLOOD AND SAND*

Episode 110 ("Party Favors") of the first season reworks Draba and Spartacus' fight with best friends Varro and Spartacus.[18] Batiatus hosts an exhibition to celebrate the fifteenth birthday of the magistrate Calavius' son Numerius and offers his *ludus*, at no additional expense, as a "favor between friends." Batiatus will match the current star, Spartacus, against the previous one, Crixus, as selected by Numerius. Batiatus emphasizes that blood is "only for show," threatening them otherwise, and privately asks Spartacus not to make Crixus look too bad. Spartacus "will give Numerius a show, nothing more," while Crixus tells Naevia that he will kill Spartacus, although against instructions, to regain his position as champion.

But Ilithyia's scheming prompts a last-minute substitution. Still reeling from her murder of her friend Licinia (episode 109), who had mocked her for committing adultery (unknowingly) with Spartacus, her husband's mortal enemy, Ilithyia notes the friendship between Varro and Spartacus and aims to strike a similar blow against him. After she seduces Numerius in the baths, he replaces Crixus with Varro, just as Crixus has been announced. This offends the former champion Crixus, who is struggling to recover from his wounds, but is a compliment to Varro, who has recently experienced both glory in the arena and reunion with his wife Aurelia.

Spartacus and Varro joke as they await the exhibition. Doctore instructs them, "Honor the boy, honor the *ludus*." Their exhibition lasts several minutes, and both enjoy the mock rivalry, even when Varro draws blood. As the more skilled of the pair, Spartacus gains the upper hand; with Varro kneeling on the ground, Spartacus places his sword against his shoulder. Although this is an exhibition, Batiatus has appointed Numerius as *editor*, whom he now calls upon. Numerius extends his hand, turns his thumb down, to the gasps of the audience, and glances at Ilithyia. Batiatus questions Calavius, as this was not the arrangement, but instructs Spartacus to kill Varro after Calavius promises reimbursement.

Spartacus hesitates, even as guards approach him. The camera focuses on Spartacus' face, his tears, and his emotions. Varro, to Spartacus' dismay, starts the sword into his shoulder, with Spartacus finishing him off. As Varro's body hits the floor and his blood pools, the audience laughs and applauds, while Spartacus' vision goes hazy.

The few spectators in the corresponding scene from the film have been replaced in the TV episode by a larger crowd of both upper-class Romans, including certain high-ranking individuals whom Lucretia forced Ilithyia to invite, and slaves from Batiatus' house and business. This audience's greater enthusiasm and engagement in the fight than their film counterparts appropriately reflects the lighthearted nature of the occasion. The greater number of Romans, however, implicates more of them in the eventual cruel turn of events.

The audience size also necessitates a change in location for the fight and thus eliminates the film's visual differentiation of slaves and Romans. Everyone appears on the same level in the villa's interior. The transfer of the fight from outside to inside and the mix of free Romans and slaves highlight the lack of spatial segregation and again stress the festive atmosphere and that this is an exhibition. The removal of the visual hierarchy, however, proves deceptive.

So too does ethnicity, which replaces the film's emphasis on Draba's race. Varro is Roman, dying for his own people's pleasure, and in a telling way he differs little from Batiatus himself. Because of heavy debts, Varro has sold himself for two years to earn money to feed his wife and son (episode 102). He chose to enslave himself instead of running away, which Aurelia suggests would have been better, but which Varro views as dishonorable (episode 107). Moments after Varro's revelation of his status as a debt-slave, a scheming Batiatus deals with his own debts; the series thereby establishes a deadly connection between the two men. A man who has enslaved himself to pay off his debts must die because another man, also burdened with debts and of lower status, is seeking the magistrate's support for political office. Varro's choice to sell himself, in contrast with the captured Spartacus, not only reflects his agency but, with a limited contract, the likelihood of freedom and reunion with his family. Varro took, and will take, a more honorable course than Batiatus.

In contrast to Draba's refusal of Spartacus' friendship, Spartacus and Varro are best friends. The moments before the fight differentiate the two pairs and the matches' intended purposes. While Spartacus and Draba sit opposite each other in solemn silence, Spartacus and Varro stand next to each other. We repeatedly see them practicing together and joking, and Ilithyia's observation of them, and these scenes emphasize their closeness, a bond that extends back to the beginning of the series. Since they are both new to the *ludus*, Varro sits with Spartacus at mealtime and strikes up a conversation, even though Spartacus has been defiant during training (episode 102). The two become each other's support system. Varro emerges as the voice of reason for Spartacus during the search for his wife Sura. Spartacus does the same for Varro after he learns of Aurelia's pregnancy by another man, and he attempts to curb Varro's return to gambling and to reunite him with his wife.[19] Varro is Spartacus' only friend; Spartacus, in his defiance and reclusiveness, resembles the distant Draba.

Draba and Spartacus were to fight to the death, but Spartacus and Varro were not. Like Draba, Spartacus hesitates when called upon to kill Varro, but he is in a worse position. Draba was expected to kill his so-called enemy, while Spartacus unexpectedly must kill a brother or die. He wants to refuse and, as he looks back and forth between Varro and the approaching guards, Varro speaks up:

VARRO: Don't. They will kill us both. There is no choice.
SPARTACUS: There is always a choice.
BATIATUS: Spartacus! [Batiatus scowls; Spartacus shakes his head]
VARRO: Not this time. [He thrusts the sword into himself] Live, and see my family provided for. And know I would have done the same.

This exchange recalls two of their earlier conversations. When the Vulcanalia pairings are announced (episode 103), although they object more to the low status and minimal money that will result from being matched first, they also address the issue of fighting each other:

VARRO: May the gods see us both survive.
SPARTACUS: There are many I would see dead in this place. You are not among them.
VARRO: You may not have a choice.
SPARTACUS: There is always a choice.

When Spartacus objects to killing fellow Thracians in the arena (episode 107), Varro tells him to do what Batiatus commands because "he is your master, his demands your duty, unreasonable or other-wise." Spartacus disagrees. Varro responds, "You act as if you have free will in the matter. You are a gladiator." While Spartacus empha-sizes that he is "a Thracian," Varro counters that he is "a slave."

Varro himself makes the decision to die and prevents Spartacus from endangering himself. Varro has denied the existence of choice, but he exerts agency over what happens to himself and, by extension, Spartacus and his family. On the DVD audio commentary, Andy Whitfield notes that he insisted that Spartacus would not just kill Varro at Batiatus' command; the writers changed the script so that Varro would choose to die. The "what if" scenario posed by Crixus in the film plays out here, emphasizing the practicality of Draba's anti-friendship attitude, and Varro's claim that gladiators have no choice recalls the scene.[20] As Winkler notes of Draba, "The man who refused to be anyone's friend has displayed greater nobility of spirit than any other gladiator."[21] Although Varro loses the fight, by adopting Draba's freedom of choice he too saves Spartacus with his self-sacrifice. Varro participates in the Romans' demand for blood but perverts it with his agency. The man who called himself "the worst of the lot" (episode 102) proves the noblest of the Romans.

Both scenes linger on Spartacus' face, as he responds to what the Romans did or watches the Romans react. Spartacus' emotions are stronger in the series, with the added sounds of the Romans laughing and the camera panning the crowd. Instead of us/the Romans look-ing at Spartacus, we also see the audience through his shocked and teary perspective and share in his anguish. The sight of both Draba's and Varro's deaths greatly impacts Spartacus, but Varro's death is just as, if not more, shocking and violent than Draba's. The end of the episode stresses Spartacus' mental state as he wrecks his cell and breaks down in Mira's arms.

The film alluded to the women's unfulfilled sexual desires, as the men chat about litter-bearers and the women objectify the gladiators. The gladiators in STARZ *Spartacus* are not explicitly objectified, but Ilithyia satisfies her desires, though not with the gladiator she expected, and she then turns the tables on him. Her desire for venge-ance as a result of (unknowingly) having sex with Spartacus, and her anger at his slights against her husband Glaber, motivate her actions. She has a personal vendetta, blaming Spartacus for Licinia's murder, and uses her sexuality to accomplish it. A close-up of her smile, emphasizing her role in Varro's death, closes the scene.

But the choice of death ultimately lies with a fifteen-year-old boy, who is easily convinced to do Ilithyia's bidding. The Roman audience, although surprised at first by Numerius' decision, applauds and laughs as Varro dies. Numerius tells Aurelia (episode 113) that Varro "deserved to die. He was nothing." Spartacus expresses his contrasting view to Doctore (episode 111) that Varro's "heart was stilled for a boy's amusement – where's the honor in that?," and condemns the bloodthirsty Romans.

The film Batiatus hesitated and protested before the gladiators were chosen, but he was merely greedy. The TV Batiatus, looking uncomfortable with Numerius' decision, remarks that death was not part of the arrangement. After Numerius' plea to his father, recalling Helena's influence on Crassus to win over Batiatus, Calavius promises reimbursement, in front of everyone including Varro. His question, "Do we have a problem Batiatus?" when Spartacus does not obey Batiatus' orders, echoes Helena's remark, "What's the matter now?" when Draba too would not kill on command. But Calavius' direct address of Batiatus highlights their connection. While Calavius will do anything to please his son, Batiatus will do anything for Calavius' support, even going against his own instructions to the gladiators. Political support trumps replacement cost. The episode repeatedly stresses their need to please Calavius via Numerius. As Batiatus tells Lucretia, upset over the substitution, "the magistrate's happiness is our only concern." Afterwards Batiatus calls the show, and thus Varro's death, "a favor for a dear friend," as Calavius praises his son's unwavering demand for blood.

Varro's life matters little to either man. Batiatus' attitude has changed since Spartacus killed his fellow gladiator Gnaeus, whose physical and sexual abuse led to Pietros' suicide. Batiatus claims that Pietros was "nothing" compared to the cost of a gladiator, while Spartacus argues the opposite (episode 107). After striking Spartacus, Batiatus yells, "I alone decide who lives, not you, not a . . . slave!" But for the purposes of the exhibition, Batiatus equates Varro's life with Pietros' and shares Numerius' estimation. However, Batiatus only fully realizes Varro's worthlessness when Calavius tells him he lacks the pedigree for politics. The exhibition was all for nothing. Although Batiatus claims outrage at the loss (episode 111), the insult and his obsession with advancement prompt him to pursue vengeance against Calavius and obtain Glaber's patronage, thereby worsening conditions around the *ludus*. Batiatus' agreement to Varro's death illustrates how his opinions and options have shifted with his rising ambitions.

The scene is dramatic, highly emotional, unexpected. Unlike the limited screen time of Draba, the slow build of a television series has

allowed the viewer to get to know and root for Varro. Fans were outraged when Varro died. DeKnight notes in an interview:

> His death was crafted to not only force Spartacus to reject the Roman way
> he had embraced, but also to highlight a complete and utter disregard for
> human life that permeated Roman culture . . . That such a good man could be
> sentenced to death for the amusement of a fifteen-year-old boy was a serious
> wake up call for Spartacus – and the audience.[22]

On the DVD commentary, Andy Whitfield remarks that the writers
told him "this is the kind of thing that's gonna send Spartacus on
to do what he does . . . so we have to go there." Batiatus' need to
please Calavius and Ilithyia's desire for vengeance force Spartacus to
destroy the one thing making his life in the *ludus* bearable, his only
friend. The first in a series of revelations, as Varro's ghost guides a
hallucinating Spartacus to the truth about the murder of his wife
Sura, it will lead to revolt. As Draba motivated the film Spartacus, so
Varro fulfills the same role of noble sacrifice and inspiration.

SPARTACUS VERSUS CRIXUS: *BLOOD AND SAND*

The first season finale (episode 113, "Kill Them All") offers another celebration and private fight. With elite Capuans in attendance, Batiatus
will celebrate Glaber's patronage with "a gift of blood": Crixus and
Spartacus will fight to the death. In a flashback to two days earlier,
Lucretia proposes that Batiatus reinforce his position with the elite
through such a fight. Since they have already unsuccessfully tried this
with Numerius' exhibition, Batiatus hesitates. He finally agrees with
her reasoning to have Crixus killed "for offenses committed against
the House of Batiatus." Batiatus reasserts his power, but personal
vendettas dictate their choices. Lucretia, furious after learning that
Crixus and Naevia are romantically involved, wants revenge, like
Ilithyia, against a former lover, but also the supposed father of her
unborn child. Batiatus is thinking politically; Crixus' attack on Ashur
because of Naevia (episode 112) threatened Glaber's patronage, and
Batiatus realizes the advantage of using Spartacus as he campaigns.
To ensure that Spartacus wins, they arrange to have Crixus drugged.
Spartacus, however, plans to rebel, if he can convince Crixus to join
forces with him.[23]

The flashback style breaks up the fight between Spartacus and
Crixus into several scenes, increasing the tension as Spartacus awaits
both a signal from Mira and Crixus' agreement to help. As Crixus

holds his own, then begins to fade, the scene alternates between them fighting, the audience shouting ("Kill that Gaul!", "Stuff that pig!"), and Spartacus revealing the truth to him: "You're weakened because they have poisoned you. They wish you dead." Locked in close combat, Spartacus exclaims, "Join me brother, and we shall see the House of Batiatus fall." Spartacus knocks Crixus down; as he pulls himself to his knees, he looks up at Lucretia. He turns, whispers Spartacus' name, and taps his shield. Spartacus then uses Crixus' shield as a springboard to the balcony. Doctore attempts to stop Spartacus in mid-leap by grabbing his wrist with his whip. But Crixus cuts the whip, knocking Doctore down and allowing Spartacus to finish his leap to the balcony, where he thrusts his sword through a magistrate's head. The revolt begins, as Crixus yells to the gladiators, "Kill them! Kill them all!"

As in the scene with Varro in episode 110, a larger audience is present, including both numerous upper-class Romans and slaves and gladiators. Yet the audience members are no longer on the same level, with the gladiators below in the *ludus* and the Romans above on the balcony. The placement restores the vertical axis of the Draba scene and highlights the Romans' power, including Batiatus' and Lucretia's reassertion of control, evident in their arrangement of the match's outcome, and Crixus' look upward. The other gladiators are shackled, in contrast to the earlier exhibition, stressing their subordination and powerlessness. The shift outside to the *ludus* grounds further reflects the more serious nature of the fight.

Instead of the Romans' perspective looking down at Draba, with the audience complicit in their viewing pleasure, we see the slaves'/Spartacus' perspective, from the rear and side, as he moves forward and leaps up. The change puts us in the position of the gladiators about to take up arms and implicates us in the revolt. The scene omits Draba's trident hurl, yet offers the closest visual parallel (Figure 12.2).[24] Spartacus launches himself upwards to the balcony, just as Draba climbed up, and he himself violates the space of the Romans. Draba's decision to defy the Romans, symbolized by his trident throw, marked a turning point in the film, much as Spartacus' leap does. On the commentary to the finale episode, DeKnight notes it was their choice to stage this as a private fight rather than in the arena: "We wanted this leap coming up that was really symbolic of the lower class attacking the upper class." Spartacus ultimately inverts the axis and, instead of the slave Draba, a Roman politician dies and the revolt begins.

As with Draba and Spartacus, supposed enemies are to fight

Figure 12.2 Spartacus (Andy Whitfield) leaps to revolt in episode 103 ("Legends"). STARZ.

to the death, but they go against the script. The episode's setup heightens the drama of what Crixus will do. Before the exhibition, Crixus claimed he would kill Spartacus, although forbidden to do so. Crixus shares Draba's willingness to kill and go against instructions. Spartacus and Crixus' relationship has been antagonistic from the start. Even when the rivals are forced to work together to defeat Theokoles (episode 105), Crixus is reluctant to do so, and his arrogance almost kills him.

The start of the fight, through both their separation in line and Crixus' emphatic refusal to engage, underscores their division. In a flashback, Crixus agrees with Doctore that Spartacus is obstructing the recovery of the honor of the *ludus* and Naevia and so must be removed. But just as Draba realized what he was being forced to do in killing Spartacus, so Crixus, looking up at Lucretia, recognizes what she has compelled him to do (be her sex slave), how he has suffered (physical and public punishment, loss of Naevia), and knows what he must do since they have set him up to die. Similarly, as Spartacus fights to the death against a lesser opponent, what will he do? Will he kill as commanded or revolt? The two rivals prove not to be enemies as Crixus acknowledges their common ground at the critical moment, and his shield tap confirms his choice to join forces. They too deny the Romans the desired and expected spectacle and transform it into rebellion.

Doctore, too, has proven Draba-like in his unfriendliness to Spartacus, although the power relation and Spartacus' insolence contribute to this. Doctore reverses Draba by "serving the Roman culture of enslavement that Draba violently rejects."[25] He initially hinders Spartacus with his whip and saves Batiatus' life. Only when Crixus severs the whip, the symbol of Doctore's power over the gladiators and his own subservience to Batiatus, can they potentially work together and realize that they too are on the same side.[26]

Doctore hesitates, as did Draba, over which side to align with, and his initial position also changes course. Close to Batiatus, Doctore values honor more than anyone. Although Batiatus has promised to free Doctore and make him *lanista*, Crixus' revelations about Sura's death and Lucretia's manipulation confirm Doctore's suspicions about Batiatus and his own affinity with the other slaves. He acknowledges his commitment, like Draba with his trident, by hurling a sword to save Crixus' life. After Sura's death and Spartacus' aborted attempts at escape, Doctore tells Spartacus (episode 107), "Next time you seek escape, you'd best kill me." Like Draba, Doctore goes against his words, and Batiatus' betrayals link the two men together. Doctore sacrifices his status and advancement, his legitimately earned freedom, to help Spartacus' pursuit of freedom and vengeance. Yet he questions the extent of the slaughter and punishes himself in *Vengeance* with exile and return to the disreputable Pit before eventually joining the rebellion and taking on the essential role of training the rebels as fighters.[27]

NAEVIA VERSUS TIBERIUS: *WAR OF THE DAMNED*

In the series' penultimate episode (309), the rebels hold games to honor the fallen, including Crixus, with blood. Spartacus begins the show, and major characters fight against and kill recently captured Romans. Among the prisoners is Tiberius, Crassus' son, who killed Crixus with a spear in the back (episode 308). Naevia, alternating between shock and grief and desiring vengeance, is to face Tiberius; the reason he is still alive, Spartacus informs Naevia, is for her to kill him.

Each holds their own in the fight, with insults thrown in, as Naevia uses Tiberius' own sword. After he taunts her that he will kill her as he did Crixus, she rages and beats him, bringing him to his knees. Spartacus, however, receives news from Caesar of a possible trade: Crassus' son for five hundred men captured when Crixus was killed. As Naevia lifts the sword to strike the fatal blow, Spartacus interrupts, explaining the proposal to everyone. Naevia refuses to believe these claims, but Spartacus leaves the decision to her. After hesitating, she hits Tiberius' head with the sword and spares his life.

As a black woman and former slave fights Crassus' son, in front of other rebel slaves, the scene reverses the Draba and Varro scenes. The context of a private fight between brothers before an audience of mainly Romans has been altered. An audience of predominantly rebel slaves recalls the scene in the film when the gladiators return to the school and force Romans to fight each other. Spartacus, hearing the cheering slaves, intervenes:

> SPARTACUS: Noble Romans, fighting each other like animals. Your new masters, betting to see who'll die first. Drop your swords.
> CRIXUS: I want to see their blood right over here where Draba died. When I fight matched pairs, they fight to the death.
> SPARTACUS: I made myself a promise, Crixus. I swore that if I ever got out of this place, I'd die before I'd watch two men fight to the death again. Draba made that promise too. He kept it. So will I.

Both men invoke Draba and his link between violent spectacle and revolt. But Spartacus accuses his fellow slaves: "What are we becoming? Romans?" Ina Rae Hark notes: "The permission to become a spectator demarcates the master from the slave. Rome maintains and enforces its power through making spectacles of those it dominates."[28] Spartacus accurately questions his fellow slaves' identities as they give in to this power and role reversal.

Instead of brother against brother, or Roman against Roman – which the audio commentary notes would not have worked here – rebel slaves fight Romans. The slaves willingly partake in the spectacle as viewers and gladiators. The rebels, on the verge of becoming Romans in watching and asserting their power, attempt to distance themselves with their dual roles and the justification of honoring the dead with violence. They ostensibly subjugate both the Romans' viewing pleasure and the film Crixus' implied vengeance to a nobler cause.

Spartacus attempts to restore glory to Crixus with the games, but also to "return favor" and offer a "lesson" of what Rome has taught them. Like Varro, Crixus died unceremoniously because of a boy. When Naevia describes Crixus' death to Spartacus, she mentions an unknown boy. The repeated designation of Tiberius as a boy recalls Numerius' age and links the two young, elite, Roman males in asserting their power through bloodshed.

Spartacus ultimately leaves the choice of Tiberius' fate to Naevia: "Yet I lay choice in the one most wronged by the boy." As Naevia hesitates, with the sword to Tiberius' throat, aural echoes recall a similar moment from the first season, that of Spartacus with Varro's life in his hands. The same music from Spartacus' hesitation (entitled "Always a Choice") plays here, from when Naevia initially prepares to kill Tiberius through her final decision. The music emphasizes the theme of choice and, although a reversal (Tiberius deserves to die, the fight was meant to be to the death, no one is a slave), it increases the tension surrounding her decision. When Spartacus told her about the games, Naevia announced, "I will have his . . . life." Daniel O'Brien notes her tendency for extreme violence against the Romans: "Marked as brutalized and violated, Naevia is reconfigured as a fighter and trainer, yet this shift in identity and status is undermined by mental fragility and instability."[29] Considering her earlier displays of, and relish for, unnecessary violence and her claims of vengeance, her rage surprisingly goes unappeased. Naevia shows greater nobility as she proves Draba-like; she has a personal investment in the outcome, but she restrains herself and thus denies the audience the spectacle of blood and herself the satisfaction of vengeance. She may not lose her life, but her own self-sacrifice, in choosing the rebellion over her personal desires, restores her dignity, and her gender points to a contrast with Ilithyia's and Lucretia's selfish motivations. And the "most wronged" may not be Naevia but Kore, Crassus' former slave/lover, who kills Tiberius at the end of the episode.[30]

CONCLUSION

Instead of using their power over others for entertainment, these Romans exploit and kill others because of their political scheming, sexual desires, and personal vendettas. The *Spartacus* series' reworkings of the Draba scene highlight that these Roman women are more sexually depraved, bloodthirsty, and vengeful than their film counterparts and that Batiatus, who will do anything to advance socially and politically, is more immoral than the film's Batiatus or even Crassus. At the end of the first season, during his rallying speech among the slaughter, Spartacus exclaims, "I would not see the passing of a brother for the purpose of sport. I would not see another heart ripped from chest or breath forfeit for no cause" (episode 113). He harkens back to Varro's death and Draba's refusal to participate in such actions but also reminds us that both men's deaths were not "for no cause" but had nobler reasons and results.

The diminution of race enhances the Romans' dastardly nature; as they exploit violent spectacle for their own self-interest, race becomes irrelevant, as do any consequences for others. Batiatus and Lucretia do not hesitate to allow a fellow Roman to die to advance their interests. The racial component of the Draba scene has also shifted to those in a position of greater power. In the twenty-first century, a black man can exhibit the highest morality and discipline others, and a black woman can become a skillful fighter and decide a greater person's fate. Both Doctore and Naevia advance from their original positions and better themselves throughout the series, which offers a semblance of racial equality and updates the portrayal of race in antiquity.

Draba, Varro, Crixus, Doctore, and Naevia exercise choice, often benefitting others in the process, and sacrifice something, whether their own life or personal desires, decisions that underscore differences between slave and Roman. They choose to do what is morally right, even if against their own interests or the Romans' commands, and refuse to grant the desired spectacle and offer a different one in its place. As each determines a life's worth, their individual choices reflect agency, and they exert control over themselves. Yet their actions are for the best collectively. Individual choice and sacrifice exhibited within violent spectacle result in collective rebellion for a just cause.

NOTES

1 This chapter began as a paper presented at the Film & History Conference in Madison, WI, in November 2014. I would like to thank Meredith Safran for bringing it to the attention of Monica Cyrino and the editors for their assistance and support.
2 Cyrino (2005: 106).
3 Cyrino (2005: 107).
4 Hark (1993: 160–1), Wyke (1997: 70).
5 Cyrino (2005: 106). Contrast Winkler (2007b: 169) on the trainer's attempts at friendship, a relationship only possible among the gladiators.
6 Futrell (2001: 100).
7 Winkler (2007b: 174–5).
8 Theodorakopoulos (2010: 62).
9 Burgoyne (2008: 86).
10 Blanshard and Shahabudin (2011: 94).
11 Wyke (1997: 68), Cyrino (2005: 118–19), Winkler (2007b: 172–5).
12 Girgus (2002: 94–5), O'Brien (2014: 150).
13 DeKnight (2010).
14 See McCoskey (2012: 55) on slaves' diverse origins.
15 McCoskey (2012: 55).

16 McCoskey (2012: 24) emphasizes, in contrast with today, "the Greeks and Romans did not promote any fundamental racial opposition between 'whiteness' and 'blackness'."

17 DeKnight (2010). The historical Oenomaus was a Gaul, but the series has reconfigured him as Numidian.

18 Although I have not confirmed that the Draba scene inspired Varro's death.

19 On their friendship, and the developing bond of Spartacus and Crixus, see Augoustakis (2013).

20 A similar "what if" conversation occurs in the prequel *Gods of the Arena* (episode 2) between the champion Gannicus and Oenomaus' wife Melitta. Much to her irritation, Gannicus jokes about it but claims he would give Oenomaus "a glorious death" (Oenomaus mostly remains silent). Gannicus emphasizes their lack of choice because of their status as slaves. The opportunity presents itself in *Vengeance* (episode 205) when Gannicus is to execute Oenomaus, but, in the chaos of Spartacus' attack, he rescues him and ultimately joins the rebellion to honor him.

21 Winkler (2007b: 169).

22 DeKnight (2010) notes that Varro was supposed to die in an earlier episode.

23 Two private fights from the prequel *Gods of the Arena* (episodes 2 and 4) reveal that the women have not reached the degree of depravity evident in the first season but expose the origins of Batiatus' and Lucretia's obsession with currying the elite's favor. These "demonstrations" advance the placement of their gladiators in the games rather than themselves. The Romans Varus and Tullius request that practice swords be replaced with real ones and could not care less about the gladiators. Women (Gaia, with Crixus and Gannicus, and Lucretia, with Tullius and Gannicus) spare the defeated man or stop things from getting out of hand.

24 In *Vengeance* (episode 205), when Spartacus destroys the arena and rescues Crixus and Oenomaus from execution, he throws his spear at Glaber, scratching his cheek and killing Cossutius. The scene shows Spartacus in side view, again placing the viewer in the position of those on the arena floor.

25 O'Brien (2014: 151).

26 The whip recalls day one of training when Doctore attempts to whip Spartacus for his defiance, but Spartacus stops it with his wrist (episode 102).

27 See O'Brien (2014: 151–2) on Oenomaus' short-lived impact on, and supporting role in, the rebellion, which thus offers little advancement from the role of Draba. Although Doctore does not die for Spartacus, his role here and as trainer of Spartacus relate to Girgus' view (2002: 89) of the "black fighter as a savior and moral figure for whites."

28 Hark (1993: 155–6).

29 O'Brien (2014: 167); he further blames Naevia for the rift between Spartacus and Crixus that leads to Crixus' death.
30 Earlier in the episode, Naevia lectures Kore on responsibility for what one does and does not do, referring to her not killing Crassus, and emphasizes "choices" and "balance scale," words which Kore uses when she stabs Tiberius from behind.

13 *Violence and Voyeurism in the Arena*

Hunter H. Gardner and Amanda Potter

In describing the level and quality of violence in the first season of the STARZ series *Spartacus*, show creator Steven S. DeKnight emphasized the appeal of the network's invitation to develop an "R-rated action series" and "unleash the violent part" of the hero's legend.[1] He further clarified the show's representation of violence in an online interview:

> We often say we take the Spartacus legend, we turn it on its side, and we beat the crap out of it. It is bloody and brutal. This was a very brutal time. The Romans had a completely different view of violence than we do. They were brought up that flinching away from blood and violence was a sign of weakness.[2]

This chapter explores the different forms of violence presented in the series, with special emphasis on its attempt to distinguish between retributive violence, motivated by a cause perceived as just, and exploitative violence, enacted primarily for its value as entertainment. We consider discourses of retributive violence in STARZ *Spartacus* initially as a departure from representations of violence in Stanley Kubrick's *Spartacus* (1960). We then turn to examine how recently developed cinematographic techniques encourage viewers of the series to adopt various – often competing – perspectives on bloodshed, perspectives that result in viewer identifications that are better understood through internet tracking of responses to egregious acts of violence represented in the series. In order to garner viewer responses, we analyzed online reviews posted on IMDb, and also obtained comments directly from viewers via an online survey and face-to-face questionnaires and interviews. Links to the online survey were posted to *Spartacus* fan sites, and face-to-face feedback was received following a public screening of the episode "Libertus"

(episode 5 of the prequel season, *Gods of the Arena*) at University
College London in 2014, and from a viewing group of five women
who watched the first season, *Blood and Sand*, together in 2010.

Throughout this discussion we evaluate what characters in the
series have to say about the appropriate application of violence,
and also consider scenes in the final season that engage with discourses of violence in the 1960 film. Two scenes in particular from
the final season of the *Spartacus* series, *War of the Damned*, in
which the assembled slave army forces captured Roman citizens and
soldiers to fight before an audience, echo the episode in the film
when Kirk Douglas' Spartacus criticizes his fellow gladiators for
compelling Roman citizens to fight each other in the abandoned
ludus. The historical record attests to Spartacus' army compelling
captured Romans to fight,[3] but we argue that each of these modern
productions appropriates the episode to comment on the proper uses
and limits of violence, as well as on the problems of attempting to
distinguish justified violence from its more exploitative counterpart.

The violent deeds committed by Spartacus throughout the history
of his representation as the leader of a slave revolt against an unjust
Roman aristocracy are ostensibly retributive; that is, such deeds are
a form of punishment that is "morally justified" and in some sense
made "obligatory by the actions of the guilty."[4] Within discussions
of violence in contemporary media, we often find a distinction made
between retributive violence, grounded in a morally authorized perspective, and what Tom Wolfe once categorized as "porno-violence,"
that is, a form of "mediated violence in American entertainment"
not confined to a single point of view or moral perspective.[5] Other
scholars distinguish between retributive violence and a more "sadistic" (that is, pleasure-seeking) variety.[6] We have chosen to polarize
retributive bloodshed with "exploitative" violence because of the
term's connotations of profit and enjoyment gleaned from staged
violence, with no apparent moral perspective offered by the agents
of that violence, as being appropriate to the production of gladiatorial *munera* ("shows"). However, all three qualifiers of violence –
"porno-," "sadistic," and "exploitative" – when used in opposition to
retributive violence, maintain a general distinction between violence
as revenge for wrongdoing and violence that is unmotivated by any
perceived wrongdoing on the part of the victim.

Within the framework of this dichotomy, we also find both the
1960 film and the STARZ series addressing the thorny issue of quantity: should agents of morally justified violence observe limits on
the extent of their retribution? If so, how are those limits deter-

mined? While few ancient sources observe Spartacus' awareness of the proper limits of retributive violence,[7] such heightened sensitivity becomes a touchstone of the Hollywood hero, who chastises his fellow slaves for moving beyond these limits of violence in their treatment of the captured Roman citizens of Capua. As Joanna Paul has noted, the violence enacted by Kirk Douglas' idealizing portrait of the hero in the film has proven a useful measure for evaluating whether the blood shed by an epic hero is justifiable.[8] At the same time, violence in the film was a point of contention for its director Kubrick and its screenwriter Dalton Trumbo, and to some extent reflects on the acceptable limits of brutality for productions of the Hollywood historical epic of the late 1950s, prior to the MPAA's loosening of its restrictions on violence in 1966.[9]

Violence in the televisual *Spartacus* is doubly warranted, since the Roman cruelties in need of avenging spring first from a personal injury to the eponymous hero, whose wife is killed on the orders of the treacherous *lanista* Batiatus; later in the series such violence is fueled by the collective plight of the slave population. Yet visual representation of violent deeds has been qualitatively transformed through the use of green-screen and CGI (computer generated imagery), which aestheticize bloodshed and enlarge its scale,[10] prompting viewers to recognize the pleasure derived from violence as a spectacle, as this recognition is heightened by dialogue interrogating whether or not violence is justified. Promotional posters, memes, and DVD packaging celebrate bloodshed, but the production self-consciously questions the ethics of violence as spectacle and evaluates the levels of realism that viewers demand of a twenty-first-century "sword and sandal" production. Such questions emerge in particular when the *Spartacus* series makes explicit allusions to the 1960 film.

FRAMING VIOLENCE IN *SPARTACUS* (1960) AND STARZ *SPARTACUS*

Violence in the 1960 *Spartacus* is repeatedly touted as retributive and morally grounded, although certain moments in the film blur the boundaries between retributive and exploitative varieties: when Spartacus leads the initial revolt at the *ludus*, the camera lingers on a shot of the hero drowning Marcellus in a steaming pot of gruel. The scene was one of many cut from the theatrical release after previews suggested unfavorable audience reactions. Other last-minute cuts, a few of which were recovered in the 1991 restoration effort, include blood spraying on Crassus' face when Draba is killed after hurling a spear at the Romans watching him perform, as well as some gory dismemberments in the final battle between the slave and Roman armies.[11] As the film stands in its current restoration, a contradiction appears between the way that *Spartacus'* spectacular widescreen format occasionally prompts viewers to consume aestheticized violence, and the message of resistance to spectacular bloodshed that its titular hero hopes to convey.

That message is demonstrated in particular when Spartacus, after walking through the *ludus* following the outbreak of revolution, comes upon a group of slaves, led by Crixus, and their Roman captives. The Romans are gray-haired and haggard, clad only in tunics, though their elite status is signaled when Spartacus addresses them with some irony as "noble Romans." The hero's disdain for the behavior of their slave captors is equally pronounced. The slaves are positioned on the fence and at the edge of the viewing box, peering down at the Romans, in a visual inversion of an earlier scene in which Crassus and his retinue observe the match between Draba and Spartacus. Here Spartacus addresses the elevated slaves who encircle the Romans as "new masters betting to see who'll die first":

> I swore that if I ever got out of this place I'd die before I watched two men fight to the death again. Draba made that promise too; he kept it; so will I . . . What are we? . . . What are we becoming? Romans?

After rejecting collective identification with the Romans, the hero then encourages the group to assemble as an "army of gladiators." On the one hand, Spartacus explicitly condemns the voyeuristic gaze. On the other hand, the film offers the visual pleasures afforded by the epic film genre – including violence. In other words, and as noted by Paul Willemen, cinematic epics, like *Spartacus*, offer the pleasure of viewing the male body "mutilated and restored through violent brutality."[12]

Certain inconsistencies in the film are perhaps inevitable: *Spartacus'* production was notoriously plagued by different visions of what kind of hero Spartacus should be and what his accomplishment signified. Director Kubrick, screenwriter Trumbo, producer Douglas, and the Universal Studio executives were constantly at odds: Kubrick in particular has noted that he wanted to convey the darker aspects of human nature, as well as the internal conflicts that frequently plague revolutionary movements.[13] The very nature of the Spartacan revolt compels us to grapple with the notion that bloodshed may have certain applications that are justified. Douglas' hero may dream of a world that eludes the violent, imperialist grasp of Rome, but to get there he must rely on violence – an "army of gladiators" is an army no less.[14] Much of that violence is only implicit in the film's diegesis, since Universal ultimately cut the majority of the battle scenes depicting victories for the slave army.

Robert Burgoyne considers the problem of Spartacus' attitude toward violence in his analysis of the redemptive, restorative role of violence in Ridley Scott's *Gladiator* (2000), a film in which the blood of the gladiator symbolizes the germs of new life planted in the sands of the arena. *Spartacus*, by contrast, advocates a "Christological alternative" to the plight of the slaves rather than emancipation through violence.[15] However, as suggested by the final duel between Antoninus and Spartacus, in which one of the men is required to kill the other in order to save the other from crucifixion, all for Crassus' viewing pleasure, generic and historic contingencies impose limits on alternatives to violence. For all its virtues the film cannot consistently practice what it has preached.

It would not be apt to suggest that STARZ *Spartacus* preached or practiced a message of peace: these gladiators smile at the prospect of a good kill and the prestige earned through it. All the same, the series and its titular hero do grapple with justifying their violent deeds and frequently indicate that violence has exceeded the limits of appropriate retribution, or that the line between retributive violence and its exploitative counterpart has been blurred. Executive producer Rob Tapert implicitly classifies the bulk of the violence in the second season, *Vengeance*, as retributive, claiming in a DVD featurette: "All [characters] are operating from this one base emotion of vengeance." At the same time, series creator DeKnight complicates attempts to label violence as either retributive or exploitative by emphasizing the personal reasons behind the violence, so that it appears justifiable in terms of a gladiator ethos or even the human condition, even when not strictly retributive: "There's an emotional element; the character needs something, wants something beyond just staying alive."[16]

In the sixth episode of *Vengeance*, Gannicus and Spartacus discuss the hero's cause, at which point Gannicus disparagingly attributes Spartacus' motive to the death of his "woman," to which Spartacus responds that love and loss alone justify his cause (episode 206). This exchange, however, constitutes part of a process by which personal retributive violence against the former owner Batiatus and the treacherous praetor Glaber is gradually transformed into a shared, communal retributive violence against Rome. And yet the series' fixation on arena culture, and at least partial endorsement of characters who derive some pleasure from killing, makes its orientation

toward violence harder to gauge. Exploitative violence, which may or
may not be enjoyed by the show's twenty-first-century spectators, is
offered, we argue, in part as a foil for its retributive counterpart; that
is, as an inappropriate use of violence allowing us to evaluate other
uses as appropriate or at least relatively justified.

VIEWERS, VIOLENCE, AND MULTIPLE PERSPECTIVES

There has been no shortage of attempts to explain violence and
spectatorship in both ancient and contemporary contexts. In his
2011 book *The Lure of the Arena*, Garrett Fagan has suggested that
similar social and psychological processes drive modern and ancient
fascinations with spectacles of violence, implying that explorations
of violence in the two distinct historical contexts can shine reciprocal light on each other. We should first, however, note a crucial
difference between ancient and modern contexts for violence: the
slave system in Rome, which legitimized the absolute power held
by one human over another, helped inure all its members to a culture of violence, especially violence enacted on members of society
who were afforded less than human status. As Ina Rae Hark has
demonstrated, Douglas' *Spartacus* regularly draws attention to this
subhuman status as he attempts to distinguish his former animalistic
performance as a gladiator from the autonomous human status he
attains in the film.[17] The more plentiful slave population that served
as fodder for violent entertainment for the commanding Roman gaze
does not make the Roman propensity for such spectacles an anom-
aly altogether: the subhuman status of the slave was assumed in
later epochs by the criminal, as well as a host of other marginalized
individuals. Fagan thus argues that fascination with violent spectacles and crowd participation in watching them is universal, though
its specific articulations (the guillotine, the arena, the electric chair)
are determined by sociocultural context. Fagan's work thus usefully
redirects the question of violence in the arena from why it was a
useful mechanism of empire to why audiences so readily assumed
their positions within that mechanism.

Just as STARZ *Spartacus* offers competing visions of justified and
exploitative violence, it offers similarly duplicitous representations
of the effects of violence, that is, of violence's realistic or aestheticizing portrayal. The impact of realistic bloodshed, as one source of
its appeal, has been evaluated differently among scholars of media
studies and social psychologists.[18] Realism may be defined as the

likelihood of a given filmic scenario occurring in the real world and of anatomically correct portrayal of gore; it was controversially promoted by auteur-directors like Sam Peckinpah and Arthur Penn, who in the later 1960s used blood squibs and slow-motion camera work to capture vividly the consequences of violence. Such techniques were an attempt to divert audiences from such behaviors by showing the "real" consequences of violent deeds. Both directors have stated more or less explicitly that such techniques were offered in ostensible contrast to those films of the 1940s and 1950s, produced under a stricter Hollywood production code, that did not allow viewers to observe the blood, pain, or suffering that should logically follow from a spray of gunfire. Peckinpah in particular has stressed that his depictions of violence have been part of a larger effort to address and counter it: "to negate violence, it must be shown for what it is, a horrifying, brutalizing, destructive, ingrained part of humanity."[19] The realism of Penn and Peckinpah, however, in many ways heightened its appeal.

Part of the problem, of course, is that realism is not reality: as Fagan observes of realism in modern media violence, "realism" applies increasingly not to how blood and gore are generated, but to how they appear after the fact.[20] Perhaps more importantly, the contextual medium of film inevitably aestheticizes scenes of carnage, through soundtrack, rapid cutting, montage techniques, differential rates of slow motion – and, one might add, through the very narrative structure that recognizes the chaos and horror of life, but also allows such forces to be observed, controlled, and contained within a two-hour viewing period. Studies on the socio-psychological effects of watching violence stress how the vividness of film as a medium exerts an emotional possession over viewers as filmmakers stylize violence and heighten its visceral impact.[21]

In light of the differential between "realism" as opposed to "reality" in screen representations of violence, it is worth considering remarks made by the producers of the series *Spartacus*: commenting on the final episode of the first season, where the violence of the arena dramatically permeates the upper strata of the House of Batiatus and nearly all of the Roman citizens – including women and children – are murdered by the gladiators, DeKnight notes that the show's cinematographers increased the level of stylization in order to please network executives offended by graphic, un-stylized bloodshed.[22] In another "making of" featurette from the second season, a special effects designer comments on the level of realism achieved in any of the show's various dismemberments:

> Chances are audience members have never seen a decapitation ... so audiences don't really know what to expect ... we don't want you looking away for too long or you'll miss what comes next.

In other words, the creators of violent spectacles in the series aim to captivate and enact the sort of emotional possession that critics of media violence warn us about. Psychologists have also demonstrated viewer tendency to identify with and enjoy the success of positively portrayed characters, while taking pleasure in the demise and punishment of negatively portrayed characters; here violence is deemed pleasurable because it is retributive and deserved by a character who has behaved unjustly. The notion that we enjoy the success or defeat of characters we like or dislike respectively, and the study of those circumstances contributing to that enjoyment, is known as disposition theory. The theory has been used to explain why we find satisfaction in the violent deaths of agents we are negatively disposed toward, and is invoked by Fagan as one explanation for why the Romans enjoyed the games.[23]

Similar "dispositions" encourage us as viewers to cheer on a favored gladiator as he defeats his opponents on screen, even as we might be repelled by the slicing off of limbs and heads. And yet data gathered from viewer surveys, tracking views of clips available on YouTube, and responses posted on websites like IMDb indicate that the series becomes most compelling when it depicts violence of the most exploitative kind. For example, "The Thing in the Pit" (episode 104), where Spartacus, disgraced as a gladiator, is forced to fight in a subterranean venue rather than the arena and builds his reputation by slicing off the face of his opponent, proved to be the episode that first captured the attention of some viewers.[24] More squeamish viewers might look away from the screen at this point, but many others are fascinated, so that one YouTube clip of Spartacus cutting off the face of a fellow slave when the rebels have assembled in an abandoned temple outside of Capua has garnered over 200,000 views.[25]

The series has proved extremely popular, so that it is rated at 8.7/10 with over 150,000 votes on IMDb, a useful though underutilized resource on global viewer opinions.[26] There is a common understanding among IMDb viewers that *Spartacus* gets us closer to what it may have been like to live in ancient Rome, a period characterized by frequent (and often unmediated) access to violence: viewers comment that "there is a lot of blood and guts [in the series] but that was the way they lived in Rome," and that "ancient Rome was a cesspit, home to extraordinary violence in the name of entertainment." Fans of the series who responded to a short online survey echo DeKnight's comments cited at the start of this chapter in giving similar justifications for the use of violence in the show: "those were brutal times, particularly in so far as the gladiatorial games and slavery were concerned"; and one viewer opined, "in the real Roman world things were far worse."

This view of ancient Rome as a place of excessive violence was itself propagated through earlier onscreen representations of antiquity, films like the silent classic *Cabiria* (1914), through the popular historical epics of the 1950s, including *Quo Vadis* (1951) and *Ben-Hur* (1959), and the 1970s BBC television miniseries *I, Claudius* (1976).[27] However, recent technological advances in cinematography, especially the digital compositing of visual elements – techniques referred to collectively as CGI and developed with increasing sophistication since their explosion in the 1990s – have allowed the spectacle of the arena to be brought into our homes: close up, slowed down, and digitally enhanced. CGI has also facilitated the creation of "impossible points of view," not available through optical compositing and traditional cinematography. Unlike the conditions of spectatorship created in the ancient amphitheater, a good deal of post-production work in the television series encourages vantage points not available to the ancient Roman spectator.[28]

STARZ *Spartacus* is described by many as an emotional or almost physical experience, offering "enormous excitement," "pure raw and enthralling spectacle," "a wild ride" that "makes your heart race" and is "so viscerally evocative it gets to you." This is perhaps the response elicited from the spectators at the actual games, but viewers of *Spartacus* are perfectly positioned to experience the violence in close up and at wide angles, not restricted by a seated position. At crucial moments the action is slowed down and blood splatters are digitally enhanced to allow us to experience the prolonged death of a gladiator, which, if recorded in real time, would have been over in an instant.[29] While some viewers found such devices distracting, many commented positively on their use. According to one enthusiastic IMDb reviewer:

> On the level of gore and blood it is more than satisfying. Blood pours, blood squirts, blood sprays in all directions ... The use of slow motion during the fights is extensive and it makes you almost feel the taste of blood as the screen catches the drips of it.

The heightened artificiality of combat scenes in the series and their stylistic resemblance to graphic novels have evoked comparisons

with Zack Snyder's *300*.[30] Susanne Turner describes the heavily cho-
reographed and digitally enhanced fight scenes in *300* as "battle as
ballet . . . an aestheticization of the body-in-motion and the body-in-
death," a visualization of the Homeric *aristeia*.[31] DeKnight specifically describes the violence as "operatic" and "stylized." While the
production team "didn't want to shy away from the violence," a key
part of the story about "gladiators and war," they also "didn't want
[the series] to be a horror show"; as he states: "We didn't want to
turn people off . . . every now and then we would do something super
realistic and gruesome, but we try to pick our moments for that."[32]
These moments are not unlike Homer's descriptions of the death of
warriors, which describe in detail spears going through heads and
cheeks, piercing through bone, tendons smashed, sinews unstrung,
and bodies crashing to the ground.

Classicists have commented that the epic film set in ancient Rome
allows viewers to "have our cake and eat it," so that we can enjoy
the vicarious pleasure of the violent spectacle of the arena while
condemning it on moral grounds.[33] As the camera allows viewers
to get closer to the action than would have been possible for actual
spectators at the games, so it also offers opportunities to adopt different perspectives. The template for enjoying multiple perspectives
was already inscribed in various historical epics, including Kubrick's
Spartacus, which presents competing views of the private match
between Spartacus and Draba that spawns the rebellion. In this
match, put on for the entertainment of two Roman noblewomen,
we have a view from the loggia above the ring, where the nobles sit,
as well as an eye-level view with the two gladiators on the sand. The
view of the fight is also interspersed with close-ups of Spartacus' love
interest Varinia, standing on a separate balcony, intently watching the
fight with a pained expression in contrast to the words of the bored
noblewomen: "Oh, what's the matter now?" and "Kill him." STARZ
Spartacus also allows us to take these different viewing positions in
relation to the violent spectacle. Unlike the Romans in the seats of
the arena who, with a few exceptions, would never find themselves
on the sand, we can identify with both voyeurs among the crowd
and the gladiators fighting on the sand. And yet, as such scenes are
incorporated into a long-running television series with an interest in
developing sympathetic characters and relationships, they encourage
us to share not just in different physical perspectives offered through
the camera, but also in the subjective experiences of the different
gladiators, allowing viewers a more nuanced understanding of their
motives and values.

A pivotal moment for the character of Spartacus in *Blood and Sand* is the fight with Theokoles in "Shadow Games" (episode 105). This episode provides a range of perspectives on the gladiatorial combat. Camera angles align viewers variously with individuals whose stories have intersected with those of the men fighting on the sand, as well as with the relatively detached spectators watching from the *cavea* at Capua: Lucretia, sitting among the nobles in the loggia hopes that her lover Crixus will prevail, not knowing that her body-slave Naevia, also erotically entangled with Crixus, desires the same outcome. We also see the fight through the bars of the holding cells with the gladiators, as the hopes of Varro, Spartacus' friend, and Ashur, his enemy, are revealed in close-up shots of their responses. Finally, we are offered the vantage points of Spartacus and Crixus on the sand, who view their monstrous opponent, Theokoles, at close quarters (Figure 13.1). It is perhaps the adoption of these personal viewing positions on the violent spectacle, as well as the visually enhanced presentation of that spectacle, that elicits the viewers' emotional response. According to one IMDb reviewer:

> *Spartacus* can actually make you feel what it was like to live there – feel the fierce joy of trouncing your opponent in the arena, the pain of murdering your best friend on the order of your master, the smoldering passion of forbidden love, and the dull ache of being a slave with no will of your own.

If we can choose from these viewing positions, then we can choose not to adopt the perspectives of the more bloodthirsty spectators at

Figure 13.1 Theokoles (Reuben De Jong) in the arena in episode 105 ("Shadow Games"). STARZ.

the games. We can enjoy the spectacle from a position of comfort, in our own homes and on our own sofas, like members of the Roman elite in the best seats, while emotionally allying ourselves with the slaves and gladiators.

For all the devices used by the series to offer competing perspectives on violent acts and endorse some of them as relatively justified through narrative content, its showcasing of exploitative violence and the characters who produce it has proven equally popular: the *lanista* Batiatus proved to be a favorite character of many viewers of the first season, according to IMDb reviews. Also, viewers occasionally choose to take a viewing position that seems to be reading against the grain. For example, some comments on the fan-authored *Spartacus* Wiki page on the character of the slave-girl Diona are disturbing.[34] The story of Diona highlights the potential plight of a slave in ancient Roman society with no control over her own body, and who lives or dies at the whims of her masters. Diona is brutally raped as entertainment in the house of Batiatus, as Lucretia is somewhat unwillingly maneuvered into offering a sex show to gain favor with Cossutius, a member of the Roman elite. Diona finally escapes, only to be captured and executed in the arena. Batiatus could have saved her life, but because he has just been betrayed by his friend Solonius, he allows Diona to die as an example to those who betray him.

As with the Wiki pages of other characters, Diona's page, written by fans, includes details of her appearance and a summary of her story. Fans who comment on the page include expressions of being "upset" at Diona's story; one fan even states, "that particular storyline kinda soured me for a few episodes." Two viewers' comments, however, have a different focus, based partly on admiration for the actress:

> The sight of her ample arse when she was being rammed by the "bull" during the orgy at the house of Batiatus, made me wet myself. When her lifeless form was being taken away (in the arena when she was executed) I could not help but marvel at the beautiful swell of her delicious thighs.

The response to this comment from another viewer is "You're sick." The next comment from another viewer is more ambiguous:

> She is really one of the most beautiful girls that I have ever seen. I remember the moment which she was raped by [a] filthy gladiator, it made me terribly upset. I wish I had been in his shoes.

In light of such comments, we should ask ourselves to what extent the series' vivid presentation of violence, allowing some viewers the visceral thrill of playing the gladiator, also offers the opportunity for viewers to (almost) feel what it is like to be a rapist?

DISCOURSES OF VIOLENCE: REFRAMING THE QUESTION OF JUSTIFICATION

While comments like these suggest that the aesthetics of *Spartacus* evoke disturbing levels of viewer identification, discourses concerning the production of gore and the generation of special effects, such as the comments just quoted from the special-effects team and proliferated in periodicals on the horror film genre (such as *Fangoria* and *Rue Morgue*), underscore the artificiality and conventionality of bloodshed in the "sword and sandal" genre. Technical virtuosity combined with generic expectations threaten to strip the violence committed on screen of any moral weight, any implications beyond the limits of a 48-inch flat-screen television, fostering an ideology of entertainment, according to which:

> The spectator is invited to become aware of . . . [certain] conventions and to think of them as defining a hermetic, autonomous world which has no bearing and no tendency and which relates to other social practices only by being different from them.[35]

While Andrew Britton's analysis is applied here to the cinema of the 1980s, especially the bloodshed of the so-called "slasher film," we argue that STARZ *Spartacus* also extends the invitation to buy into an ideology of entertainment, but does so with overt discourse about the difference between a hermetically sealed world where violence is fun and the endorsement of violence in the "real" world of historical change.

Part of this discourse emerges from the competing cinematic conventions that shape the series' ethos of violence – in STARZ *Spartacus*, the conventions of violence that define the epic film, such as the 1960 *Spartacus*, are played in constant counterpoint to those that have shaped recent incarnations of "sword and sandal" bloodshed, as well as various horror subgenres. STARZ *Spartacus*, of course, is not a film, though its producers and actors do not hesitate to describe it as "epic." Just as Kirk Douglas' character constantly negotiates, and by some standards epitomizes, the appropriate behavior of an epic hero in the "sword and sandal" genre, Andy Whitfield and later Liam McIntyre, in dialogue with their fellow gladiator-heroes, constantly re-evaluate the code of behavior that should govern their cause. In the scene of carnage that opens *Vengeance*, the rebel Agron zealously beats in the head of a Roman mercenary soldier, while his comrades nearby note that "the fellow's dead already." Spartacus observes Agron's overly enthusiastic retribution and quickly redirects his attention to the more useful, productive work of gathering supplies. The line between justified retribution and exploitative violence is crossed repeatedly in the series, but not without a constant reminder of the crossing.

The line is perhaps most evident in scenes that reference Kubrick's film; and in fact the series performs a double-take on the scene discussed above from the 1960 *Spartacus* when slaves and former gladiators assume the role of voyeurs and compel captured Romans to fight. For its initial take on the earlier film, STARZ *Spartacus* presents rebel slaves behaving badly in Sinuessa where, led by Crixus, they generally abuse the captured citizens, repeatedly raping some of the women and at one point compelling two men to fight to the death for a piece of bread. Among the crowd of rebels cheering on the fight, only Gannicus cynically questions, "So we fall to fucking games now?" His friend Attius, a free Sinuessan cautiously enlisted as a blacksmith by the rebel cause, similarly observes the irony by asking how the rebels, who encourage the compulsory match and then slice off the hand of the winner claiming his prize, differ from the villainous Romans. At first, Spartacus knows nothing about the ill treatment of the Sinuessans, but his condemnation of it will soon force him to part ways with Crixus.

In the final season's second take on the episode, however, and in sharp contrast to Douglas' hero, McIntyre's Spartacus organizes *munera* to honor the memory of Crixus, who has been slain by Tiberius, son of Crassus, in a recent battle. Tiberius is captured when, acting as envoy to Pompey for his father, he is ambushed by slaves disguised as Pompey's men. He and his soldiers, waiting as captives to perform in the funeral games of Crixus, are especially sensitive to the threat that performing in a spectacle poses to their status as free Romans. Tiberius commands them, saying: "Do not raise weapons; we will not give entertainment in death. Remember that we are Romans." Of course, the first Roman who follows this advice in the arena with Spartacus finds his throat promptly slit.

From a non-Roman perspective, however, a different kind of status can be recovered, even elevated in the arena. In homage to Scott's *Gladiator*, Spartacus opens the games with a handful of sand, suggesting the regenerative power of the arena. Gannicus, in response to his lover Sibyl, who has never seen gladiatorial combat before and looks at him in confusion, explains the appeal of the spectacle before them: he lauds the glory gained from fighting in the sand and the clear sense of purpose that attends it. In a similar exchange, by which the show self-consciously asks us to interpret the value of violence as entertainment, Spartacus discusses his cause with his tentative love interest Laeta. This former Roman *matrona* has never viewed the games before, but assures him, "I may flinch from gory sight, and yet know that I revel in its meaning." The immediate significance of the reference is the triumph of the slave-gladiators over their former Roman masters, though the implications of her comment may well extend to the series' entire three-and-a-half-season attempt to theatricalize but also interrogate the meaning and propriety of violent deeds.

For all its apparent celebration of violence and violent spectacles, the show posits (hypothetical if not definitive) limits to bloodshed. It is worth noting that this crowd of mostly sympathetic slaves, in their role as spectators, reflects the Capuan audiences we disapproved of in earlier seasons. Similarities between unruly Capuans and former slaves attending the *munera* in honor of Crixus indicate the emotionally possessive and transformative effects of staged violence. The body of one Roman soldier forced to fight a gladiator opponent provocatively transgresses the bounds of the arena as it is hurled into the *cavea*, to the delight of greedy spectators eager to take part in the violence. Yet, just as such chaos forcibly muddles the distinction between exploitative violence and just retribution, Spartacus announces an offer from Crassus to spare his son in exchange for five hundred captured slaves, prompting us as viewers along with the internal audience to redefine the relationship between exploitative violence and its morally authorized counterpart. The announcement comes at the moment when Naevia is finally granted the opportunity to kill Tiberius, and thereby gain vengeance for the death of her lover Crixus. She is forced to pause before inflicting a final sword thrust, and initially resists the offer, ostensibly on the basis that it constitutes "another Roman lie." She ultimately spares Tiberius, however, after Spartacus grants power of life and death to her alone, as the one "most wronged by the boy." In effect, the mishandling of justice in Sinuessa has been corrected through Naevia's decision to forgo the fulfillment of a private vendetta in light of a greater good, the lives of five hundred rebel slaves, a decision legitimized through the very public and visible context of the arena in which it is made.[36]

More than any other twenty-first-century hero born from the epic tradition since Maximus in Scott's *Gladiator*, the series Spartacus "questions(s) the appropriate application of violence";[37] he prompts viewers to ask whether the end justifies the violent means by which it is attained. And this is where we suggest that the series asks our intellect – guided perhaps by a set of epic, heroic conventions – to engage in productive combat with whatever socio-psychological forces immerse us in the *jouissance* of blood, guts, and gore. Despite digital image compositing and special effects wizardry that make atrocious actions palatable or even fun, and create complicity between spectators and spectacle, STARZ *Spartacus* questions the impact of exploitative violence within both the ancient and con-temporary contexts that foster it. Through a discourse negotiating the limits of retributive bloodshed and the difficulties of disentan-gling it from exploitative violence, the series projects the image and meaning of Spartacus well beyond the closed circuit of the arena.

NOTES

1 These comments and the following quote are from the DVD featurette "*Spartacus: Blood and Sand*, Behind the Scenes" and from an online interview in Loggins (2010).
2 See note 1.
3 Paulus Orosius, *History Against the Pagans* 5.24.
4 See Morris (2012: 45), who relies on Kant's theory of retributive justice in order to distinguish retributive violence from "sadistic" violence.
5 On Wolfe's coinage in light of the conventionalization of horror movie violence, see Kendrick (2009: 3). For the "redemptive" role of vio-lence in Ridley Scott's *Gladiator*, see Burgoyne (2008: 83–97). It is worth noting that "retributive" is a less morally implicated term than Burgoyne's "redemptive." Not all retributive violence is equally justified, but retribution does imply justification from some character's perspec-tive, however unsympathetic that character may be.
6 For "sadism" as opposed to retributive violence in torture-horror, see Morris (2012: 48–52).
7 With the exception of some suggestive fragments of the third book of Sallust's *Histories*, cited in Winkler (2007a: 242).
8 Paul (2013: 203).
9 On the MPAA's restrictions on violence, see Prince (2000a: 2, 6–8); see Cooper (2007b: 57) for the disagreements of Kubrick and Trumbo over violence represented in the film.
10 See Sobchack (1990) on excesses of epic production.
11 A great deal of cut footage was disposed of in 1975 by Universal Pictures and is therefore irrevocably lost; see Cooper (2007a).

12 Willemen (1981), cited in Burgoyne (2008: 83–4).
13 The competing visions of Spartacus are often dubbed the "large" and "small" versions; see esp. Cooper (2007a: 22–9).
14 See Hark (1993: 160–1) on Spartacus' "army of gladiators" and the problems faced by the hero in attempting to renounce phallic aggression.
15 Burgoyne (2008: 92).
16 Faye (2011).
17 Hark (1993).
18 On realism and empathetic response, see Tamborini (1996); see also Sparks and Sparks (2000: 73–91) for a useful overview of social, psychological, and aesthetic approaches to explaining the appeal of onscreen violence.
19 From an interview cited in Prince (2000b: 177–8).
20 Fagan (2011: 234).
21 See Prince (2000a: 11–13, 17–18) on "emotional possession"; see also Sobchack (2000: 117–19).
22 STARZ *Spartacus*, audio commentary on episode 113.
23 Fagan (2011: 241–73).
24 The viewing group of five women who provided feedback on their viewing experience had initially committed to watch the episodes to take part in research and had found the pilot laughable, one describing the series as "porn." After watching "The Thing in the Pit," however, they found that they were enjoying the series.
25 The YouTube clip is entitled "Spartacus Gives Sedullus a Shave."
26 On infrequent citation of IMDb by academics, see Sobchack (2013).
27 The miniseries *I, Claudius* includes some notably shocking scenes (including Caligula's apparent consumption of the fetus of his child by Drusilla), although it varies from other depictions of the ancient world in its lack of visual spectacle; see Joshel (2001).
28 For the expanding field of post-production work done in films relying on CGI, as well as the unique vantage points offered by image compositing, see Moana Thomson (2011: 41); see also Cyrino (2011) for the advantages of CGI in the creation of a similarly "graphic novel" style of Zack Snyder's *300*.
29 Such slow-motion frames are usually matched by accelerated action, creating a slow-to-fast-motion photographic technique known as "bullet time"; see Cyrino (2011: 21).
30 See, for example, O'Neill's review (2010).
31 Turner (2009: 135).
32 Quotes from DeKnight in this paragraph are from a YouTube interview with him entitled "*Spartacus: Vengeance* – Limits to Sex & Violence?"
33 See, for example, Winkler (2004: 97–8) and Fitzgerald (2001: 26).
34 See www.spartacus.wikia.com/wiki/Diona; on Diona's rape, see Strong in this volume.
35 Britton (1986), cited in Kendrick (2009: 137).

36 Although he is spared by Naevia, Tiberius ironically dies at the hands of
   Kore, who fulfills her own private vendetta against the boy who raped
   her; see also Strong in this volume.
37 Quoted from Paul (2013: 202), in a remark originally referring to Kirk
   Douglas.

Filmography

FEATURE FILMS

12 Years a Slave (2013). Directed by Steve McQueen. 20th Century Fox.

300 (2007). Directed by Zack Snyder. Legendary Pictures, Warner Bros.

A Funny Thing Happened on the Way to the Forum (1966). Directed by Richard Lester. United Artists.

Cabiria (1914). Directed by Giovanni Pastrone. Italia Film Company.

Cleopatra (1934). Directed by Cecil B. DeMille. Paramount Pictures.

Cleopatra (1963). Directed by Joseph L. Mankiewicz. 20th Century Fox.

Conan the Barbarian (1982). Directed by John Milius. Universal Pictures. 20th Century Fox.

Alien³ (1992). Directed by David Fincher. 20th Century Fox.

Belle (2013). Directed by Amma Assante. DJ Films.

Ben-Hur: A Tale of the Christ (1925). Directed by Fred Niblo. Metro-Goldwyn-Mayer.

Ben-Hur (1959). Directed by William Wyler. Metro-Goldwyn-Mayer.

Django Unchained (2012). Directed by Quentin Tarantino. Columbia Pictures.

Fabiola (1949). Directed by Alessandro Blasetti. Universalia.

The Fall of the Roman Empire (1964). Directed by Anthony Mann. Paramount Pictures.

The Fall of Troy (1911). Directed by Luigi Romano Borgnetto and Giovanni Pastrone. Italia Film Company.

Gladiator (2000). Directed by Ridley Scott. DreamWorks Pictures, Universal Pictures.

Hercules (1997). Directed by Ron Clements and John Musker. Walt Disney Pictures.

In & Out (1997). Directed by Frank Oz. Paramount Pictures.

Intolerance: Love's Struggle Throughout the Ages (1916). Directed by D. W. Griffith. Triangle Film Corporation.

Lincoln (2012). Directed by Steven Spielberg. 20th Century Fox.

Mad Max Beyond Thunderdome (1985). Directed by George Miller and George Ogilvie. Warner Bros.

The Mask of Zorro (1998). Directed by Martin Campbell. TriStar Entertainment.

The Matrix Revolutions (2003). Directed by Andy and Lana Wachowski (as The Wachowski Brothers). Warner Bros.

Monty Python's Life of Brian (1979). Directed by Terry Jones. HandMade Films.

The Mummy (1997). Directed by Stephen Sommers. Universal Pictures.

The Mummy Returns (2001). Directed by Stephen Sommers. Universal Pictures.

The Mummy: Tomb of the Dragon Emperor (2008). Directed by Rob Cohen. Universal Pictures.

Punchline (1988). Directed by David Seltzer. Columbia Pictures.

The Queen of Sheba (1921). Directed by J. Gordon Edwards. Fox Film Corporation.

Quo Vadis (1912). Directed by Enrico Guazzoni. Società Italiana Cines.

Quo Vadis (1951). Directed by Mervyn LeRoy and Anthony Mann. Metro-Goldwyn-Mayer.

The Robe (1953). Directed by Henry Koster. 20th Century Fox.

The Slave (1962). Created by Sergio Corbucci. Titanus.

Spartaco (1913). Directed by Giovanni Enrico Vidali. Pasquali e C.

Spartaco (1953). Directed by Riccardo Freda. API Film.

Spartacus (1960). Directed by Stanley Kubrick. Bryna Productions, Universal Pictures.

That Thing You Do! (1996). Directed by Tom Hanks. 20th Century Fox.

Theodora (1921). Directed by Leopoldo Carlucci. Ambrosio-Zanotta.

Troy (2004). Directed by Wolfgang Petersen. Warner Bros.

TELEVISION SERIES AND FILMS

Blackadder Goes Forth (1989). Written by Richard Curtis and Ben Elton. BBC.

Blackadder II (1986). Written by Richard Curtis and Ben Elton. BBC.

The Black Adder (1983). Written by Richard Curtis and Rowan Atkinson. BBC.

Blake's 7, Series Four (1981). Created by Terry Nation. BBC.

Bones (2005–present). Created by Hart Hanson. Fox.

Breaking Bad (2008–13). Created by Vince Gilligan. AMC.

COPS (1989–present). Created by John Langley and Malcolm Barbour. Fox.

Criminal Minds (2005–present). Created by Jeff David. CBS / ABC.

CSI: Crime Scene Investigation (2000–15). Created by Anthony E. Zuiker. CBS.

Das Boot (1985). Directed by Wolfgang Petersen. Bavaria Film, BBC, RAI.

Dexter (2006–13). Developed by James Manos Jr. Showtime.

Doctor Who, Series Four (new series) (2007). Produced by Russell T. Davis. BBC.

Hercules: The Legendary Journeys (1995–99). Created by Christian Williams. MCA Television.

I, Claudius (1976). Produced by Martin Lisemore. BBC.

Law and Order (1990–present). Created by Dick Wolf. NBC.

Lockdown (2007–present). Created by David Ross Smith. National Geographic.

Rome, Season One (2005). Created by Bruno Heller, William J. MacDonald, and John Milius. HBO BBC.

Rome, Season Two (2007). Created by Bruno Heller, William J. MacDonald, and John Milius. HBO BBC.

Sons of Anarchy (2008–present). Created by Kurt Sutter. FX.

The Sopranos (1999–2007). Created by David Chase. HBO.

Spartacus (2004). Created by Robert Dornhelm. Nimar Studios, USA Network Pictures.

Spartacus: Blood and Sand (2010). Created by Steven S. DeKnight. STARZ.

Spartacus: Gods of the Arena (2011). Created by Steven S. DeKnight. STARZ.

Spartacus: Vengeance (2012). Created by Steven S. DeKnight. STARZ.

Spartacus: War of the Damned (2013). Created by Steven S. DeKnight. STARZ.

Star Trek (1966–69). Created by Gene Roddenberry. NBC.

True Detective (2014–present). Created by Nic Pizzolatto. HBO.

Up Pompeii (1969–70). Written by Sid Colin and Talbot Rothwell. BBC.

The Walking Dead (2010–present). Created by Frank Darabont. AMC.

Xena: Warrior Princess (1995–2001). Created by Rob Tapert. Studios USA, Universal Television.

Bibliography

Adcock, Frank E. (1966). *Marcus Crassus Millionaire*. Cambridge: Cambridge University Press.

Allen, Alena (2008). "Staging Interiors in Rome's Villas," in Monica S. Cyrino (ed.), *Rome Season One: History Makes Television*. Oxford: Blackwell, 179–92.

Alonso, Juan J., Jorge Alonso, and Enrique A. Mastache (2008). *La Antigua Roma en el Cine*. Madrid: T & B Editores.

Alston, Richard (1998). "Soldiers, Masculinity and Power in Republican and Imperial Rome," in Lin Foxhall and John Salmon (eds.), *When Men Were Men: Masculinity, Power and Identity in Classical Antiquity*. London: Routledge, 205–23.

Amiel, Maurice (2014). "The Residential Balcony as Urban Loge and Stage," *Cultural Weekly*, 8 January.

Arieti, James A. (1997). "Rape and Livy's View of Roman History," in Susan Deacy and Karen F. Pierce (eds.), *Rape in Antiquity*. London: Duckworth, 209–29.

Arnott, Peter D. (1970). *The Romans and their World*. New York: St. Martin's Press.

Augoustakis, Antony (2008). "Women's Politics in the Streets of Rome," in Monica S. Cyrino (ed.), *Rome Season One: History Makes Television*. Oxford: Blackwell, 117–29.

Augoustakis, Antony (2010). *Motherhood and the Other: Fashioning Female Power in Flavian Epic*. Oxford: Oxford University Press.

Augoustakis, Antony (2013). "Partnership and Love in *Spartacus: Blood and Sand* (2010)," in Monica S. Cyrino (ed.), *Screening Love and Sex in the Ancient World*. New York: Palgrave Macmillan, 157–65.

Augoustakis, Antony (2015). "Effigies of Atia and Servilia: Effacing the Female Body in *Rome*," in Monica S. Cyrino (ed.), *Rome, Season Two: Trial and Triumph*. Edinburgh: Edinburgh University Press, 117–27.

Bacon-Smith, Camille (1992). *Enterprising Women: Television Fandom and the Creation of Popular Myth*. Philadelphia: University of Pennsylvania Press.

Barsam, Richard, and David Monahan (2010). *Looking at Movies: An Introduction to Film*. 3rd edn. New York: W. W. Norton & Co.

Beard, Mary (2007). *The Roman Triumph*. Cambridge, MA: Harvard University Press.

Bedford, Briand (2015). *Spartacus International Gay Guide*. Berlin: Bruno Gmünder.

Bennett, Tara (2010). "Starz's *Spartacus*: Blood, Sand, and CGI," *Newsarama. com*, 22 January.

Bianco, Robert (2010). "*Spartacus: Blood and Sand*: Preview," *USA Today*, 22 January: 9D.

Bird, Robert M. (1966 [1831]). "The Gladiator," in Richard Moody (ed.), *Dramas from the American Theatre, 1762–1909*. Boston: Houghton Mifflin.

Blanshard, Alastair J. L., and Kim Shahabudin (2011). *Classics on Screen: Ancient Greece and Rome on Film*. London: Bristol Classical Press.

Bomgardner, David L. (2002). *The Story of the Roman Amphitheatre*. London: Routledge.

Britton, Andrew (1986). "Blissing Out: The Politics of Reaganite Entertainment," *Movie* 31–2: 1–42.

Brown, Shelby (1992). "Death as Decoration: Scenes from the Arena on Roman Domestic Mosaics," in Amy Richlin (ed.), *Pornography and Representation in Greece and Rome*. New York: Oxford University Press, 180–211.

Brownmiller, Susan (1976). *Against Our Will: Men, Women, and Rape*. New York: Bantam Books.

Burgoyne, Robert (2008). *The Hollywood Historical Film*. Oxford: Blackwell.

Burgoyne, Robert (2011). "Bare Life and Sovereignty in *Gladiator*," in Robert Burgoyne (ed.), *The Epic Film in World Culture*. New York: Routledge, 82–97.

Burgoyne, Robert (2014). "Colour in the Epic Film: *Alexander* and *Hero*," in Andrew Elliot (ed.), *The Return of the Epic Film: Genre, Aesthetics and History in the 21st Century*. Edinburgh: Edinburgh University Press, 95–109.

Burkert, Walter (1985). *Greek Religion*. Trans. John Raffan. Oxford: Blackwell.

Cadoux, Theodore J. (1956). "Marcus Crassus: A Reevaluation," *Greece and Rome* 3.2: 153–61.

Calhoun, John (2000). "Circus Maximus: Production Designer Arthur Max Takes Filmgoers to the Arena in Gladiator," *Livedesignonline.com*, 1 July.

Campbell, Joseph (1968). *The Hero with a Thousand Faces*. Princeton: Princeton University Press.

Cantarella, Eva (2002). *Bisexuality in the Ancient World*. New Haven: Yale University Press.

Carruthers, Mary (1990). *The Book of Memory: A Study of Memory in Medieval Culture*. New York: Cambridge University Press.

Cooper, Duncan L. (2007a). "Who Killed the Legend of Spartacus? Production, Censorship, and Reconstruction of Stanley Kubrick's Epic Film," in Martin M. Winkler (ed.), *Spartacus: Film and History*. Oxford: Blackwell, 14–55.

Cooper, Duncan L. (2007b). "Dalton Trumbo vs. Stanley Kubrick: The Historical Meaning of Spartacus," in Martin M. Winkler (ed.), *Spartacus: Film and History*. Oxford: Blackwell, 56–64.

Cornelius, Michael G. (2015). "*Spartacus* and the Shifting Sands of Sacred Space," in Michael G. Cornelius (ed.), *Spartacus in the Television Arena: Essays on the Starz Serie*s. Jefferson, NC: McFarland, 130–51.

Cuklanz, Lisa M. (2000). *Rape on Prime Time: Television, Masculinity, and Sexual Violence*. Philadelphia: University of Pennsylvania Press.

Cyrino, Monica S. (2005). *Big Screen Rome*. Oxford: Blackwell.

Cyrino, Monica S. (ed.) (2008a). *Rome Season One: History Makes Television*. Oxford: Blackwell.

Cyrino, Monica S. (2008b). "Atia and the Erotics of Authority," in Monica S. Cyrino (ed.), *Rome Season One: History Makes Television*. Oxford: Blackwell, 130–40.

Cyrino, Monica S. (2011). "'This is Sparta!': The Reinvention of Epic in Zack Snyder's *300*," in Robert Burgoyne (ed.), *The Epic Film in World Culture*. New York: Routledge, 19–38.

Cyrino, Monica S. (2014). "Ancient Sexuality on Screen," in Thomas K. Hubbard (ed.), *A Companion to Greek and Roman Sexualities*. Malden, MA: Blackwell, 612–28.

Cyrino, Monica S. (2015). "Introduction: The Trials and Triumph of *Rome* Season Two," in Monica S. Cyrino (ed.), *Rome, Season Two: Trial and Triumph*. Edinburgh: Edinburgh University Press, 1–12.

Darling, Cary (2010). "Television Review: *Spartacus: Blood and Sand* Borders on Camp," *The Dallas Morning News*, 22 January.

DeKnight, Steven (2010). "*Spartacus: Blood and Sand*: Interview," Whedon. info, 23 April.

Dickson, Robert K., and Michael G. Cornelius (2015). "(Re)presenting the Phallus: Gladiators and their 'Swords'," in Michael G. Cornelius (ed.), *Spartacus in the Television Arena: Essays on the Starz Serie*s. Jefferson, NC: McFarland, 170–85.

Doherty, Thomas (2002). *Teenagers and Teenpics: Juvenilization of American Movies*. Philadelphia: Temple University Press.

Douglas, Kirk (1988). *The Ragman's Son*. New York: Simon and Schuster.

Drake, David (1986). *Ranks of Bronze*. New York: Bain.

Driscoll, Catherine (2006). "One True Pairing: The Romance of Pornography and the Pornography of Romance," in Karen Hellekson and Kristina Busse (eds.), *Fan Fiction and Fan Communities in the Age of the Internet*. Jefferson, NC: McFarland, 79–96.

Duggan, Alfred (1956). *Winter Quarters*. London: Faber and Faber.

Dunkle, Roger (2014). "Overview of Roman Spectacle," in Paul Christesen and Donald G. Kyle (eds.), *A Companion to Sport and Spectacle in Greek and Roman Antiquity*. Oxford: Blackwell, 381–94.

Eldridge, David (2006). *Hollywood's History Films*. London: I. B. Tauris.

Elliot, Andrew (ed.) (2013). *The Return of the Epic Film: Genre, Aesthetics and History in the 21st Century*. Edinburgh: Edinburgh University Press.

Fagan, Garrett G. (2011). *The Lure of the Arena: Social Psychology and the Crowd at the Roman Games*. Cambridge: Cambridge University Press.

Fagan, Garrett G. (2014). "Gladiatorial Combat as Alluring Spectacle," in Paul Christesen and Donald G. Kyle (eds.), *A Companion to Sport and Spectacle in Greek and Roman Antiquity*. Oxford: Blackwell, 465–77.

Fast, Howard (1951). *Spartacus*. New York: Published by the Author.

Favro, Diane (1996). *The Urban Image of Augustan Rome*. Cambridge: Cambridge University Press.

Faye, Denis (2011). "Blood, Starz, Sex and CGI Magic." www.wga.org/writers-room/features-columns/the-craft.

Fejfer, Jane (2008). *Roman Portraits in Context*. Berlin: Walter de Gruyter.

Fitzgerald, William (2001). "Oppositions, Anxieties and Ambiguities in the Toga Movie," in Sandra R. Joshel, Margaret Malamud, and Donald T. McGuire, Jr. (eds.), *Imperial Projections: Ancient Rome in Modern Popular Culture*. Baltimore: Johns Hopkins University Press, 23–49.

Flower, Harriet I. (1996). *Ancestor Masks and Aristocratic Power in Roman Culture*. Oxford: Clarendon Press.

Flower, Harriet I. (2006). *The Art of Forgetting: Disgrace and Oblivion in Roman Political Culture*. Chapel Hill: University of North Carolina Press.

Foka, Anna (2015a). "Redefining Gender in Sword and Sandal: The New Action Heroine in *Spartacus* (2010–13)," *Journal of Popular Film and Television* 43.1: 39–49.

Foka, Anna (2015b). "Queer Heroes and Action Heroines," in Michael G. Cornelius (ed.), *Spartacus in the Television Arena: Essays on the Starz Serie*s. Jefferson, NC: McFarland, 186–206.

Fowler, Matt (2010). "Lawless and Hannah Talk *Spartacus: Gods of the Arena*," *IGN.com*, 7 August.

Fredal, James (2006). *Rhetorical Action in Ancient Athens: Persuasive Artistry from Solon to Demosthenes*. Carbondale: Southern Illinois University Press.

Fredrick, David (2003). "Grasping the Pangolin: Sensuous Ambiguity in Roman Dining," *Arethusa* 36.3: 309–43.

Freiman, Ray (1959). *The Story of the Making of Ben-Hur: A Tale of the Christ, from Metro-Goldwyn-Mayer*. New York: Random House.

Frensham, Ray (2003). *Teach Yourself Screenwriting*. London: Hodder Education.

Futrell, Alison (1997). *Blood in the Arena: The Spectacle of Roman Power*. Austin: University of Texas Press.

Futrell, Alison (2001). "Seeing Red: Spartacus as Domestic Economist," in Sandra R. Joshel, Margaret Malamud, and Donald T. McGuire, Jr.

(eds.), *Imperial Projections: Ancient Rome in Modern Popular Culture*. Baltimore: Johns Hopkins University Press, 77–118.

Futrell, Alison (2006). *The Roman Games*. Oxford: Blackwell.

Garraffoni, Renata S., and Pedro Paolo A. Funari (2009). "Reading Pompeii's Walls: A Social Archaeological Approach to Gladiatorial Graffiti," in Tony Wilmott (ed.), *Roman Amphitheatres and Spectacula: A 21ˢᵗ Century Perspective*. Oxford: Archeopress, 185–93.

Gantz, Timothy (1993). *Early Greek Myth: A Guide to Literary and Artistic Sources*. Baltimore: Johns Hopkins University Press.

Garron, Barry (2010). "*Spartacus*: A Bloody Spectacle," *Reuters Review*, 21 January.

Gérôme, Jean-Léon (1904). "Notes et Fragments de Jean-Léon Gérôme," *Les Arts: Revue mensuelle des musées, collections, expositions* 26: 22–32.

Gilbert, Matthew (2010). "*Spartacus* Offers Swords, Sandals, Sex, and Silliness," *The Boston Globe*, 22 January.

Giovagnoli, Raffaello (1874). *Spartaco: Racconto storico dell saeculo VII dell'era Romana*. Rome: Tipografia del Giornale l'Italie.

Girgus, Sam B. (2002). *America on Film: Modernism, Documentary, and a Changing America*. Cambridge: Cambridge University Press.

Golvin, Jean-Claude (1988). *L'amphithéâtre romain*. Paris: E. de Boccard.

Goodman, Tim (2010). "*Spartacus: Blood and Sand*," *San Francisco Chronicle*, 22 January.

Gowing, Alain M. (2000). "Memory and Silence in Cicero's *Brutus*," *Eranos* 98: 39–64.

Gowing, Alain M. (2005). *Empire and Memory: The Representation of the Roman Republic in Imperial Culture*. Cambridge: Cambridge University Press.

Grant, Michael (1967). *Gladiators*. New York: Delacorte.

Grimes, Tom, James A. Anderson, and Lori Bergen (2008). *Media Violence and Aggression: Science and Ideology*. Thousand Oaks, CA: Sage.

Gruen, Eric S. (1977). "M. Licinius Crassus: A Review Article," *American Journal of Ancient History* 2.2: 117–28.

Gruen, Eric S. (2011). *Rethinking the Other in Antiquity*. Princeton: Princeton University Press.

Gunter, Barrie, Jackie Harrison, and Maggie Wykes (2003). *Violence on Television*. London: Routledge.

Hall, Sheldon (2010). *Epics, Spectacles, and Blockbusters: A Hollywood History*. Detroit: Wayne State University Press.

Halterman, Jim (2013). "Interview: Dan Feuerriegel Says 'It's All About Love' With The Possible End Of Nagron," Thebacklot.com, 23 March.

Hammer, Jessica (2012). "Geek Media – What's With All the Rape?," Gamingaswomen.com, 31 May.

Hark, Ina Rae (1993). "Animals or Romans: Looking at Masculinity in *Spartacus*," in Steven Cohan and Ina Rae Hark (eds.), *Screening the Male:*

Exploring Masculinities in Hollywood Cinema. London: Routledge, 151–72.

Haugen, David M. (ed.) (2007). *Is Media Violence a Problem?* Detroit: Greenhaven.

Hellekson, Karen, and Kristina Busse (eds.) (2006). *Fan Fiction and Fan Communities in the Age of the Internet*. Jefferson, NC: McFarland.

Hibberd, James (2011a). "*Spartacus* Hunts for Star for Season 2," *Entertainment Weekly.com*, 21 January.

Hibberd, James (2011b). "Cancer Claims Life of *Spartacus* Star," *Entertainment Weekly.com*, 16 September.

Hibberd, James (2013). "Spartacus Series Finale Gains Victorious Ratings," *Entertainment Weekly.com*, 15 April.

Hinckley, David (2010). "Starz' *Spartacus: Blood and Sand* Starring Andy Whitfield Is Orgy of Sex, Violence, and Swearing," *New York Daily News*, 22 January.

Holliday, Peter J. (2002). *The Origins of Roman Historical Commemoration in the Visual Arts*. New York: Cambridge University Press.

Hopkins, Keith (1983). *Death and Renewal*. Cambridge: Cambridge University Press.

Iggulden, Conn (2004). *Emperor: The Death of Kings*. New York: Delacorte.

Itzkoff, Dave (2014). "For 'Game of Thrones,' Rising Unease Over Rape's Recurring Role," *The New York Times*, 3 May.

Jacobelli, Luciana (2003). *Gladiators at Pompeii*. Rome: L'Erma.

Jenkins, Henry (1992). *Textual Poachers: Television Fans and Participatory Culture*. London: Routledge.

Jenkins, Henry (2006). *Fans, Bloggers and Gamers: Exploring Participatory Culture*. New York: New York University Press.

Jones, Nick (2015). *Hollywood Action Films and Spatial Theory*. London: Routledge.

Joshel, Sandra R. (1992). "The Body Female and the Body Politic: Livy's Lucretia and Verginia," in Amy Richlin (ed.), *Pornography and Representation in Greece and Rome*. Oxford: Oxford University Press, 112–30.

Joshel, Sandra R. (1997). "Female Desire and the Discourse of Empire: Tacitus' Messalina," in Judith P. Hallett and Marilyn B. Skinner (eds.), *Roman Sexualities*. Princeton: Princeton University Press, 221–54.

Joshel, Sandra R. (2001). "*I, Claudius*: Imperial Projections and Soap Opera," in Sandra R. Joshel, Margaret Malamud, and Donald T. McGuire, Jr. (eds.), *Imperial Projections: Ancient Rome in Modern Popular Culture*. Baltimore: Johns Hopkins University Press, 119–61.

Joshel, Sandra R. (2010). *Slavery in the Roman World*. Cambridge: Cambridge University Press.

Joshel, Sandra R., and Lauren H. Petersen (2014). *The Material Life of Roman Slaves*. Cambridge: Cambridge University Press.

Kaplan, Fred (1999). *Gore Vidal: A Biography*. New York: Doubleday.

Kendrick, James (2009). *Hollywood Bloodshed: Violence in 1980s American Cinema*. Carbondale: Southern Illinois University Press.

Keppie, Lawrence (2000). *Legions and Veterans: Roman Army Papers 1971–2000*. Stuttgart: Franz Steiner.

Kerbel, Matthew (2000). *If it Bleeds, it Leads: An Anatomy of Television News*. Boulder: Westview.

Kiefer, Otto (1934). *Sexual Life in Ancient Rome*. New York: AMS.

Koestler, Arthur (1939). *The Gladiators*. New York: Macmillan.

Konstantarakos, Myrto (2000). *Spaces in European Cinema*. Exeter: Intellect Books.

Kyle, Donald G. (1998). *Spectacles of Death in Ancient Rome*. London: Routledge.

Lear, Andrew (2014). "Ancient Pederasty: An Introduction," in Thomas K. Hubbard (ed.), *A Companion to Greek and Roman Sexualities*. Malden, MA: Blackwell, 102–27.

Lewis, Jon (2013). *Essential Cinema: An Introduction to Film Analysis*. Boston: Wadsworth, Cengage Learning.

Lloyd, Robert (2010). "*Spartacus: Blood and Sand* on Starz," *LA Times*, 22 January.

Loggins, Emma (2010). "Interview: Steven S. DeKnight and Robert Tapert from *Spartacus: Blood and Sand*," Fanbolt.com, 5 January.

Lowry, Brian (2010). "Review: *Spartacus: Blood and Sand*," *Variety Magazine*, 17 January.

McCoppin, Rachel S. (2015). "Spartacus' Entrapment in the Underworld in *Blood and Sand*," in Michael G. Cornelius (ed.), *Of Muscles and Men: Essays on the Sword and Sandal Film*. Jefferson, NC: McFarland, 97–117.

McCoskey, Denise Eileen (2012). *Race: Antiquity and its Legacy*. London: I. B. Tauris.

McCullough, Colleen (1993). *Fortune's Favourites*. London: Random House.

McGovern, Joe (2015). "Kirk Douglas: A Life in Film," *Entertainment Weekly*, 27 February: 50–1.

McGrath, Charles (2010). "'Spartacus' Returns to a New Arena: The Small Screen," *New York Times*, 15 January.

McLaughlin, Raoul (2010). *Rome and the Distant East: Trade Routes to the Ancient Lands of Arabia, India and China*. London: Continuum.

Malamud, Margaret (2001). "Brooklyn-on-the-Tiber: Roman Comedy on Broadway and in Film," in Sandra R. Joshel, Margaret Malamud, and Donald T. McGuire, Jr. (eds.), *Imperial Projections: Ancient Rome in Modern Popular Culture*. Baltimore: Johns Hopkins University Press, 191–208.

Mammel, Kathryn (2014). "Ancient Critics of Roman Spectacle and Sport," in Paul Christesen and Donald G. Kyle (eds.), *A Companion to Sport and Spectacle in Greek and Roman Antiquity*. Oxford: Blackwell, 603–16.

Mañas, Alfonso (2013). *Gladiadores: El gran espectáculo de Roma*. Barcelona: Editorial Planeta.

Marshall, Bruce A. (1976). *Crassus: A Political Biography*. Amsterdam: A. M. Hakkert.

Masterson, Mark (2014). "Studies of Ancient Masculinity," in Thomas K. Hubbard (ed.), *A Companion to Greek and Roman Sexualities*. Malden, MA: Blackwell, 17–30.

Maxfield, Valerie (1981). *The Military Decorations of the Roman Army*. Berkeley: University of California Press.

Moana Thompson, Kirsten (2011). "'Philip Never Saw Babylon': 360-vision and the Historical Epic in the Digital Era," in Robert Burgoyne (ed.), *The Epic Film in World Culture*. New York: Routledge, 39–62.

Mollo, Luigi, and Paola Pesaresi (2010). "Restoring Archaeological Structures Using Regional Traditional Building Techniques," in Alessandro Bucci and Luigi Mollo (eds.), *Regional Architecture in the Mediterranean Area*. Florence: Alinea, 404–15.

Morris, Jeremy (2012). "The Justification of Torture-Horror: Retribution and Sadism in *Saw*, *Hostel*, and *The Devil's Rejects*," in Thomas Fahy (ed.), *The Philosophy of Horror*. Lexington: The University Press of Kentucky, 42–56.

Müller, Jürgen (2004). *Movies of the 60s*. Cologne: Taschen.

Nagy, Gregory (1999). *The Best of the Achaeans*. Baltimore: Johns Hopkins University Press.

Nisbet, Gideon (2009). "'Dickus Maximus': Rome as Pornotopia," in Dunstan Lowe and Kim Shahabudin (eds.), *Classics for All: Reworking Antiquity in Mass Culture*. Newcastle: Cambridge Scholars, 150–71.

O'Brien, Daniel (2014). *Classical Masculinity and the Spectacular Body on Film: The Mighty Sons of Hercules*. New York: Palgrave Macmillan.

O'Brien, Geoffrey (1993). *The Phantom Empire: Movies in the Mind of the 20th Century*. New York: W. W. Norton & Co.

O'Leary, Tim (2010). "What Worked and Didn't Work about *Spartacus*' Shocking Gay Twist," Thebacklot.com, 8 March.

O'Neill, Phelim (2010). "Have You Been Watching . . . *Spartacus: Blood and Sand*?," TheGuardian.com, 29 June.

Osborne, Robin (1985). "The Erection and Mutilation of the Hermai," *Proceedings of the Cambridge Philological Society* 25: 45–73.

Overbeck, Johannes A., and August Mau (1884). *Pompeii*. Leipzig: Wilhelm Engelmann.

Parker, Holt (1999). "The Observed of All Observers: Spectacle, Applause, and Cultural Poetics in the Roman Theater Audience," in Bettina Bergmann and Christine Kondoleon (eds.), *The Art of Ancient Spectacle*. Washington, DC: National Gallery of Art, 163–80.

Paul, Joanna (2013). *Film and the Classical Epic Tradition*. Oxford: Oxford University Press.

Paul, Joanna (2014). "When it Comes to Ancient Rome, Hollywood Sticks to the Same Tired Old Formula," TheConversation.com, 21 May.

Penley, Constance (1992). "Feminism, Psychoanalysis and Popular Culture," in Laurence Grossberg, Cary Nelson, and Paula A. Treichler (eds.), *Cultural Studies*. London: Routledge, 479–500.

Picón, Carlos A. (2007). *Art of the Classical World in the Metropolitan Museum of Art: Greece, Cyprus, Etruria, Rome*. New York: The Metropolitan Museum of Art.

Pierce, Jerry B. (2011). "To Do or Die Manfully: Performing Heteronormativity in Recent Epic Films," in Michael G. Cornelius (ed.), *Of Muscles and Men: Essays on the Sword and Sandal Film*. Jefferson, NC: McFarland, 40–57.

Plass, Paul C. (1995). *The Game of Death in Ancient Rome: Arena Sport and Political Suicide*. Madison: University of Wisconsin Press.

Potter, Amanda (2015). "Slashing *Rome*: Season Two Rewritten in Online Fan Fiction," in Monica S. Cyrino (ed.), *Rome, Season Two: Trial and Triumph*. Edinburgh: Edinburgh University Press, 219–30.

Potter, David S. (2010). "Entertainers in the Roman Empire," in David S. Potter and David J. Mattingly (eds.), *Life, Death, and Entertainment in the Roman Empire*, 2nd edn., Ann Arbor: University of Michigan Press, 280–349.

Potter, James W. (1999). *On Media Violence*. London: Sage.

Pournelle, Jeri (1979–). *Janissaries*. New York: Ace Books.

Prince, Stephen (2000a). "Graphic Violence in the Cinema: Origins, Aesthetic Design, and Social Effects," in Stephen Prince (ed.), *Screening Violence*. New Brunswick, NJ: Rutgers University Press, 1–46.

Prince, Stephen (2000b). "The Aesthetic of Slow-Motion Violence in the Films of Sam Peckinpah," in Stephen Prince (ed.), *Screening Violence*. New Brunswick, NJ: Rutgers University Press, 175–201.

Projansky, Sarah (2001). *Watching Rape: Film and Television in Postfeminist Culture*. New York: New York University Press.

Pugh, Sheenagh (2004). "The Democratic Genre: Fan Fiction in a Literary Context," *Refractory* 5 (blogs.arts.unimelb.edu.au/refractory).

Quinn, Josephine C. (2007). "Herms, Kouroi and the Political Anatomy of Athens," *Greece and Rome* 54: 82–105.

Ramirez, Juan Antonio (2004). *Architecture for the Screen: A Critical Study of Set Design in Hollywood's Golden Age*. Jefferson, NC: McFarland.

Raucci, Stacie (2013). "The Order of Orgies: Sex and the Cinematic Roman," in Monica S. Cyrino (ed.), *Screening Love and Sex in the Ancient World*. New York: Palgrave Macmillan, 143–55.

Richards, Jeffrey (2008). *Hollywood's Ancient Worlds*. London: Continuum.

Rodrigues, Nuno Simões (2010). "A Antiguidade no Cinema: *Spartacus* de Stanley Kubrick (1960)," *Boletim de Estudos Clássicos* 54: 91–8.

Rodrigues, Nuno Simões (2012). "*Least that's what Plutarch says*. Plutarco no Cinema," in Luisa N. Ferreira, Nuno S. Rodrigues, and Paulo S. Rodrigues (eds.), *Plutarco e as Artes: Pintura, Cinema e Artes Decorativas*. Coimbra: Imprensa da Universidade de Coimbra, 139–272.

Rodrigues, Nuno Simões (2013). "Roma Antiga no Cinema: Utopia,

Distopia e Pornotopia," in Margarida Acciaiuoli, Ana D. Rodrigues, Maria J. Castro, Paula André, and Paulo S. Rodrigues (eds.), *Arte & Utopia*. Lisbon: CHAIA, 55–69.

Rodrigues, Nuno Simões (2014). "A Antiguidade no Cinema: *Caligula* de Tinto Brass e Bob Guccione (1979)," *Boletim de Estudos Clássicos* 59: 137–52.

Ross, Dalton (2012). "He. Is. *Spartacus*," *Entertainment Weekly*, 13 January: 26–9.

Ross, Dalton (2013). "*Spartacus* Bids Farewell," *Entertainment Weekly*, 12 April: 64.

Roush, Matt (2010). "From Swords to Cyborgs," *TV Guide Magazine Online*, 22 January.

Ryan, Maureen (2010). "The 'Spartacus' Season 1 Finale: Were You Not Entertained?," *Chicago Tribune*, 16 April.

Sampson, Gareth C. (2008). *The Defeat of Rome: Crassus, Carrhae, and the Invasion of the East*. Barnsley: Pen & Sword Military.

Saurin, Bernard-Joseph (1772). *Oeuvres de théâtre*. Paris: Librairie Duchesne.

Schiavone, Aldo (2013). *Spartacus*. Cambridge, MA: Harvard University Press.

Schwartz, John (2015). "Highlights from the Supreme Court Decision on Same-Sex Marriage," *New York Times*, 8 June.

Scott, A. O. (2011). "Tattooed Heroine Metes Out Slick, Punitive Violence," *New York Times*, 19 December.

Sebesta, Judith L., and Larissa Bonfante (2001). *The World of Roman Costume*. Madison: University of Wisconsin Press.

Sepinwall, Alan (2014). "Review: Game of Thrones – Breaker of Chains: Uncle Deadly?," Hitflix.com, 20 April.

Shaw, Brent D. (2001). *Spartacus and the Slave Wars: A Brief History with Documents*. Boston: Bedford.

Sheldon, Rose Mary (2010). *Rome's Wars in Parthia*. London: Valentine Mitchell.

Shiel, Mark (2001). "Cinema and the City in History and Theory," in Mark Shiel and Tony Fitzmaurice (eds.), *Cinema and the City: Film and Urban Societies in a Global Context*. Oxford: Blackwell, 1–18.

Shillock, Larry T. (2015). "Single Combat, the Semiotics of the Arena, and Martial Intimacy," in Michael G. Cornelius (ed.), *Spartacus in the Television Arena: Essays on the Starz Series*. Jefferson, NC: McFarland, 77–96.

Signorielli, Nancy (2005). *Violence in the Media: A Reference Handbook*. Oxford: ABC-Clio.

Sobchack, Vivian (1990). "Surge and Splendor: A Phenomenology of the Hollywood Historical Epic," *Representations* 29: 24–49.

Sobchack, Vivian (2000). "The Violent Dance: A Personal Memoir of Death in the Movies," in Stephen Prince (ed.), *Screening Violence*. New Brunswick, NJ: Rutgers University Press, 110–24.

Sobchack, Vivian (2013). "Why I Love IMDb: What the Number One Film Website Tells Us About 'Those Wonderful People in the Dark'," *Film Comment* 49.2: 38–40.

Solomon, Jon (2001). *The Ancient World in the Cinema*. New Haven: Yale University Press.

Sorin, Gerald (2012). *Howard Fast: Life and Literature in the Left Lane*. Bloomington: Indiana University Press.

Sparks, Glenn G., and Cheri W. Sparks (2000). "Violence, Mayhem, and Horror," in Dolf Zillmann and Peter Vorderer (eds.), *Media Entertainment: The Psychology of Its Appeal*. Mahwah, NJ: Lawrence Erlbaum Associates, 73–92.

Stasi, Mafalda (2006). "The Toy Soldiers from Leeds: The Slash Palimpsest," in Karen Hellekson and Kristina Busse (eds.), *Fan Fiction and Fan Communities in the Age of the Internet*. Jefferson, NC: McFarland, 115–33.

Stransky, Tanner (2011). "*Spartacus: Gods of the Arena*: New Drama," *Entertainment Weekly*, 14 January: 56.

Strauss, Barry (2009). *The Spartacus War*. New York: Simon and Schuster.

Strong, Anise K. (2013). "Objects of Desire: Female Gazes and Male Bodies in *Spartacus: Blood and Sand*," in Monica S. Cyrino (ed.), *Screening Love and Sex in the Ancient World*. New York: Palgrave Macmillan, 167–82.

Sumi, Geoffrey (2009). "Monuments and Memory: The *Aedes Castoris* in the Formation of Augustan Ideology," *Classical Quarterly* 59.1: 167–86.

Tamborini, Ron (1996). "A Model of Empathy and Emotional Reactions to Horror," in James B. Weaver, III and Ron Tamborini (eds.), *Horror Films: Current Research on Audience Preferences and Reactions*. Mahwah, NJ: Lawrence Erlbaum Associates, 103–24.

Tatum, Jeffrey W. (2007). "The Character of Marcus Licinius Crassus," in Martin M. Winkler (ed.), *Spartacus: Film and History*, Oxford: Blackwell, 128–43.

Theodorakopoulos, Elena (2010). *Ancient Rome at the Cinema: Story and Spectacle in Hollywood and Rome*. Exeter: Bristol Phoenix Press.

Toner, Jerry (2014). "Trends in the Study of Roman Spectacle and Sport," in Paul Christesen and Donald G. Kyle (eds.), *A Companion to Sport and Spectacle in Greek and Roman Antiquity*, Oxford: Blackwell, 451–62.

Treggiari, Susan (1991). *Roman Marriage: Iusti Coniuges from the Time of Cicero to the Time of Ulpian*. Oxford: Clarendon Press.

Tschen-Emmons, James B. (2014). *Artifacts from Ancient Rome*. Santa Barbara: ABC-Clio.

Tucker, Ken (2010). "*Spartacus: Blood and Sand*: Preview," *Entertainment Weekly*, 29 January: 59.

Turner, Susanne (2009). "'Only Spartan Women Give Birth to Real Men': Zack Snyder's *300* and the Male Nude," in Dunstan Lowe and Kim Shahabudin (eds.), *Classics for All: Reworking Antiquity in Mass Culture*. Newcastle: Cambridge Scholars, 128–49.

Urbainczyk, Theresa (2004). *Spartacus*. London: Bristol Classical Press.

Vogler, Charles (1998). *The Writer's Journey: Mythic Structure for Writers*. Studio City: Michael Wiese Productions.

Ward, Allen (1977). *Marcus Crassus and the Late Roman Republic*. Columbia: University of Missouri Press.

Welch, Katherine E. (2007). *The Roman Amphitheater: From its Origins to the Colosseum*. New York: Cambridge University Press.

Whitlock, Cathy (2010). *Designs on Film: A Century of Hollywood Art Direction*. New York: Harper Collins.

Wiedemann, Thomas (1992). *Emperors and Gladiators*. London: Routledge.

Willemen, Paul (1981). "Anthony Mann: Looking at the Male," *Framework* 15–17: 16–20.

Williams, Craig A. (2010). *Roman Homosexuality: Ideologies of Masculinity in Classical Antiquity*. Oxford: Oxford University Press.

Winkler, Martin M. (2004). "*Gladiator* and the Colosseum: Ambiguities of Spectacle," in Martin M. Winkler (ed.), *Gladiator: Film and History*. Oxford: Blackwell, 87–110.

Winkler, Martin M. (ed.) (2007a). *Spartacus: Film and History*. Oxford: Blackwell.

Winker, Martin M. (2007b). "The Holy Cause of Freedom: American Ideals in *Spartacus*," in Martin M. Winkler (ed.), *Spartacus: Film and History*. Oxford: Blackwell, 154–88.

Winner, David (2005). "A Blow to the Temples," *Financial Times*, 28 January.

Wistrand, Magnus (1992). *Entertainment and Violence in Ancient Rome: The Attitudes of Roman Writers of the First Century A.D.* Göteburg: Göteburg University Press.

Wyke, Maria (1997). *Projecting the Past. Ancient Rome, Cinema and History*. London: Routledge.

Zanker, Paul (1998). *Pompeii*. Cambridge, MA: Harvard University Press.

Zillmann, Dolf (1991). "Empathy: Affect from Bearing Witness to the Emotions of Others," in Jennings Bryant and Dolf Zillmann (eds.), *Responding to the Screen: Reception and Reaction Processes*. London: Routledge, 135–68.

Zillmann, Dolf (2000). "Mood Management in the Context of Selective Exposure Theory," in Michael E. Roloff (ed.), *Communication Yearbook* 23. Thousand Oaks, CA: Sage, 103–33.

Zillmann, Dolf, and Joanne Cantor (1977). "Affective Responses to the Emotions of a Protagonist," *Journal of Experimental Social Psychology* 13: 155–65.

Zoller Seitz, Matt (2012). "TV Review: The Sexy, Gory, Low-Rent Spectacle of *Spartacus: Vengeance*," *Vulture*, 27 January.

Index